GOD'S PLANS FOR YOU

Other Crossway books by J. I. Packer

Growing in Christ
Life in the Spirit
A Passion for Faithfulness
A Quest for Godliness

GOD'S PLANS *for* YOU

J. I. PACKER

CROSSWAY BOOKS • WHEATON, ILLINOIS
A DIVISION OF GOOD NEWS PUBLISHERS

Library of Congress Cataloging-in-Publication Data
Packer, J. I. (James Innell)
  God's plans for you / J. I. Packer.
    p.   cm.
  Includes bibliographical references.
  ISBN 1-58134-290-X (alk. paper)
    1. Christian life—Anglican authors. I. Title.
BV4501.3.P32   2001
248.4—dc21   2001003934
                                   CIP

15	14	13	12	11	10	09	08	07	06	05	04	03	02
15	14	13	12	11	10	9	8	7	6	5	4	3	2

I know the plans I have for you,
declares the LORD,
plans for wholeness and not for evil,
to give you a future and a hope.

JEREMIAH 29:11 ESV

CONTENTS

PREFACE   9

1   DANGER! THEOLOGIAN AT WORK   11
What These Chapters Are Meant to Do

2   THE PLAN OF GOD   17
The Basic Christian Orientation

3   MEETING GOD   35
The Basic Christian Relationship

4   HOT TUB RELIGION   47
Toward a Theology of Enjoyment

5   A CHRISTIAN STYLE OF LIFE   73
Managing our Labor, Leisure, Pleasure, and Treasure

6   GUIDANCE   89
How God Leads Us

7   JOY   107
A Neglected Discipline

8   SCRIPTURE AND SANCTIFICATION   127
How the Bible Helps Us to Holiness

9   THE TRANSFORMATION TRACK   143
What It Means to Follow Christ

10   POOR HEALTH   149
Physical Cures and Healing

11   DISAPPOINTMENT, DESPAIR, DEPRESSION   157
How the Great Physician Touches Troubled Minds

12   KNOW YOURSELF   167
Identity and Self-Image

13   POWER PATH   181
Taking the Holy Spirit Seriously

14   MUSINGS ON THE LIFE OF FAITH   193
Double-Mindedness, Seriousness, Balance, Dying

15   CHURCH REFORMATION   205
Outward Reordering and Inward Renewal

NOTES   221

Preface

I hope the title of this book does not upset you. I can see that it might seem altogether too bold, as if I were laying claim to the sort of advance knowledge that astrologers and fortune-tellers offer and that Christians emphatically do not have. But, as the epigraph on the previous page shows, my title is no more than an echo of God's own words addressed to the deported Jews in Babylon and relayed to them in Jeremiah's letter; and my purpose in choosing it was simply to set before our minds the certainty that God, who is Lord of both his own future and ours, is taking his people somewhere wonderful.

The note on the text in the *New Living Translation* declares, rightly: "As long as God, who knows the future, provides our agenda and goes with us as we fulfill his mission, we can have boundless hope. This does not mean that we shall be spared pain, suffering, or hardship, but it does mean that God will see us through to a glorious conclusion."

So John Ryland's lyric is fully justified:

> *Sov'reign Ruler of the skies,*
> *Ever gracious, ever wise,*
> *All my times are in thy hand,*
> *All of events at thy command.*

> *His decree who form'd the earth*
> *Fix'd my first and second birth;*
> *Parents, native place, and time,*
> *All appointed were by him.*

> *He that form'd me in the womb,*
> *He shall guide me to the tomb;*
> *All my times shall ever be*
> *Order'd by his wise decree.*

> *Times of sickness, times of health,*
> *Times of penury and wealth;*

Times of trial and of grief,
Times of triumph and relief;

Times the tempter's power to prove,
Times to test the Saviour's love;
All must come, and last, and end
As shall please my heavenly Friend.

Plagues and deaths around me fly;
Till he bids, I cannot die.
Not a single shaft can hit
Till the love of God sees fit.

The chapters that follow seek to illuminate and apply all this in a variety of different connections. The aim throughout is to show how life looks and feels when lived by faith in the sovereign God of the Bible, and to help in forming attitudes, focusing values, and making decisions amid the perplexing cross-currents of decadence in the culture and the church. The plans of God in which we shall take soundings cover, first and fundamentally, his agenda for leading us from where we are into fullness of fellowship and perfection of life with himself, and within this frame, second and specifically, his agenda for drawing out of us—which means, working in us—the cooperation with him of humble heart, helping hand, and holy hope that is integral to this process. My ideal reader, the "you" of my title, is someone who shares my certainty that in life, in death, and for eternity our relationship with God is what matters most, and therefore should be our main concern here and now. Are you with me? I hope so.

So let us together get down to business.

1

DANGER!
THEOLOGIAN AT WORK
What These Chapters Are Meant to Do

A favorite picture book for three-year-olds, *I Am a Bunny*, looks at life from a rabbit's point of view. On that basis, this book could well be called *I Am a Theologian*. Such a title would sound conceited, elitist, and stuffy to the last degree. Like a lead balloon, it would sink the book and its author straight into oblivion. Yet, as a declaration of commitment rather than a claim to competence, it would not be wholly unfit. My goal is to pinpoint some problems that a theologian cannot help but see and to fulfill in relation to them, as best I can, the theologian's proper and distinctive role.

What is that? Well, what is theology? (Always begin at the beginning!) Theology is one of those terms (there are not too many of them) whose meaning is clear from its derivation. Theology comes from two Greek words, *theos* (God) and *logos* (discourse, speech, line of argument), and means simply God-talk or, more fully, thoughts about God expressed in statements about God. God-thoughts are only right when they square with God's own thoughts about himself; theology becomes good only when we let God's revealed truth—that is, Bible teaching—penetrate our minds. So theology is an exercise of listening before it is one of talking. It is the attempt to hear what the Westminster Confession I.x calls "the Holy Spirit speaking in the Scripture" and then to apply what Scripture says to correct and direct our lives. We bring our doubts and questions to the Bible's teaching for resolution, and we allow God in and through that same teaching to question us about the way we think and live. The name of theologian is given to those who help with this process.

There is a sense in which every Christian is a theologian. Simply by speaking of God, whatever you say, you become a theologian, just as by hitting the keys you become a pianist, whatever it sounds like. (My twenty-three-month-old grandson was fulfilling the role of pianist even as I wrote the first draft.) The question then is whether you are good or bad at what you are doing. But as in secular speech the word *pianist* is normally kept for competent performers, so in Christian speech the word *theologian* is kept for those who in some sense specialize in the study of God's truth.

What use are such people? Is there a particular job that we should look to them to do for us? Yes, there is. By the lake in a resort I know stands a building grandly labeled Environmental Control Center. It is the sewage plant, there to ensure that nothing fouls the water; its staff is comprised of water engineers and sewage specialists. Think of theologians as the church's sewage specialists. Their role is to detect and eliminate intellectual pollution and to ensure, so far as man can, that God's life-giving truth flows pure and unpoisoned into Christian hearts.

Their calling obliges them to act as the church's water engineers, seeking by their preaching, teaching, and biblical exposition to make the flow of truth strong and steady; but it is particularly as disposers of spiritual sewage that I want to portray them. They are to test the water and filter out anything that confuses minds, corrupts judgments, and distorts the way that Christians view their own lives. If they see Christians astray, they must haul them back on track; if they see them dithering, they must give them certainty; if they find them confused, they must straighten them out. That is why this book might be called *I Am a Theologian*, for this is precisely what I am attempting to do.

The chapters that follow deal with some crucial questions about which Christians often feel hesitant and uncertain. These questions all have a directly personal twist. What is God up to in his world, bewildering and agonizing as it so often proves to be? Who is entitled to claim his acquaintance? What will holiness require of me? How will

God guide me? Will he guide me at all? Is there such a thing as divine healing? What should I expect from God when I am sick or when I feel broken into little pieces? How should I react to my own reactions to things, and to the present condition of the church? These are some of the questions on which I add my mite to the treasury of Christian discussion. They are important questions that often receive wrong answers, and I want to say what I can about them.

MAP MAKING

What should a theologian do when facing questions of this sort? Picture it thus: He should make a map of each problematical life situation, with all the human factors involved, and then superimpose all the relevant biblical teachings and Bible-based considerations. The scale of the map will need to be fairly large. The map is to be used when walking cross-country, so correctness of detail is important.

The Christian life is cross-country travel all the way, with hedges and ditches, ups and downs, rough places and smooth places, deserts and swamps. There are storms and fogs periodically punctuating the sunshine. The purpose of the map is to enable the walker to find his way at all times, whatever the terrain and whatever the weather. With a good map he will recognize the terrain around him, relate the features he observes to the larger landscape, and see at each stage where he should go. Theology's proper goal is to equip the disciples of Jesus Christ for obedience. The maps theologians draw are meant, not simply to be possessed as so much intellectual wealth, but rather to be used for the believer's route-finding in his personal pilgrimage of following his Lord.

Technicalities (sometimes unavoidable in theology, as in any field of scientific study) will be pursued only for the sake of simplicity. Simplicity of principle, once it is achieved, makes for straightforwardness of practice. The best theological maps are clear and have seven basic qualities.

First, they are accurate in their presentation of material, both human and biblical. Nothing can compensate for failure here.

Second, they are God-centered, recognizing divine sovereignty at the heart of everything and showing God's control of problematical events, both actual and imaginable.

Third, they are doxological, giving God glory for his glorious achievements in creation, providence, and grace, and encouraging a spirit of joyous, trustful worship and adoration in all circumstances.

Fourth, they are future-oriented, for Christianity is a religion of hope. Often the only sense theology can make of present trends, conditions, and behavior patterns, as they both mark society and touch individuals, is to diagnose them as fruits of sin and hold forth the promise that God will one day wipe them out and unveil something better.

Fifth, they are Christ-related in two ways. On the one hand, they proclaim the centrality of Jesus our mediator, prophet, priest, and king, in all God's present dealings with, and future plans for, the human race. On the other hand, they reformulate our notional perplexities by turning them into practical issues of faithfully following the Savior whom we love along the path of self-denial and cross-bearing, according to his own explicit call (see Luke 9:23). They show us how to walk patiently with him through experiences that defeat our minds and feel like death, into the experienced reality of personal internal resurrection. This is the biblical way to live the Christian life, and good theological maps lead us right into it.

Sixth, such maps are church-centered. The New Testament presents the church as central in God's plan. Christians are not meant to journey through life in isolation but in company with fellow believers, supporting them and being supported by them.

Seventh, good theological maps are freedom-focused. They are tuned in to the decision-making processes of authentically Christian men and women—that is, people who know themselves to be free from the law as a system of salvation, yet desire to live by it, first, out of love for their Lord who wills this; second, out of love for the law itself, which now delights them with its vision of righteousness; and third, out of self-love, since they know that there is no real happiness for them either here or hereafter without holiness. Freedom from what restricts and enslaves is the negative aspect of freedom for the fulfillment and contentment that constitute true happiness, and it is this positive reality of holy, happy freedom in Christ that theology must always seek to promote.

Good theology constantly calls for deliberate, responsible decisions about how we are going to live, and it never forgets that Christian decisions are commitments to action on principle (not out of mindless conformity), undertaken in freedom (not from external pressure or bullying), and motivated primarily by love of God and of justice (not by fear). Good theology thus molds Christian character, neither demeaning nor diminishing us but rather enhancing our God-given dignity.

Is theology dangerous, as my title for this chapter might seem to suggest? Not in itself, unless it is done on false principles—but dangers certainly exist for those who take theology seriously, though the dangers are greater for those who don't. Neglect theology, and sooner or later, however well-intentioned you are, you will make big practical blunders that you may never recognize as blunders. The outcome will be sad, perhaps the saddest imaginable.

Attend to theology, however, and you will find yourself lured toward the Pharisaic downfall of the arrogant know-all who tells others what to do while forgetting that he needs to do the same himself. Those who work hard theologizing, whether as professionals or from general interest, have to battle these twin temptations. The first is to see themselves as superior Christians because they know more than others, and the second is to exempt themselves from obligations that bind others, as if their expertise puts them in a class by themselves to which ordinary rules do not apply.

Every member of our fallen race is tempted to indulge pride in some form, for pride is of the essence of our heritage of original sin; and this is the recurring form in which would-be theologians, clergy and layfolk, academics and pastors alike, have to encounter that temptation. God's ideal for us, however, is that we should always think and speak and live in the manner shown in the previous paragraphs, and humble honesty in seeking to conform to that ideal is the only godly way for any of us to go. Theological discussion of questions involved in knowing God's plans for us must always seek to point us along that road.

There is no denying that many theological treatments of problem areas fail to measure up to these criteria. Authoritarianism within the church, secularism from outside, and a restless Athenian cast of mind in universities and seminaries have constantly combined to contaminate theology, both past and present. But that need not concern us now. I have written this chapter only so that you will know the standards to which I am trying to work. I may well fail; you shall be the judge of that. But if I do, please remember that, like the pianist whom the wild Westerners in a certain famous cartoon planned to shoot, I am doing my best.

The foregoing paragraphs were drafted in 1987, and it is now 2001. I am often asked whether over the years I have changed my mind about anything in Christianity. The answer is no, at least not consciously; if there is a difference, it is in the way I respond to positions that deviate from my own. The Chilean pianist Claudio Arrau, when asked how aging had affected his playing, replied: "The fingers grow wiser." I hope something like that might be said of the items in this book, carefully reviewed and sometimes enlarged, that have appeared before.

Now let us move on.

2

THE PLAN OF GOD

The Basic Christian Orientation

IS THERE A PLAN?

People today feel lost and astray. Modern art, poetry, and novels, or five minutes' conversation with any sensitive person will assure us of that. It may seem odd that this is so in an era when we have more control over the forces of nature than ever before. But it really is not. It is God's judgment, which we have brought down on ourselves by trying to feel too much at home in this world.

For that is what we have done. We refuse to believe that one should live for something more than this present life. Even if we suspect the materialists are wrong in denying that God and another world exist, we have not allowed our belief to keep us from living on materialistic principles. We have treated this world as if it were the only home we shall ever possess and have concentrated exclusively on arranging it for our comfort. We thought we could build heaven on earth.

Now God has judged us for our impiety. During the past century we had two "hot" world wars and one "cold" one, the latter in some respects still continuing. We find ourselves today in the age of nuclear warfare, racism, tribalism, global racketeering, torture, terrorism, and all sorts of brainwashing. In such a world it is not possible to feel at home. It is a world that has disappointed us. We expected life to be friendly. Instead, it has mocked our hopes and left us disillusioned and frustrated. We thought we knew what to make of life. Now we are baffled as to whether anything can ever be made of it. We thought of ourselves as wise men. Now we find ourselves like benighted children, lost in the dark.

Sooner or later this was bound to happen. God's world is never friendly to those who forget its Maker. The Buddhists, who link their atheism with a thorough pessimism about life, are to that extent correct. Without God, man loses his bearings in this world. He cannot find them again until he has found the One whose world it is. It is natural that nonbelievers feel their existence is pointless and miserable. We should not wonder when these bitter, frustrated souls turn to drugs and drink or when teenagers respond to the traumatic chaos around them by committing suicide. God made life, and God alone can tell us its meaning. If we are to make sense of life in this world, then, we must know about God. And if we want to know about God, we must turn to the Bible.

READ THE BIBLE

So let us read the Bible—if we can. But can we? Many of us have lost the ability. When we open our Bibles, we do so in a frame of mind that forms an insurmountable barrier to reading it at all. This may sound startling, but it is true. Let me explain.

When you read a book, you treat it as a unit. You look for the plot or the main thread of the argument and follow it through to the end. You let the author's mind lead yours. Whether or not you allow yourself to "dip" before settling down to absorb the book, you know that you will not have understood it till you have read it from start to finish. If it is a book that you want to master, you set aside time for a careful, unhurried journey through it.

But when we come to Holy Scripture, our behavior is different. To start with, we are not in the habit of treating it as a book—a unit—at all; we approach it simply as a collection of separate stories and sayings. We take it for granted that these items represent either moral advice or comfort for those in trouble. So we read the Bible in small doses, a few verses at a time. We do not go through individual books, let alone the two Testaments, as a single whole. We browse through the rich old Jacobean periods of the King James Version or the informalities of the *New Living Translation,* waiting for something to strike us. When the words bring a soothing thought or a pleasant picture, we believe the Bible has done its job. We have come to view the Bible not as a book, but as a collection of beautiful and suggestive snippets, and it is as such that we use it. The result is that, in the ordinary sense of "read," we never read the Bible at all. We take it for granted that we are handling Holy Writ in the truly religious way, but this use of it is in fact merely superstitious. It is, I grant, the way of natural religiosity. But it is not the way of true religion.

God does not intend Bible reading to function simply as a drug for fretful minds. The reading of Scripture is intended to awaken our minds, not to send them to sleep. God asks us to approach Scripture as his *Word*—a message addressed to rational creatures, people with minds, a message we cannot expect to understand without thinking about it. "Come now, and let us reason together," said God to Judah through Isaiah (Isa. 1:18 KJV), and he says the same to us every time we take up his book. He has taught us to pray for divine enlightenment as we read. "Open thou mine eyes, that I may behold wondrous things out of thy law" (Ps. 119:18 KJV). This is a prayer for God to give us insight as we think about his Word. But we effectively prevent God from answering this prayer if after praying we blank out and stop thinking as we read.

God wants us to read the Bible as a *book*—a single story with a single theme. I am not forgetting that the Bible consists of many separate units (sixty-six to be exact) and that some of those units are themselves composites (such as the Psalter, which consists of 150 separate prayers and hymns). For all that, however, the Bible comes to us as the product of a single mind, the mind of God. It proves its unity over and over again by the amazing way it links together, one part throwing light on another part. So we should read it as a whole. And as we read, we are to ask: What is the plot of this book? What is its subject? What is it about? Unless we ask these questions, we will never see what it is saying to us about our lives.

When we reach this point, we shall find that God's message to us is more drastic and at the same time more heartening than any that human religiosity could conceive.

THE MAIN THEME

What do we find when we read the Bible as a single, unified whole, with our minds alert to observe its real focus?

We find just this: The Bible is not primarily about man at all. Its subject is God. He (if the phrase may be allowed) is the chief actor in the drama, the hero of the story. The Bible is a factual survey of his work in this world—past, present, and future, with explanatory comments from prophets, psalmists, wise men, and apostles. Its main theme is not human salvation, but the work of God vindicating his purposes and glorifying himself in a sinful and disordered cosmos. He does this by establishing his kingdom and exalting his Son, by creating a people to worship and serve him, and ultimately by dismantling and reassembling this order of things, thereby rooting sin out of his world.

It is into this larger perspective that the Bible fits God's work of saving men and women. It depicts God as more than a distant cosmic architect, or a ubiquitous heavenly uncle, or an impersonal life-force. God is more than any of the petty substitute deities that inhabit our twentieth-century minds. He is the living God, present and active everywhere, "glorious in holiness, fearful in praises, doing wonders" (Exod. 15:11 KJV). He gives himself a name—Yahweh (Jehovah: see Exod. 3:14-15; 6:2-3), which, whether it be translated "I am that I am" or "I will be that I will be" (the Hebrew means both), is a proclamation of his self-existence and self-sufficiency, his omnipotence and his unbounded freedom.

This world is his, he made it, and he controls it. He works "all things after the counsel of his own will" (Eph. 1:11 KJV). His knowledge and dominion extend to the smallest things: "The very hairs of your head are all numbered" (Matt. 10:30). "The Lord reigns"—the psalmists make this unchangeable truth the starting point for their praises again and again (see Ps. 93:1; 96:10; 97:1; 99:1). Though hostile forces rage and chaos threatens, God is King. Therefore his people are safe.

Such is the God of the Bible. And the Bible's dominant conviction about him, a conviction proclaimed from Genesis to Revelation, is that behind and beneath all the apparent confusion of this world lies his plan. That plan concerns the perfecting of a people and the restoring of a world through the mediating action of Jesus Christ. God governs human affairs with this end in view. Human history is a record of the outworking of his purposes. History is in truth his story.

The Bible details the stages in God's plan. God visited Abraham, led him into Canaan, and entered into a covenant relationship with him and his descendants—"an everlasting covenant between me and you and your descendants after you for the generations to come, to be your God and the God of your descendants after you. . . . I will be their God" (Gen. 17:7ff.). He gave Abraham a son. He turned Abraham's family into a nation and led them out of Egypt into a land of their own. Over the centuries he prepared them and the Gentile world for the coming of the Savior-King, "who verily was foreordained before the foundation of the world, but was manifest in these last times for you, who by him do believe in God" (1 Pet. 1:20ff. KJV).

At last, "when the fullness of the time was come, God sent forth his Son, made of a woman, made under the law, to redeem them that were under the law, that we might receive the adoption of sons" (Gal. 4:4ff. KJV). The covenant promise to Abraham's seed is now fulfilled to all who put faith in Christ: "If you are Christ's, then you are Abraham's seed, and heirs according to the promise" (Gal. 3:29 NKJV).

The plan for this age is that this Gospel should be known throughout the world, and "a great multitude . . . of all nations, and kindreds, and people, and tongues" (Rev. 7:9 KJV) be brought to faith in Christ; after which, at Christ's return, heaven and earth will in some unimaginable way be remade. Then, where "the throne of God and of the Lamb" is, there "his servants will serve him. They will see his face . . . and they will reign for ever and ever" (Rev. 22:3-5).

This is the plan of God, says the Bible. It cannot be thwarted by human sin, because God made a way for human sin itself to be a part of the plan, and defiance of God's revealed will is used by God for the furtherance of his will. Joseph's brothers, for instance, sold him into Egypt. "You thought evil against me," observed Joseph afterwards, "but God meant it for good . . . to save much people alive" (Gen. 50:20 KJV); "So it was not you that sent me hither, but God" (Gen. 45:8 KJV). The cross of Christ itself is the supreme illustration of this principle.

"Him, being delivered by the determinate counsel and foreknowledge of God," said Peter in his Pentecost sermon, "ye . . . by wicked hands have crucified and slain" (Acts 2:23 KJV). At Calvary God overruled Israel's sin, which he foresaw, as a means to the salvation of the world. Thus it appears that man's lawlessness does not thwart God's plan for his people's redemption; rather, through the wisdom of omnipotence, it has become the means of fulfilling that plan.

ACCEPTING THE PLAN

This, then, is the God of the Bible—a God who reigns, who is master of events, and who works out through the stumbling service of his people and the impudence of his foes his eternal purpose for his world. Now we begin to see what the Bible has to say to our generation that feels so utterly lost and bedeviled in an inscrutably hostile order of events. There is a plan, says the Bible. There is sense in circumstances, but you have missed it.

Turn to Christ. Seek God. Give yourself to the fulfillment of his plan, and you will have found the elusive key to living. "Whoever follows me," Christ promises, "will never walk in darkness, but will have the light of life" (John 8:12). You will have a motive: God's glory. You will have a rule: God's law. You will have a friend in life and death: God's Son. You will have found the answer to the doubting and despair triggered by the apparent meaninglessness, even malice, of circumstances: You will know that "the Lord reigns," and that "in all things God works for the good of those who love him, who have been called according to his purpose" (Rom. 8:28). And you will have peace.

The alternative? We may defy and reject God's plan, but we cannot escape it. For one element in his plan is the judgment of sin. Those who reject the gospel offer of life through Christ bring upon themselves a dark eternity. Those who choose to be without God shall have what they choose: God respects our choice. This also is part of the plan. God's will is done no less in the condemnation of unbelievers than in the salvation of those who put faith in the Lord Jesus.

Such are the outlines of God's plan, the central message about God that the Bible brings us. Its exhortation to us is that of Eliphaz to Job:

"Now acquaint yourself with Him, and be at peace; thereby good will come to you" (Job 22:21 NKJV). Since we know that "the Lord reigns," working out his plan for his world without hindrance, we can begin to appreciate both the wisdom of this advice and the glory that lies hidden in this promise.

"ALL THINGS FOR GOOD"?

"The Lord reigns." This, we now see, is the first fundamental truth we must face. The Creator is King in his universe. God "works all things after the counsel of his own will" (Eph. 1:11 KJV). The decisive factor in world history, the purpose that controls it and the key that interprets it, is God's eternal plan. The sovereign lordship of God is the basis of the biblical message and the foundation fact of Christian faith, and we have noted that on it is built the great assurance that "all things work together for good to them that love God." If this is so, it is marvelously good news.

But can this assurance stand? The claim it makes raises problems for sensitive and thoughtful souls at many points. It does not admit of rational demonstration, and circumstances on occasion prompt painful doubts. Some of the things that happen to Christians in particular hurt and bewilder us. How can these misfortunes, these frustrations, these apparent setbacks to God's cause, be any part of his will? In response to these things, we find ourselves inclined to deny either the reality of God's government or the perfect goodness of the God who governs. To draw either conclusion would be easy—but it would also be false. When we are tempted to do this, we should stop and ask ourselves certain questions.

THE SECRET THINGS

Ought we to be surprised when we find ourselves baffled by what God is doing? No! We must not forget who we are. We are not gods; we are creatures, and no more than creatures. As creatures, we have no right or reason to expect that at every point we shall be able to comprehend the wisdom of our Creator. He himself has reminded us: "My thoughts are not your thoughts. . . . As the heavens are higher than the earth, so are . . . my thoughts than your thoughts" (Isa. 55:8-9 NKJV). Furthermore, the King has made it clear to us that it is not his pleasure to disclose all the details of his policy to his human subjects. As Moses declared when he had finished expounding to Israel what God had revealed of his will for them: "The secret things belong unto the LORD our God: but those things which are revealed belong unto us . . . that we may do all the words of this law" (Deut. 29:29 KJV).

The principle illustrated here is that God has disclosed his mind and will, so far as we need to know them for practical purposes, and we are to take what he has disclosed as a complete and adequate rule for our faith and life. But there still remain "secret things" that he has not made known and that, in this life at least, he does not intend us to discover. And the reasons behind God's providential dealings sometimes fall into this category.

Job's case illustrates this. Job was never told about the challenge God met by allowing Satan to plague his servant. All Job knew was that the omnipotent God was morally perfect and that it would be blasphemously false to deny his goodness under any circumstances. He refused to "curse God" even when his livelihood, his children, and his health had been taken from him (Job 2:9-10). Fundamentally he maintained this refusal to the end, though the well-meant platitudes that his smug friends churned out at him drove him almost crazy and at times forced out of him wild words about God (for which he later repented). Though not without struggle, Job held fast his integrity throughout the time of testing and maintained his confidence in God's goodness.

Job's confidence was vindicated. For when the time of testing ended, after God had come to Job in mercy to renew his humility (40:1-5; 42:1-6) and Job had obediently prayed for his three maddening friends, "the LORD gave Job twice as much as he had before" (42:10 KJV). "You have heard of the perseverance of Job," writes James, "and seen the end intended by the Lord—that the Lord is very compassionate and merciful" (James 5:11 NKJV). Did the bewildering series of catastrophes that overtook Job mean that God had abdicated his throne or abandoned his servant? Not at all, as Job proved by experience. But the reason God had plunged him into darkness was never revealed to him. Now may not God, for wise purposes of his own, treat others of his followers as he treated Job?

But there is more to be said than that. There is a second question to ask.

Has God left us entirely in the dark as to what he is doing in his providential government of the world? No! He has given us full information as to the central purpose that he is executing and a positive rationale for the trying experiences of Christians.

What is God doing? He is "bringing many sons unto glory" (Heb. 2:10 KJV). He is saving a great company of sinners. He has been engaged in this task since history began. He spent many centuries preparing a people and a setting of world history for the coming of his Son. Then he sent his Son into the world in order that there might be a Gospel, and now he sends his Gospel through the world in order that there may be a church. He has exalted his Son to the throne of the universe, and Christ from his throne now invites sinners to himself, keeps them, leads them, and finally brings them to be with him in his glory.

God is saving men and women through his Son. First he justifies and adopts them into his family for Christ's sake as soon as they believe, and thus restores the relationship between them and himself that sin had broken. Then, within that restored relationship, God continually works in and upon them to renew them in the image of Christ, so that the family likeness (if the phrase may be allowed) shall appear in them more and more. It is this renewal of ourselves, progressive here and to be perfected hereafter, that Paul identifies with the "good" for which "all things work together . . . to them that love God . . . the called according to his purpose" (Rom. 8:28 KJV). God's purpose, as Paul explains, is that those whom God has chosen and in love has called to himself should "be conformed to the likeness of his Son, that he [the Son] might be the firstborn among many brothers" (Rom. 8:28-29). All God's ordering of circumstances, Paul tells us, is designed for the fulfillment of this purpose. The "good" for which all things work is not the immediate ease and comfort of God's children (as is, one fears, too often supposed), but their ultimate holiness and conformity to the likeness of Christ.

Does this help us to understand how adverse circumstances may find a place in God's plan for his people? Certainly! It throws a flood of light upon the problem, as the writer to the Hebrews demonstrates. To Christians who had grown disheartened and apathetic under the pressure of constant hardship and victimization, we find him writing: "Have you forgotten the exhortation which addresses you as sons?— 'My son, do not regard lightly the discipline of the Lord, nor lose courage when you are punished [better, *reproved*, RV] by him. For the Lord disciplines him whom he loves, and chastises every son whom he receives.' It is for discipline that you have to endure. God is treating you as sons; for what son is there whom his father does not discipline? . . . We have had earthly fathers to discipline us and we respected them. Shall we not much more be subject to the Father of spirits and live? . . . He disciplines us *for our good, that we may share his holiness.* For the moment all discipline seems painful rather than pleasant; later it yields the peaceful fruit of righteousness to those who have been trained by it" (Heb. 12:5-11 RSV, quoting Prov. 3:11-12, emphasis added).

It is striking to see how this writer, like Paul, equates the Christian's "good," not with ease and quiet, but with sanctification. The passage is so plain that it needs no comment, only frequent rereading whenever we find it hard to believe that the rough handling that circumstances (or our fellow Christians) are giving us can possibly be God's will.

THE PURPOSE OF IT ALL

However, there is still more to be said. A third question we should ask ourselves is: What is God's ultimate end in his dealings with his children? Is it simply their happiness, or is it something more? The Bible indicates that it is the glory of God himself.

God's end in all his acts is ultimately himself. There is nothing morally dubious about this. If we say that man can have no higher end than the glory of God, how can we say anything different about God himself? The idea that it is somehow unworthy to represent God as aiming at his own glory in all that he does reflects a failure to remember that God and man are not on the same level. It shows lack of realization that, while sinful man makes his own well-being his ultimate end at the expense of his fellow creatures, our gracious God has determined to glorify himself by blessing his people. His end in redeeming man, we are told, is "the praise of his glory" (Eph. 1:6, 12, 14). He wills to display his resources of mercy (the "riches" of his grace and of his glory—"glory" being the sum of his attributes and powers as he reveals them: Eph. 2:17; 3:16) in bringing his saints to their ultimate happiness in the enjoyment of himself.

But how does this truth, that God seeks his own glory in all his dealings with us, bear on the problem of providence? In this way: It gives us insight into the way in which God saves us, suggesting to us the reason why he does not take us to heaven the moment we believe. We now see that he leaves us in a world of sin to be tried, tested, belabored by troubles that threaten to crush us—in order that we may glorify him by our patience under suffering and in order that he may display the riches of his grace and call forth new praises from us as he constantly upholds and delivers us. Psalm 107 is a majestic declaration of this truth.

Is it a hard saying? Not to those who have learned that their chief end in this world is to "glorify God and [in doing so] to enjoy him forever." The heart of true religion is to glorify God by patient endurance and to praise him for his gracious deliverances. It is to live one's life through smooth and rough places alike in sustained obedience and thanksgiving for mercy received. It is to seek and find one's deepest joy, not in spiritual lotus-eating, but in discovering through each successive storm and conflict the mighty adequacy of Christ to save. It is the sure knowledge that God's way is best, both for our own welfare and for his glory. No problems of providence will shake the faith of the one who has truly learned this.

THE GLORY OF GOD

The crucial fact we need to grasp, then, is that God the Creator rules his world for his own glory. "To him are all things" (Rom. 11:36); he himself is the end of all his works. He does not exist for our sake, but we for his. It is the nature and prerogative of God to please himself, and his revealed good pleasure is to make himself great in our eyes.

"Be still," he says to us, "and know that I am God: I will be exalted among the heathen, I will be exalted in the earth" (Ps. 46:10 KJV). God's overriding goal is to glorify himself.

Or is it? Because the claim is so crucial and is so often found offensive and dismissed, I want now to sharpen the focus on it and spell it out more fully. Once this concept is clear in our minds beyond any shadow of doubt, everything else in Christianity will fall into place and make sense. However, as long as we are uncertain about it, the rest of the biblical faith will set us constant problems. Look again, then, at the thing that is being said here about the Maker of us all.

Its reasonableness. That God aims always to glorify himself is an assertion we at first find hard to believe. Our immediate reaction is an uncomfortable feeling that such an idea is unworthy of God, that self-concern of any sort is incompatible with moral perfection and in particular with God's nature as love. Many sensitive and morally cultured people are shocked by the thought that God's ultimate end is his own glory, and they strongly oppose such a concept. To them, it depicts God as essentially no different from an evil man or even the devil himself! To them it is an immoral and outrageous doctrine, and if the Bible teaches it, so much the worse for the Bible! They often draw this conclusion explicitly with regard to the Old Testament. A volume, they say, that depicts God so persistently as a "jealous" Being, concerned first and foremost about his "honor," cannot be regarded as divine truth. God is not like that. It is blasphemy, real even if unintentional, to think that he is! Since these convictions are widely and strongly held, it is important to consider what validity, if any, they have.

We begin by asking: Why are these convictions asserted with so much heat? On other theological matters people can disagree calmly enough. But protests against the doctrine that God's chief end is his glory are made with passion and often angry rhetoric. The answer is not difficult to see, and it does credit to the moral earnestness of the speakers. These people are sensitive to the sinfulness of continual self-seeking. They know that the desire to gratify self is at the root of moral weaknesses and shortcomings. They are themselves trying as best they can to face and fight this desire. Hence they conclude that for God to be self-centered would be equally wrong. The vehemence with which they reject the idea that the holy God would exalt himself reflects their acute sense of the guiltiness of human self-absorption.

Is their conclusion valid? We repeat: It is in fact a complete mistake. If it is right for man to have the glory of God as his goal, can it be wrong for God to have the same goal? If man can have no higher purpose than God's glory, how can God? If it is wrong for man to seek a lesser end than this, it would be wrong for God, too. The reason it cannot be right for man to live for himself, as if he were God, is because he is not God. However, it cannot be wrong for God to seek his own glory, simply because he is God. Those who insist that God should not seek his glory in all things are really asking that he cease to be God. And there is no greater blasphemy than to will that.

If the objectors' line of reasoning is so clearly false, why do so many today believe it? The plausibility of the argument derives from our habit of making God in our image and thinking of him as if he and we stood on the same level. In other words, his obligations to us and ours to him correspond—as if he were bound to serve us and further our well-being with the same selflessness with which we are obligated to serve him. This is, in effect, to think of God as if he were a man, albeit a great one. If this way of thinking were right, then for God to seek his own glory in everything would indeed make him comparable to the worst of men and to Satan himself.

But our Maker is not a man, not even an omnipotent superman, and this way of thinking of him is gross idolatry. (You do not have to make a graven image picturing God as a man to be an idolater; a false mental image is all that is needed to break the Second Commandment.) We must not imagine, then, that the obligations that bind us creatures to him, bind him as Creator equally to us. Dependence is a one-way relationship and carries with it one-way obligations. Children, for instance, ought to obey their parents—not vice versa! Our dependence upon our Creator binds us to seek his glory without committing him to seek ours. For us to glorify him is a duty; for him to bless us is grace. The only thing that God is bound to do is the very thing that he requires of us—to glorify himself.

We conclude, then, that it is the reverse of blasphemy to speak of God as self-centered; on the contrary, not to do so would be irreligious.

It is the glory of God to make all things for himself and to use them as a means for his exaltation. The clearheaded Christian will insist on this. He also will insist that it is the glory of man that he is privileged to function as a means to this end. There can be no greater glory for man than to glorify God. "Man's chief end is to glorify God"—and it is in so doing that man finds true dignity for himself.

The humanist, who believes man is at his noblest and most god-like when he has thrown off the shackles of religion, will say that we rob human life of all real worth by asserting that man is no more than a means to God's glory. The truth, however, is the opposite. Life without God has no real worth; it is a mere monstrosity. When we say that human beings are no more than a means to God's glory, we also say that they are no less than that—thus showing how life can have meaning and value. The only person in this world who enjoys complete contentment is the person who knows that the only worthwhile and satisfying life is to be a means, however humble, to God's chief end—his own glory and praise. The way to be truly happy is by being truly human, and the way to be truly human is to be truly godly.

Its meaning. But what does it mean to say that God's chief end is his glory? To many of us the phrase "the glory of God" is rather empty. What significance does Scripture give it?

In the Old Testament the word translated "glory" originally expressed the idea of weight. Glory came to be applied to any characteristic of a person that makes him "weighty" in other people's eyes and prompts them to honor and respect him. Jacob's gains and Joseph's wealth are called "glory" (Gen. 31:1; 45:13). Then the word was extended to mean honor and respect itself.

Accordingly, the Bible uses glory with reference to God in a double connection. On the one hand, it speaks of the glory that belongs to God—the divine splendor and majesty attached to all God's revelations of himself. On the other hand, it speaks of glory that is given to God—the honor and blessing, praise and worship that God has a right to receive, the only fit response to his holy presence. Ezekiel 43:2ff. reflects the link here: "The glory of the God of Israel came . . . and I fell upon my face." The term *glory* thus connects the thoughts of God's praiseworthiness—the majesty of his power and presence—and of the worship that is the right response when God stands before us and we before him.

Take these two thoughts separately for a moment.

In revelation God shows us his glory. *Glory* means deity in manifestation. Creation reveals him. "The heavens are telling the glory of God" (Ps. 19:1). "The whole earth is full of his glory" (Isa. 6:3). In Bible times God disclosed his presence by means of theophanies, which were termed his "glory" (the shining cloud in the tabernacle and temple, Exod. 40:34, 1 Kings 8:10ff.; Ezekiel's vision of the throne and the wheels, Ezek. 1:28; etc.). Believers now behold his glory fully and finally displayed "in the face of Jesus Christ" (2 Cor. 4:6). Wherever we see God in action, there we see his glory. He presents himself before us as holy and adorable, summoning us to bow down and worship.

We give God glory. We do this by all our responses to his revelation of grace:

1. By worship and praise. "Whoso offereth praise glorifieth me" (Ps. 50:23 KJV); "Give to the LORD the glory due His name" (Ps. 96:8 NKJV); "Glorify God for his mercy" (Rom. 15:9 KJV).

2. By believing his word. "Thy word is true" (Ps. 119:160 KJV); "Thy words are true" (2 Sam. 7:28 RSV).

3. By trusting his promises (that was how Abraham gave glory to God, Rom. 4:20ff.).

4. By confessing Christ as Lord, "to the glory of God the Father" (Phil. 2:11).

5. By obeying God's law. "The fruits of righteousness" are to "the glory and praise of God" (Phil. 1:11).

6. By bowing to his just condemnation of our sins (so Achan gave God glory, Josh. 7:19ff.).

7. By seeking to make him great (which means making self small) in our daily lives.

Now we can see the meaning of the statement that God's chief end is his glory. It means that his unchanging purpose is to display to his rational creatures the glory of his wisdom, power, truth, justice, and love so that they come to know him and, knowing him, to give him glory for all eternity by love and loyalty, worship and praise, trust and obedience. The kind of fellowship that he intends to create between us and him is a relationship in which he gives of his fullest riches, and we give of our heartiest thanks—both to the highest degree. When he declares himself to be a "jealous" God and proclaims: "My glory will I not give to another" (Isa. 42:8 KJV; 48:11), his concern is to safeguard the purity and richness of this relationship. Such is the goal of God.

All God's works are a means to this end. The only answer that the Bible gives to questions that begin: "Why did God . . . ?" is: "For his own glory." It was for this that God decreed to create and for this he willed to permit sin. He could have kept man from transgression. He could have barred Satan from the garden or confirmed Adam so that he became incapable of sinning (as he will do to the redeemed in heaven). But he did not. Why? For his own glory. It is often said that nothing in God is so glorious as his redeeming love—the mercy that wins back transgressors through the bloodshed of God's own Son. But there would be no revelation of redeeming love had sin not been permitted first.

Again, why did God choose to redeem? He need not have done so. He was not bound to take action to save us. His love for sinners, his resolve to give his Son for them, was a free choice that he did not have to make. Why did he choose to love and redeem the unlovely? The Bible tells us: "To the praise of the glory of his grace . . . to the praise of his glory . . ." (Eph. 1:6, 12, 14 KJV).

We see the same purpose determining point after point in the plan of salvation. Some he elects to life; others he leaves under merited judgment, "choosing to show his wrath and make his power known . . . to make the riches of his glory known to the objects of his mercy . . ." (Rom. 9:22ff.). He chooses to make up the bulk of his church from the riff-raff of the world—persons who are "foolish . . . weak . . . base . . . despised." Why? "That no flesh should glory in His presence. . . . that, as it is written, 'He who glories, let him glory in the LORD'" (1 Cor. 1:29-31 NKJV). Why does God not root indwelling sin out of his saints in the first moment of their Christian life, as he will do the moment they die? Why, instead, does he carry on their sanctification with a painful slowness so that all their lives they are troubled by sin and never reach the perfection they desire? Why is it his custom to give them a hard passage through this world?

The answer is again that he does all this for his glory—to expose to us our own weakness and impotence so that we may learn to depend upon his grace and the limitless resources of his saving power. "We have this treasure in earthen vessels," wrote Paul, "that the excellency of the power may be of God, and not of us" (2 Cor. 4:7 KJV). Once for all, let us rid our minds of the idea that things are as they are because God cannot help it. God "worketh all things after the counsel of his own will" (Eph. 1:11 KJV), and all things are as they are because God has chosen that they should be, and the reason for his choice in every case is his glory.

THE GODLY MAN

Let us now define what godliness is. We can say at once that it is not simply a matter of externals but a matter of the heart; and it is not a natural growth, but a supernatural gift; and it is found only in those who have admitted their sin, who have sought and found Christ, who have been born again, who have repented. But this is only to circumscribe and locate godliness. Our question is: What essentially is godliness? Here is the answer: It is the quality of life that exists in those who seek to glorify God.

The godly person does not object to the thought that one's highest vocation is to be a means to God's glory. Rather, he or she finds it a source of great satisfaction and contentment. His ambition is to follow the great formula in which Paul summed up the practice of Christianity—"glorify God in your body. . . . Whether therefore ye eat, or drink, or whatsoever ye do, do all to the glory of God" (1 Cor. 6:20 KJV; 10:31). The dearest wish of the godly is to exalt God with all that they are, in all that they do. They follow in the footsteps of Jesus their Lord, who affirmed to his Father at the end of his life here: "I have glorified thee on the earth" (John 17:4 KJV), and who told the Jews: "I honor my Father . . . I seek not mine own glory" (John 8:49ff. KJV). They think of themselves in the manner of George Whitefield the evangelist, who said: "Let the name of Whitefield perish, so long as God is glorified."

Like God himself, the godly are supremely jealous that God, and only God, should be honored. This jealousy is a part of the image of God in which they have been renewed. There is now a doxology written on their hearts, and they are never so truly themselves as when they are praising God for the glorious things that God has already done and pleading with him to glorify himself yet further. We may say that it is by their prayers that they are known—to God, if not to men. "What a man is alone on his knees before God," said Robert Murray M'Cheyne, "that he is, and no more."

In this case, however, we should say, "and no less." For secret prayer is the veritable mainspring of the godly person's life. When we speak of prayer, we are not referring to the prim, proper, stereotyped, self-regarding formalities that sometimes pass for the real thing. The godly do not play at prayer. Their hearts are in it. Prayer to them is their chief work. Their prayer is consistently the expression of their strongest and most constant desire—"Be thou exalted, LORD, in thine own strength. Be thou exalted, O God, above the heavens. . . . Father, glorify thy name. . . . Hallowed be thy name" (Ps. 21:13; Ps. 57:5; John 12:28; Matt. 6:9 KJV). By this God knows his saints, and by this we may know ourselves.

3

MEETING GOD

The Basic Christian Relationship

A young lady asked a friend of mine, "Did you ever meet C. S. Lewis?"

"Yes," replied my friend. "As a matter of fact, I had quite a bit to do with him."

The young lady stood silent for a moment and then shyly said, "May I touch you?"

As Humpty-Dumpty said to Alice, "There's glory for you!" To have met C. S. Lewis—wow! But, as Lewis would have been the first and my friend the second to point out, a far greater thing than meeting C. S. Lewis is meeting God.

Someday we shall all meet God. We shall find ourselves standing before him for judgment. Should we leave this world unforgiven, it will be a dire event. There is, however, a way of meeting God on earth that removes all terror from the prospect of that future meeting. It is possible for imperfect people like ourselves to live and die in the knowledge that our guilt has gone and that love—both God's love for us and our love for him—has already established a joyful togetherness that nothing can destroy. The mode of meeting that introduces us to this great grace, however, often has traumatic beginnings. It was so for Isaiah, as we shortly shall see.

Who may claim that they have met God? Certainly not those who resolutely deny his reality or his knowability, nor those who go no further than acknowledging that there is "Somebody up there." The simple answer is that we meet God as a loving heavenly Father through coming to recognize his Son, Jesus Christ, as the Way, the Truth, and the Life. We meet God through entering into a relationship both of dependence on Jesus as our Savior and Friend and of discipleship to him as our Lord and Master.

The exposition of this answer obliges us to say that no one meets God—no one meets Christ—until Isaiah's watershed experience begins to become reality in one's life. Isaiah 6 is thus not only of historic interest as a great man's account of what set the direction of his own ministry. The passage is significant for everyone. Its contents serve as a checklist of the conscious perceptions that indicate whether we have truly met God or not. We need to understand what Isaiah learned through his vision.

He saw the vision in the temple. What was he doing there? The answer is provided by the opening phrase of the first verse of chapter 6: "In the year that King Uzziah died." Uzziah had reigned fifty-two years, but now he had either just died or was about to die, and this was a traumatic event for Judah to face. Judah was under political pressure. Powerful enemies, namely the resurgent Assyrians, lived just over the border. There was anxiety about the future. Trauma of any kind drives people to prayer, and it is natural to suppose that Isaiah was in the temple to pray about the future of his people.

The fact that this is chapter 6 of the prophecy, not chapter 1 where Isaiah tells us that the word of the Lord came to him during Uzziah's reign as well as the reigns that followed (see 1:1), suggests that he was an active prophet already. Possibly it was his desire to know what his message to the people was now to be that had led him into the temple on this occasion. Though that cannot be proved, it seems likely and will be assumed in what follows.

Uzziah, as 2 Chronicles emphasizes (see 26:8, 15-16), had been a strong king, under whom Judah had enjoyed safety and prosperity. Now the kingdom was to pass to his son Jotham, who was in his mid-twenties. No one knew what sort of a king Jotham would make. For this reason also all of Judah, Isaiah included, must have felt anxiety about national well-being. When Isaiah entered the temple, that was the big thing on his mind. But God showed himself to Isaiah in a manner that forced the prophet to think about himself and his own relationship to God in a way that he had never done before.

We too often think of God as simply there to help us. We seek gifts and strength from God to cope with external pressures when the real need is to have our distorted relationship with him set straight. It is mercy on God's part when he cracks through our attempts to harness him to our purposes and compels us to put first things first. But such mercy can have a fearsome aspect, as Isaiah discovered.

Isaiah was shown a vision of God's *holiness*. He saw the Lord on his throne, so he tells us, and the angels worshiping him as they hovered before the throne. They called to one another: "Holy, holy, holy, is the LORD of hosts; the whole earth is full of his glory" (6:3 RSV). Like all repetition in the Bible, the threefold "holy" is for rising emphasis.

What was being conveyed to Isaiah by what he saw and heard? If you look up *holy* in a dictionary of theology, you find that in both Testaments it is a word that applies primarily to God and expresses everything that sets him apart from us, making him different; everything that sets him above us, making him worshipful and awesome; and everything that sets him against us, making him an object of actual terror. The basic thought that the word carries is of God's separateness from us and of the contrast between what he is and what we are. If you think of holiness as a circle embracing everything about God that is different from what we are, the center of the circle is God's moral and spiritual purity, which contrasts painfully with our twisted sinfulness. It was just this contrast that Isaiah perceived.

A bad hymn (by the Anglican, Bishop Mant) starts thus:

> *Bright the vision that delighted*
> *Once the sight of Judah's seer,*
> *Sweet the countless tongues united*
> *To entrance the prophet's ear.*

As if Isaiah had been attending the Grand Ole Opry! The truth is that Isaiah found God's holiness terrible to contemplate. Facing it convinced him there was no hope for him with God because of his sin. But meantime the angels celebrated God's holiness in the widest sense of that word, bringing before Isaiah an awareness of God's "endless wisdom, boundless power" as well as his "awful purity" (I quote these words from Frederick W. Faber's hymn, "My God, How Wonderful Thou Art").

Focus now on God's holiness in its full and inclusive sense. As the spectrum of colors constitute light, a spectrum of distinct qualities combine to constitute holiness. Isaiah's narrative sets before us five realities about God in a blend for which holiness is the proper name.

Lordship—or to use a long word that theologians love, *sovereignty*—is the first of these realities. The English Bible puts it in short words: "The Lord reigns; God is King!" Isaiah saw a visual symbol of lordship: God seated on a throne. Other people in Scripture are on record as having been shown that same symbol. Ezekiel, for instance, saw God's throne coming at him out of a storm cloud, with living creatures acting as a kind of animated chariot for it and whirling wheels at all sorts of angles in relationship to each other below the seat, where you would have expected the legs of the throne to be. The living creatures and wheels were both emblems of endless energy; God on the throne is infinitely and eternally powerful. Ezekiel tells us that the throne was high above him, and huge, and his impression was that a figure like a man sat on it. (See Ezekiel 1.) So, too, the throne that Isaiah saw was high and huge; "the train of his [God's] robe filled the temple," he tells us, and the "holy place" of the temple was approximately sixty feet by thirty feet and forty-five feet high.

The vision of God as King, whether perceived visually or only with the mind's eye, recurs frequently in the Bible. Psalm after psalm proclaims that God reigns. John saw "a throne in heaven with someone sitting on it" (Rev. 4:2). And 1 Kings 22 tells us of Micaiah, the faithful prophet whom Ahab had imprisoned because he had threatened Ahab with God's judgment. At Jehoshaphat's urging Micaiah was brought from prison to answer the question that the two kings together were posing: Should Ahab, with Jehoshaphat's help, attempt to recapture Ramoth Gilead from the Syrians?

The scene into which Micaiah was led was an impressive one: "Dressed in their royal robes, the king of Israel and Jehoshaphat king of Judah were sitting on their thrones . . . with all the prophets [about

400] prophesying before them" (v. 10). It was a grand official occasion. No doubt an admiring crowd stood around watching all that went on. Micaiah, however, was not overawed. First he mocked Ahab by imitating the court prophets (v. 15) and then told him what really was true, that if he went to Ramoth Gilead he would die. The secret of Micaiah's boldness is in verse 19, where he declares: "I saw the LORD sitting on his throne." Therefore, Micaiah was not cowed when he saw Ahab and Jehoshaphat on their thrones in the gate of Samaria. The vision of God on the throne in heaven made plain who was in charge!

This realization of God's sovereign providence (for that is what it really is) is enormously strengthening. It strengthened Micaiah; it strengthened John; no doubt it strengthened Isaiah, too. To know that nothing happens in God's world apart from God's will may frighten the godless, but it stabilizes the saints. It assures them that God has everything worked out and that everything that happens has a meaning, whether or not we can see it at the time.

Peter reasoned about the cross this way in the first Christian evangelistic sermon, preached on Pentecost morning. "This man [Jesus] was handed over to you *by God's set purpose and foreknowledge;* and you, with the help of wicked men, put him to death . . . " (Acts 2:23, emphasis added). You did it of your own free will, says Peter. You are guilty of doing it and need to repent, but don't imagine that it happened apart from the will of God. Knowing that God is on the throne upholds one under pressure and in the face of bewilderment, pain, hostility, and events that appear not to make sense. It is a supportive truth for believers, and it is the first element or ingredient in the holiness of God.

Greatness is the second element. The vision was of God high and exalted, with the six-winged seraphs hovering before him in worship. Note their posture; the description has something to teach us. The two wings covering each angel's face is a gesture that expresses reverent restraint in God's presence. We should not pry into his secrets. We are to be content to live with what he has told us. Reverence excludes speculation about things that God has not mentioned in his Word. Augustine's reply to the man who asked him, "What was God doing before he made the world?" was, "Making hell for people who ask questions like that"—a sharp use of shock tactics to make the questioner see the irreverence behind his curiosity.

One of the attractive things (to me anyway) about John Calvin is his sensitivity to the mystery of God—that is, the reality of the unrevealed—and his unwillingness to go a step beyond what Scripture says. He and Augustine combine to assure us that we must be content not to know what Scripture does not tell us. When we reach the outer limits of what Scripture says, it is time to stop arguing and start worshiping. This is what the angels' covered faces teach us.

Two wings also covered each angel's feet. That expresses the spirit of self-effacement in God's presence, another aspect of true worship. Genuine worshipers want to blot themselves out of the picture, calling no attention to themselves, so that all can concentrate without distraction on God alone. A Christian communicator has to learn that he cannot present himself as a great preacher and teacher if he also wants to present God as a great God and Christ as a great Savior. There is a pair-of-scales effect here. Only as one's assertion of self sinks will God be exalted and become great in one's estimate. Self-effacing humility before God is the only way to uplift him—that is the lesson of the angels' covered feet.

Another aspect of the angels' posture was that each was hovering on two wings, as hummingbirds hover, ready to dart away—to go for God, to run his errands just as soon as the command was given. Such readiness also belongs to the spirit of true worship, worship that acknowledges the lordship and greatness of God.

Our worship, like the angels' worship, must include the elements of reverent restraint, self-effacement, and readiness to serve, or we shall really be diminishing God, losing sight of his greatness and bringing him down to our level. We must examine ourselves: Irreverence, self-assertion, and spiritual paralysis frequently disfigure our so-called worship. We must recover the sense of God's greatness that the angels expressed. We need to learn afresh that greatness is number two in the spectrum of qualities that make up the holiness of God.

Nearness, or in long words, omnipresence in manifestation, is the third element in God's holiness. "The whole earth is full of his glory" (v. 3). *Glory* means God's presence shown forth so that his nature and power are made evident. Nowhere can you escape the presence of God, and we, like Isaiah, must reckon with that fact. For those who love to be in God's presence, this is good news. It is bad news, however, for those who wish God could not see what they do.

Psalm 139 celebrates God's nearness and his exhaustive knowledge of who and what each believer is. It ends with a plea that God, the searcher of hearts, would show the psalmist any sin that was in him so that he might eliminate it. "Search me, O God . . . see if there is any offensive way in me, and lead me in the way everlasting" (vv. 23-24). Nothing goes unnoticed so far as God is concerned; all our "offensive ways" are evident to him however much we may try to hide them, shrug them off, or forget about them. This third aspect of God's holiness will be an uncomfortable truth to anyone who is not willing to pray the psalmist's prayer.

Purity is the fourth quality that contributes to God's holiness. "Your eyes are too pure to look on evil; you cannot tolerate wrong," says Habakkuk to God (1:13). Most people think of purity first when they hear of the holiness of God. What was said earlier about purity as the center of the circle shows that they are right to do so. Isaiah perceived this purity without a word being spoken. The sense of being defiled and unfit for God's fellowship overwhelmed him. "Woe to me!" Isaiah cried. "I am ruined! For I am a man of unclean lips, and I live among a people of unclean lips, and my eyes have seen the King, the LORD Almighty" (Isa. 6:5). Just as sin is rebellion against God's authority and brings guilt in relation to God as lawgiver and judge, so sin also is uncleanness in relation to God's purity. Isaiah felt unclean before God when he recognized his sin, as every God-centered person will. A sense of defilement before God is not morbid, neurotic, or unhealthy in any way. It is natural, realistic, healthy, and a true perception of our condition. We are sinners in fact. It is our wisdom to admit it.

"I am a man of unclean lips," says Isaiah. He is thinking of particular sins of speech. The Bible has much to say about such sins, for they reflect what is in a person's heart. "Out of the overflow of [a person's] heart his mouth speaks" (Luke 6:45). We can use God's gift of speech to express malice and cut others down. Some people gossip (a practice that has been defined as the art of confessing other people's sins). Others deceive, exploit, and betray people by sweet-talking and lying. We cheapen life by disgraceful, obscene, demeaning talk; we ruin relationships by thoughtless and irresponsible chatter. When Isaiah speaks of unclean lips, he says something that touches us all.

(Perhaps there is also a reference in these words to Isaiah's prophetic ministry. In delivering God's messages he may have been more concerned about his reputation as a preacher than about glorifying God. Unfortunately, this attitude—and the defilement it engenders—still exists. Christian communicators with murky motives have unclean lips.)

"And I live among a people of unclean lips," Isaiah continues. Presumably he is acknowledging that he has gone with the crowd, taken his cue from them, talked as they talked, been foulmouthed with others who were foulmouthed, and so been led astray by bad examples. He does not offer this as an excuse, however. To do what others do when, deep down, one knows it is wrong is moral cowardice, which does not lessen guilt but increases it. Isaiah's conformity to the unclean ways of the society around him made his guilt greater. Perhaps as a prophet and preacher he had up to this point thought of himself in a different category from his fellow Jews, as if the very act of denouncing their sins excluded him from guilt when he himself behaved the same way. Now he knew better. For the first time, perhaps, he saw himself as the hypocritical conformist he really was, and he expressed his shame. God's purity had made a moral realist out of him.

The fifth element in God's holiness is mercy—the purifying, purging mercy that Isaiah experienced when he confessed his sin. A seraph flew to him, sent by God to touch his lips with a live coal from the altar and to bring him God's message: "See, this has touched your lips; your guilt is taken away and your sin atoned for" (v. 7). The altar was the place of sacrifice. The coal pictures the application of sacrifice—in new covenant terms, the application to the guilty conscience of the shed blood of Jesus Christ. The initial application is to the place of conscious guilt. Isaiah felt most keenly his sins of speech; therefore, his lips were touched. But, just as true conviction of sin is conviction of sinfulness everywhere as well as of particular wrongdoing, so the angel's words meant that all Isaiah's sin—known and unknown—was atoned for (literally, taken out of God's sight). The initiative here was God's, as it always is when people come to know his grace. P. T. Forsyth used to insist that the simplest, truest, profoundest notion of God's nature is holy love, the mercy that saves us from our sin, not by ignoring it but by judging it in the person of Jesus Christ and so justifying us justly. Isaiah would undoubtedly have agreed.

Church and society today play games. We do not acknowledge God's true nature. We do not meet and deal with him as he is. Even Christian workers can fail to grasp, or can lose touch with, the holiness of God, just as it seems Isaiah did long ago. When this happens, we, too, have to undergo the traumatic adjustment that Isaiah's temple experience brought him. Reading the story from Isaiah's standpoint, we see him making no less than four mistakes. Note them; they could be yours, too.

Mistake number one, made when he entered the temple, was to think of God as tame—there to be managed and controlled and called into action at Isaiah's request, like the genie of Aladdin's wonderful lamp. It is fair to suppose that God gave Isaiah the vision of angelic worship because he needed to learn to worship. Anyone for whom God is like Father Christmas, there simply to give presents; or like P. G. Wodehouse's Jeeves, there simply to help the young master out of trouble; or like an insurance policy or safety net, there simply to prevent one from being hurt too much, still needs to learn to worship. Isaiah, one supposes, had gone to the temple to pray in the way many today seem to do: "God, we need you to do your safety net thing for us again. All right?" To a tame deity who makes no claim on people it might make sense to say, in this fashion, "My will be done"; but Isaiah had to learn that it makes no sense to talk that way to Israel's mighty Lord.

Mistake number two was to think he was accepted—that as a prophet there could be no problem in his own personal relationship to God. He was, after all, a distinguished young man, highborn and very gifted, in a nation that was officially in covenant with God. Also he was religiously inclined, a regular worshiper at the temple, and involved in ministry. Was he not doing God a favor by thus pursuing his religious interests? What problem could God have with him? Many in our society think in similar terms. They believe they do God a favor by being interested in him in a world where so few care about him. They expect thereby to become a spiritual elite who can count on God's favor. Isaiah had to learn that something needed to happen to him before he could be accepted into God's fellowship and favor. We today have to learn the same lesson.

Mistake number three was for Isaiah to think, when he realized something of God's holiness, that not only was he outside the realm of God's friendship because of his sin (that was true), but that he was eternally lost. "Woe to me. I am ruined!" Finding that his supposed righteousness was as filthy rags, he despaired. But again he was wrong; there was mercy for him. Great as his sin was (there are no small sins against a great God), God's grace was greater. God cleansed his sin, both that of which he was aware at the time and that which he would spend the rest of his life discovering. In the same way, for the Christian all sin, known and unknown, all acts and habits of sin, and all the ramifications of sinfulness in our spiritual system, is atoned for by the death of our Lord Jesus Christ. Holy love overcomes the power of sin to condemn and ruin our souls.

Isaiah appreciated what had happened to him. His attitude changed as his conscience was cleansed. In gratitude and joy he volunteered to go for God as the angels do, as indeed the angel who brought the word of pardon to him had done. All who know themselves to be forgiven sinners, people whom grace has found when they thought themselves lost, feel the same gratitude. Isaiah's "Here am I. Send me!" will strike an echo in their hearts.

Isaiah's fourth error was to count on success in God's service. He knew, I suppose, the greatness of his natural gift of eloquence. He knew something of the power of his position as a coming young man in Israel's high society. No doubt he took it for granted that when he resumed his influential position—a new man with a new joy walking in the power of a new experience of God—he would be noticed and admired, and his ministry would bear much fruit.

I infer that Isaiah was thinking in these terms because the first divine words to him after his volunteering were a warning that his mission was not going to be conspicuously successful at all. God said, "Go and tell this people: 'Be ever hearing, but never understanding. . . .' Make the heart of this people calloused; make their ears dull and close their eyes . . ." (vv. 9-10). There is divine grief and irony here. God takes no pleasure in the death of the wicked, and the task to which he was appointing Isaiah was to recall Israelites to himself. But now God was warning Isaiah that his message was going to be rejected, so that the effect of his ministry would be to leave people less sensitive to spiritual things than before (for hearts are always calloused by saying no to God).

In the same way we who speak for Christ today must be prepared to find that what we say is disregarded, and we are laboring with little or no visible success. Like Isaiah, we are called to be faithful, not necessarily fruitful. Faithfulness is our business; fruitfulness is an issue that we must be content to leave with God. God's Word will not return to him completely void, we know, but we must be willing not to see the fruits of it ourselves, or at least not immediately. Visible success in the form of instant results is not guaranteed in Christian ministry, neither for you nor for me.

What is the conclusion of the matter? First, because God is holy, no one can ever have fellowship with him save on the basis of the atonement that God himself provides and applies. Second, no one will speak for God as he should except out of a personal awareness of the holiness of God, the sinfulness of one's own sins, the objectivity of Christ's atonement, and the graciousness of God in bringing one to faith and assuring one of pardon. Third, no one should assume that his heart or message or ministry are not as they should be because he is seeing no present success. Such a situation is a call to return to God to ask him if anything is wrong (and something may be). But lack of present success does not necessarily mean that any particular thing is wrong. The right course may simply be to persevere in faithfulness, waiting until God's time to bless comes. Fourth, personal worship— praise and devotion—must be the mainstay of the Christian's life and ministry. These thoughts are precious to me; they keep me praying, and thereby keep me going. I hope they will be precious to you, too, and work in you just the same way.

4

HOT TUB RELIGION

Toward a Theology of Enjoyment

What would you consider a fit symbol of contemporary Western culture? A hamburger? A stereo? A car? A plane? A TV? A computer? My choice is a hot tub. Why? Because a hot tub is such *fun!* Relaxing with company in water at 102 degrees Fahrenheit (36 degrees Celsius) with an air jet all to oneself is one of life's most exquisite experiences. Turkish baths and saunas are for your health, but you sit in a hot tub for no other reason than that it is a totally delightful way of unwinding and passing the time. That is why I do it when I get the chance (maybe once every two or three years). As the image of a dog facing the horn on the HMV label perfectly conveys the idea of fascinated delight at what is being heard, so the emblem of the hot tub perfectly expresses the obsessive passion of the modern West to find pleasant forms of relaxation. Our forebears rested in order to be fit for work; we work in order to be free to rest. We devote endless ingenuity to finding new ways of having fun and feeling enjoyment. Vacations, holidays, trips, sports, public entertainment, leisure arts—all of which the hot tub represents one way or another—are what our materialistic age assumes life is all about.

This has disturbing consequences for Western Christianity. Hedonism (the pleasure-seeking syndrome) bends holiness out of shape, and hedonism today has a very tight hold on our priorities. Are we in danger of losing touch with the moral essence of Christian discipleship? Perhaps. My first experience of the sweetness of the hot tub jolted me into thinking about this, which resulted in my writing the following article:

A VIEW FROM A HOT TUB

The other day I was one of a crowd who spent much of a wet Saturday afternoon in a hot tub. My student advisees, who formed the crowd, had advised me to try it; "You'll like it," they said. Previously I had thought of hot tubs as reserved for hedonists in Hollywood and sybarites in San Francisco, but now I know that under certain circumstances members of Regent College's teaching faculty may also use them. Every day, it seems, one learns something new.

As I sat there savoring hot tubness, cracking small jokes, and adjusting to the feel of being bubbled over from all angles, it struck me that the hot tub is the perfect symbol of the modern route in religion. The hot tub experience is sensuous, relaxing, floppy, laid-back—not in any way demanding, whether intellectually or otherwise, but very, very nice, even to the point of being *great fun* (especially with an advisee group like mine). Many today want Christianity to be like that, and labor to make it so. The ultimate step, of course, would be to clear church auditoriums of seats and install hot tubs in their place; then there would never be any attendance problems. Meantime, many churches, evangelists, and electronic religionists are already offering occasions which we are meant to feel are the next best thing to a hot tub—namely, happy gatherings free from care, real fun times for all. Happiness has been defined as a warm puppy. This kind of religion projects happiness in the form of a warm welcome to all who tune or drop in; a warm choir with a schmaltzy swing; a warm, back-scratching use of words in prayer and preaching; and a warm, cheerful afterglow (another hot tub touch). To the question, where is God? the answer that these occasions actually project, never mind what is said, is: In the preacher's pocket. Soothing, for sure, but is it faith? Worship? Service of God? Is godliness the real name of this game?

As I hot tubbed on, slumping deeper into uninhibited floppiness, I saw why the chromium-plated folk religion of which I am speaking has gained such a hold. Modern life strains us. We get stimulated till we are dizzy. Relationships are brittle; marriages break; families fly apart; business is a cutthroat rat race, and those not at the top feel themselves mere cogs in another's machine. Automation and computer technology have made life faster and tenser, since we no longer have to do the time-consuming routine jobs over which our grandparents used to relax their minds. We have to run more quickly than any generation before us simply to stay where we are.

No wonder, then, that when modern Western man turns to religion (if he does—most don't), what he wants is total tickling relaxation, the sense of being at once soothed, supported, and effortlessly invigorated—in short, hot tub religion. He asks for it, and up folk jump to provide it. What hot tub religion illustrates most clearly is the law of demand and supply.

What, then, should we say of hot tub religion? Certainly, a rhythm of life that includes relaxation is right; the fourth commandment shows that. Alternating hard labor with fun times is right, too; all work and no play makes Jack a dull boy, and Jesus so often went to banquets, the fun times of the ancient world, that he got called a glutton and a drunkard.

Enjoying our bodies while we can, as opposed to despising them (which is Platonism at best, Manicheism at worst, and super-spiritual conceit either way), is part of the discipline of gratitude to our Creator. And uninhibited exuberances like clapping, dancing, shouting praise, and crying out in prayer can be approved, too, provided we do not hereby stumble others. Without these hot tub factors, as we may call them, our Christianity would be less godly and less lively, for it would be less human.

But if there were no more to our Christianity than hot tub factors—if, that is, we embraced a self-absorbed hedonism of relaxation and happy feelings while dodging tough tasks, unpopular stances, and exhausting relationships—we should fall short of biblical God-centeredness and of the cross-bearing life to which Jesus calls us, and we should thus advertise to the world nothing better than our own decadence. Please God, however, we shall not settle for that.

And I could live without ever seeing a hot tub again—but I hope I won't have to. . . .

What I was expressing in that article may be nailed down in three propositions:

1. Hot tub religion is almost right. Granted, it is wrong psychologically, for the paradoxical truth is that to seek pleasure, comfort, and happiness is to guarantee that you will miss them all. On the spiritual as on the natural level, these subjective states become heart realities only as by-products that come from focusing on something else, something perceived as valuable, invigorating, and commanding. The seeds of happiness, it has been truly said, grow most strongly in the soil of service.

Often the "something else" that wins our allegiance is some*one* else, a person rather than an abstract concept. That is especially the case where spiritual happiness is concerned. This happiness comes from basking in the knowledge of the redeeming love of the Father and the Son and showing active loyal gratitude for it. You love God and find yourself happy. Your active attempts to please God funnel the pleasures of his peace into your heart. That is how it goes. Yet hot tub religion touches on a deep, sweet truth of theology when it highlights the fact that real enjoyment is integral to real godliness.

We need to emphasize the Christian's heritage of enjoyment. Unbelief makes us fear that God is a hard and unfriendly taskmaster who will begrudge us pleasure and require us to do things that we do not want to do and cannot enjoy. Scripture, however, shows us that the opposite is true. "You will fill me with joy in your presence, with eternal pleasures at your right hand" (Ps. 16:11). "You give them drink from your river of delights" (Ps. 36:8). "God, my joy and my delight" (Ps. 43:4). "I will be glad and rejoice in you" (Ps. 9:2). "The kingdom of God is . . . righteousness, peace, and joy in the Holy Spirit" (Rom. 14:17). "May the God of hope fill you with all joy and peace as you trust in him" (Rom. 15:13). A wonderful homespun hymn by the old Calvinist Isaac Watts, the songster of Puritanism, expresses the Christian's mood of exultant enjoyment with tremendous verve:

> *Come, we that love the Lord,*
> *And let our joys be known;*
> *Join in a song with sweet accord,*
> *And thus surround the throne.*

The sorrows of the mind
Be banished from the place!
Religion never was destined
To make our pleasures less.

Let those refuse to sing
Who never knew our God,
But children of the heavenly King
May speak their joys abroad.

The God that rules on high,
And thunders when he please,
That rides upon the stormy sky
And manages the seas—

This awful [awesome] God is ours,
Our Father and our love;
He shall send down his heavenly powers
To carry us above.

There we shall see his face,
And never, never sin;
There from the rivers of his grace
Drink endless pleasures in.

The sons of grace have found
Glory begun below;
Celestial fruits on earthly ground
From faith and hope may grow.

The hill of Zion yields
A thousand sacred sweets,
Before we reach the heavenly fields,
Or walk the golden streets.

Then let our songs abound,
And every tear be dry!
We're marching through Emmanuel's ground
To fairer worlds on high.

Amen! Watts is right. Christianity, which some believe breeds gloom, actually drives it out. Sin brings sorrow, but piety produces pleasure. Hot tub religion has a true instinct at its heart.

It is sad to find that neither the *Evangelical Dictionary of Theology* (1984) nor any other dictionary of theology known to me has any entry under pleasure. To be sure, their articles on joy sometimes make shrewd reference to pleasure. Look at this, for instance, from *EDT*:

> *Joy.* A delight in life that runs *deeper than pain or pleasure* . . . not limited by nor tied solely to external circumstances . . . a gift of God . . . a quality of life and not simply a fleeting emotion. . . . The fullness of joy comes when there is a deep sense of the presence of God in one's life. . . . Jesus made it clear that joy is inseparably connected to love and to obedience (John 15:9-14). . . . There can also be joy in suffering or in weakness when suffering is seen as having a redemptive purpose and weakness as bringing one to total dependency upon God (Matt. 5:12; 2 Cor. 12:9).[1]

That joy is deeper than and not dependent on pleasure is the first thing that needs to be said. Until this distinction has been established, discussion about pleasure in the Christian life is premature. But once it is established that joy does not depend on pleasure, then a positive theology of pleasure becomes possible. And such a theology is needed if we are going to speak to a generation that has learned from Freud (not to mention personal self-knowledge) that the "pleasure principle" is one of the strongest motives in life.

How would a theology of pleasure be formulated? It would have in it at least these points:

Pleasure is (I quote Webster's dictionary) "the gratification of the senses or of the mind; agreeable sensations or emotions; the feeling produced by enjoyment or the expectation of good." Pleasure, like joy, is God's gift, but whereas joy is active (one rejoices), pleasure is passive (one is pleased). Pleasures are feelings, either of stimulation or of tensions released and relaxed in the body, or of realization, remembrance, or recognition in the mind.

Pleasure is part of the ideal human condition. Adam's state was all pleasure before he sinned (Eden, God's pleasure-garden, from which

Adam was expelled, typifies that). When our redemption is complete, pleasure, total and constant, will have become our state forever. "Never again will they hunger; never again will they thirst. The sun will not beat upon them, nor any scorching heat. . . . The Lamb . . . will lead them to springs of living water. And God will wipe away every tear from their eyes" (Rev. 7:16-17ff.). As God made us for pleasure, so he redeems us for pleasure—ours, as well as his. C. S. Lewis's senior tempter Screwtape complains of God, justly from his own point of view: "He's a hedonist at heart. All those fasts and vigils and stakes and crosses are only a facade. Or only like foam on the seashore. Out at sea, out in his sea, there is pleasure, and more pleasure. He makes no secret of it; at his right hand are 'pleasures for evermore.' Ugh!"[2]

Pleasure (conscious enjoyment) has no intrinsic moral quality. What makes pleasures right, good, and valuable or wrong, bad, and sinful is what goes with them. Look at the motivation and outcome of your pleasures. How hard do you chase after them? What kind of behavior do they produce? What is your response to them when they come? If pleasure comes unsought, or as our grateful acceptance of a gift providentially set before us, and if the leisure does no damage to ourselves or others, and if the delight of it prompts fresh thanksgiving to God, then it is holy. But if the taking of one's pleasure is a gesture of self-indulgence, pleasing oneself with no concern as to whether one pleases God, then, whether or not the action itself is wasteful or harmful, one has been entrapped by what the Bible sees as the pleasures of the world and of sin (Luke 8:14; Heb. 11:25; cf. Isa. 58:13; 1 Tim. 5:6; 2 Tim. 3:4; Titus 3:3; James 4:3; 5:5; 2 Pet. 2:13). The same pleasant experience—eating, drinking, making love, playing games, listening to music, hot tubbing, or whatever—will be good or bad, holy or unholy, depending on how it is handled.

In the order of creation, pleasures are meant to serve as pointers to God. Pleasure-seeking, as such, sooner or later brings boredom and disgust (Eccles. 2:1-11). Yet we have it on the same authority that "a man can do nothing better than to eat and drink and find satisfaction in his work. This too, I see, is from the hand of God, for without him, who can eat or find enjoyment?" (v. 24ff.). So "I commend the enjoyment of life" (8:15; cf. 9:9).

A Jewish rabbi suggested that on judgment day God would take account of us for neglecting pleasures that he provided. Christian teachers have rightly insisted that contempt for pleasure, so far from arguing superior spirituality, is actually the heresy of Manicheism and the sin of pride. Pleasure is divinely designed to raise our sense of God's goodness, deepen our gratitude to him, and strengthen our hope of richer pleasures to come in the next world. That austere Anglo-Catholic moralist C. S. Lewis declares that in heaven the highest raptures of earthly lovers will be as milk and water compared with the delights of knowing God. All pleasures are sanctified and increased when received and responded to in this way.

Hot tub religion seeks after all of this, and it is right to do so. Unhappily, though, it sometimes gets hold of the wrong end of the stick with disastrous results, as we shall now see.

2. Hot tub religion is radically wrong. Why? Because it expresses both egocentricity, whereby one declines to deny oneself, and also eudaemonism, whereby one rejects God's disciplinary program for oneself. Thus it becomes doubly irreligious.

By "egocentricity" I mean the central core of the image of Satan in fallen humanity. This can be described as unwillingness to see oneself as existing for the Creator's pleasure and instead establishing oneself as the center of everything. The quest for one's own pleasure in some shape or form is the rule and driving force of the egocentric life. Pride is the classic Christian name for this self-asserting, self-worshiping syndrome, of which "my will be done" is the implicit motto. Though egocentric pride may adopt the form of Christianity, it corrupts Christianity's substance and spirit. It tries to manage God and harness him to our own goals. This, as was hinted earlier, reduces religion to magic, treating the God who made us as if he were Jeeves to our Bertie Wooster or the genie of the lamp to our Aladdin.

Theocentricity that repudiates egocentricity, recognizing that in the fundamental sense we exist for God rather than he for us and worshiping him accordingly, is basic to real godliness. Without this radical shift from self-centeredness to God-centeredness, any show of religion is phony to a greater or lesser degree.

Jesus Christ demands self-denial, that is, self-negation (Matt.

16:24; Mark 8:34; Luke 9:23), as a necessary condition of discipleship. Self-denial is a summons to submit to the authority of God as Father and of Jesus as Lord and to declare lifelong war on one's instinctive egoism. What is to be negated is not personal self or one's existence as a rational and responsible human being. Jesus does not plan to turn us into zombies, nor does he ask us to volunteer for a robot role. The required denial is of carnal self, the egocentric, self-deifying urge with which we were born, which dominates us so ruinously in our natural state.

Jesus links self-denial with cross-bearing. Cross-bearing is far more than enduring this or that hardship. Carrying one's cross in Jesus' day, as we learn from the story of Jesus' own crucifixion, was required of those whom society had condemned, whose rights were forfeit, and who were now being led out to their execution. The cross they carried was the instrument of death. Jesus represents discipleship as a matter of following him, and following him as based on taking up one's cross in self-negation. Carnal self would never consent to cast us in such a role. "When Christ calls a man, he bids him come and die," wrote Dietrich Bonhoeffer eight years before the Nazis hanged him. Bonhoeffer was right: Accepting death to everything that carnal self wants to possess is what Christ's summons to self-denial is all about.

Hot tub religion fails to face this issue and attempts to harness the power of God to the priorities of self-centeredness. Feelings of pleasure and comfort, springing from pleasant circumstances and soothing experiences, are prime goals these days. Much of popular Christianity on both sides of the Atlantic tries to oblige us by manufacturing them for us. Sometimes, as a means to this end, it invokes the idea that God's promises are like a magician's spells: Use them correctly, and you can extract from God any legitimate pleasant thing you wish.

As a student I was jolted by the title of a book of sermons by a well-known evangelist, *How to Write Your Own Check with God Today.* Fifty years later the "health-and-wealth gospel," which promises miraculous healing for the sick and material enrichment for the needy provided they act boldly on the "name it-claim it" formula (or "gab it-grab it," as it has been derisively but revealingly paraphrased), has a large and fascinated following. Many who are not full-blown health-and-wealth devotees will yet treat James 5:15 ("the prayer offered in faith will make the sick person well") as a guaranteed magic formula for miraculous healing every time that "faith" is achieved. When I speak of hot tub religion, I have in mind positions such as this.

Confidence in God's unlimited resources and high expectations of being delivered from evil are right and good. But to conceive petitionary prayer as a technique for making God dance to your tune and do your bidding is neither right nor good. In petition we should try to discern God's purpose in the life or life situation that we lay before him. We need to be able to crystallize our specific requests as a spelling out of "*Thy* will be done," which must always be our basic plea. Hot tub religion does not reach the point where it sees this. The egocentricity that spawned it is overwhelming; hence prayer as our way of managing and directing God's energies so that he serves us rather than we him is never far from its heart. Bad!

Eudaemonism is an uncommon word for which I should perhaps apologize. I use it because it is the only word I know that fits. It has nothing to do with demons. It comes from the Greek for "happy," *eudaimon,* and Webster defines it as "the system of philosophy which makes human happiness the highest object." I use the word as a label for the view that happiness means the presence of pleasure and freedom from all that is unpleasant. Eudaemonism says that since happiness is the supreme value, we may confidently look to God here and now to shield us from unpleasantness at every turn. If unpleasantness breaks in, we expect God to deliver us from it immediately, because it is never his will for us. This is a basic principle of hot tub religion. Unhappily, however, it is a false principle. It loses sight of the place of pain in sanctification, whereby God trains his children to share his holiness (see Heb. 12:5-11). Such oversight can be ruinous.

Happiness, in the sense defined, will be enjoyed in heaven. Revelation 7:16-17 shows us that. When we are glorified with Christ, our condition will be one of conscious joy and wholehearted delight in everything around (happiness at its highest), not simply of quiet contentment with the way things are (happiness at its lowest). But there is a catch. Heaven is a state of holiness, which only persons with holy tastes will appreciate, and into which only persons of holy character can enter (Rev. 21:27; 22:14ff.). Accordingly, God's present purpose is to work holiness—which means Christlikeness—into us so as to fit us for heaven. It is precisely God's concern for our future happiness that leads him to concentrate here and now on making us holy, for "without holiness no one will see the Lord" (Heb. 12:14).

Holiness is not a price we pay for final salvation, but is, rather, the road by which we reach it, and sanctification is the process whereby God leads us along that road. The New Testament shows us that in the school of sanctification many modes of pain have their place—physical and mental discomfort and pressure, personal disappointment, restriction, hurt, and distress. God uses these things to activate the supernatural power that is at work in believers (2 Cor. 4:7-11), to replace self-reliance with total trust in the Lord who gives strength (1:8ff.; 12:9ff.), and to carry on his holy work of changing us from what we naturally are into Jesus' moral likeness "with ever-increasing glory" (2 Cor. 3:18). Thus he prepares us for that which he has prepared for us, verifying Paul's statement that "God chose you to be saved through the sanctifying work of the Spirit and through belief in the truth . . . that you might share in the glory of our Lord Jesus Christ" (2 Thess. 2:13ff.; cf. Eph. 5:25-27; Titus 2:11-14; 3:4-7).

When children are allowed to do what they like and are constantly shielded from situations in which their feelings might get hurt, we describe them as spoiled. When we say that, we are saying that overindulgent parenthood not only makes them unattractive today but also fails to prepare them for the moral demands of adult life tomorrow—two evils for the price of one. But God, who always has his eye on tomorrow as he deals with us today, never spoils his children. The lifelong training course in holy living in which he enrolls us challenges and tests us to the utmost again and again. Christlike habits of action and reaction—in other words, the fruit of the Spirit: love, joy, peace, patience, kindness, goodness, faithfulness, gentleness, and self-control (Gal. 5:22ff.)—are ingrained most deeply as we learn to maintain them through experiences of pain and unpleasantness, which in retrospect appear as God's chisel for sculpting our souls.

There is more to sanctification than this, but not less. "Endure hardship as discipline; God is treating you as sons," writes the author of Hebrews. "For what son is not disciplined by his father? If you are not disciplined (and everyone undergoes discipline), then you are illegitimate children and not true sons" (Heb. 12:7ff.). Bastard offspring notoriously go uncared-for, but, says the writer, it will not be so for you who believe. Your heavenly Father loves you enough to school you in holy living. Appreciate what he is doing, then, and be ready for the rough stuff that his program for you involves.

So any form of the idea that since God really loves us, he must intend to keep us or immediately to deliver us out of all the troubles that threaten—poor health, lonely isolation, family disruption, shortage of funds, hostility, cruelty, or whatever—should be dismissed as utterly wrong. Faithful Christians will experience help and deliverance in times of trouble over and over again. But our lives will not be ease, comfort, and pleasure all the way. Burrs under the saddle and thorns in our bed will abound. Woe betide the adherent of hot tub religion who overlooks this fact!

3. Hot tub religion is a product of our time. It embodies and reflects the world's way of looking at life. It is by biblical standards both worldly and eccentric.

Pleasure, conceived and pursued in terms of this world's goods and comforts, is as we noted the central focus of hot tub religion. It is revealing to see how pleasure has been regarded at different times in Christian history and to make comparisons between earlier views and this particular syndrome. Since Christianity both affirms the world as God's good creation and renounces it as corrupt through sin, we would expect to find some historical instances of oscillation between viewing pleasure as good and as evil, and so in fact we do. The Graeco-Roman world of the first and subsequent centuries was firmly in the grip of a decadent, pleasure-seeking mentality. So we should not wonder that the New Testament and the patristic writings spend more time attacking sinful pleasures than celebrating godly ones, nor that this perspective was carried into the Middle Ages, in which the monastic type of ascetic world renunciation was thought of as the highest form of Christianity. But then, through the Reformers' and Puritans' insistence on the sanctity of secular life, the biblical theology of pleasure finally broke surface, and most of Christendom has recognized it by now.

Calvin expressed this theology with unique brilliance and wisdom. In a chapter of his *Institutes* entitled "How We Should Use This Present Life and Its Helps," he warns against the extremes of both overdone austerity and overdone indulgence. He affirms (against Augustine!) that not to use for pleasure created realities that afford pleasure is ingratitude to their Creator. At the same time, however, he enforces Paul's admonition to sit loose to the sources of pleasure (1 Cor. 7:29-31) since we may one day lose them. Calvin recommends moderation—that is, in practice, a degree of restraint—in availing ourselves of pleasures, lest our hearts be enslaved to them and we become unable cheerfully to do without them.[3] It is ironic that Calvin, supposedly the embodiment of gloomy austerity, should actually be a classic theologian of pleasure. It is no less ironic that the Puritans, supposedly professional killjoys (H. L. Mencken defined Puritanism as the haunting fear that somewhere, somehow, somebody may be happy), should have been the ones who insisted most emphatically that "religion never was designed to make our pleasures less." But such is the fact.

However, not all evangelicals followed Calvin and the Puritans in their integration of pleasure into godliness. Revivalism bred a narrow and negative otherworldliness, and in eighteenth- and nineteenth-century Britain and America many pietistic evangelicals made a point of embracing an ostentatiously frugal version of the bourgeois lifestyle as a witness against luxury and profligate living. This reactionary asceticism still survives in some circles in the form of communal taboos on alcohol, tobacco, light reading, live theater, dancing, gambling, stylish clothes, cosmetics, and similar items. Maybe there were and are good reasons for such abstinences as matters of personal decision, but communal taboos tend to blunt rather than quicken consciences. It seems plain that this blunting happened here. Worldliness was defined in terms of breaking the taboos, and more far-reaching identifications with society's sins went unnoticed.

Pietism seldom goes beyond surface-level criticism of the ways of the world, primarily because it tends to be world-denying rather than

world-affirming. Pietism separates from the world rather than studying it and seeking to change it, and is hostile to pleasure rather than
grateful for it out of fear lest the world ride into our hearts on pleasure's back. So Protestant pietists, mainstream and free church alike,
entered the twentieth century with a less positive theology of pleasure
than other Christians held and, one suspects, a less robust enjoyment
of pleasures in consequence.

What has happened in this century is that pietistic asceticism in
its various mutations, both conservative and liberal in terms of formal
theology, has cracked under the strain, with results comparable to the
bursting of a dam. Secular pressures have proved too much for it.
Materialism, particularly in its Marxist form, has cowed Christians
into forgetting heaven and proceeding on the basis that the only life
we have to think about and get pleasure from is life in this world.
Freudianism has captured Christian no less than post-Christian imaginations with its picture of the human individual driven by desperate
desires for pleasure, especially sexual pleasure, and likely to come
apart at the seams if these desires are not indulged. Humanism has
touted individual self-expression, self-discovery, self-realization, and
self-fulfillment as life's supreme goal. Christians have taken this
thought into their minds and affirmed that this is God's will, too.
Hollywood and TV have projected a fairy-tale view of life in which
pleasure is the crock of gold that you always find at the end of the rain-
bow, provided that your previous behavior has not been too utterly
outrageous. Out of this murky mix of thought has emerged hot tub
religion, preoccupied with personal pleasure in one form or another,
demanding that godliness be soothing, and insisting that whatever
eases life's tensions must for that reason be good and holy.

Now we can see hot tub religion for what it is—Christianity corrupted by the passion for pleasure. Hot tub religion is Christianity trying to beat materialism, Freudianism, humanism, and Hollywood at
their own game, rather than to challenge the errors that the rules of
that game reflect. Christianity, in short, has fallen victim yet again (for
this has happened many times before in different ways) to the allure
of this fallen world. Worldliness—that is, embracing the world's values, in this case pleasure—is the source of hot tub religion's distinc-

tive outlook. "The place for the ship is in the sea," said D. L. Moody, speaking of the church and the world, "but God help the ship if the sea gets into it." His sentiment was surely just.

Symptoms of hot tub religion today include a skyrocketing divorce-and-remarriage rate among Christians; widespread indulgence of sexual aberrations; an overheated supernaturalism that seeks signs, wonders, visions, prophecies, and miracles; constant soothing syrup from electronic preachers and the liberal pulpit; anti-intellectual sentimentalism and emotional "highs" deliberately cultivated, the Christian equivalent of cannabis and coca; and an easy, thoughtless acceptance of luxury in everyday living. These are not healthy trends. They make the church look like the world, driven by the same unreasoning desire for pleasure seasoned with magic. Thus they undermine the credibility of the Gospel of new life. If these trends are to be reversed, a new frame of reference will have to be established. To this task, therefore, we now move, following where Scripture leads.

The word from God that we need to hear on this subject was written by John the apostle: "Do not love the world or anything in the world. If anyone loves the world, the love of the Father is not in him. For everything in the world—the cravings of sinful man, the lust of his eyes and the boasting of what he has and does—comes not from the Father, but from the world. The world and its desires pass away, but the man who does the will of God lives for ever" (1 John 2:15-17).

These passionate words are crucial in the argument of John's letter. He is writing to a rump church, the faithful core that stayed loyal to his Gospel when a large segment of the congregation withdrew. The seceders had professed a higher, more modern, more intellectual version of Christianity that involved dismissing the Incarnation and the Atonement as uncertain and unnecessary and that led to contemptuous impatience with any who would not embrace the new teaching.

John starts his letter to the remnant by reminding them that he speaks with the authority of an eyewitness of Christ (1:1-4) and that the thrust of his message is and always was salvation from sin through cleansing by Jesus' blood for a holy walk with a holy God (1:5-10). Next he spells out his pastoral purpose in addressing them—to keep them from the seceders' sins (arrogance, hatred, and moral laxity) and to hold them to the path of obeying God and loving others, the path that they had faithfully and triumphantly followed thus far (2:1-14). Now comes this three-verse outburst in which John sums up his letter's negative thrust. Love of the world, he says in effect, is the root cause of the defections, as it is of all other failures among professed Christians to love God; so, whatever you do, do not love the world!

What does it mean to love the world? John analyzes this love in terms of the lust (desire) that says "I want . . ." and the pride (vainglory) that says "I have. . . ." He is speaking here of restless craving for what you do not have along with complacent crowing about what you do have (v. 16). I agree with the *New International Version*'s interpretation, quoted above, of John's terse "lust of the flesh, lust of the eyes, and pride of life." The *New English Bible* renders the last phrase "the glamour of (the world's) life," but that strains the Greek. Passion to possess and pride in possessing what the world around us has to offer is what love of the world means.

From this we see why love of the world excludes love of the Father (v. 15). Love of the world is egocentric, acquisitive, arrogant, ambitious, and absorbing, and leaves no place for any other kind of affection. Those who love the world serve and worship themselves every moment; it is their full-time job. And from this we see that anyone whose hopes are focused on gaining material pleasure, profit, and privilege is booked for a bereavement experience, since, as John says (v. 17), the world will not last. Life's surest certainty is that one day we will leave worldly pleasure, profit, and privilege behind. The only uncertainty is whether these things will leave us before our time comes to leave them. God's true servants, however, do not face such bereavement. Their love and desire center on the Father and the Son in a fellowship that already exists (cf. 1:3), and that nothing can ever disrupt.

By this analysis John diagnoses for us a disease, of which the seceders' shrugging off evangelical faith and obedience was one form and hot tub religion another. The disease is essentially a moral one. Some who suffer from it, like John's seceders and many of today's liberals, give up the truths of Incarnation, Atonement, and new birth. Others, moving in more conservative circles, do not. But in neither case does the Gospel determine the life pattern. The essence of the disease is misdirected love and hope, the syndrome of looking exclusively to the existing order of things for present and future delight. To desire and hope is natural to us all, but the snare is to center our highest valuations and expectations on people, things, and events in this world. John indicates the cure— redirection of love and hope, so that for joy and contentment here and hereafter one looks to God alone.

Two points must be appreciated if we are to understand this.

First, life should be viewed and lived in terms of two worlds, not just one. Until recently this was a common Christian perspective. Every believer knew it was true and sought to act on it. The two-world view, quaint though it sounds to modern ears, should cause no surprise. The New Testament is clearly and consistently two-worldly in its teaching. Jesus constantly taught about heaven and hell as the destinies between which men and women choose in this life by the commitments they make or fail to make (see Matt. 5:22-26, 29ff.; 6:14ff., 19ff.; 7:13ff., 21-27; 10:28-39; 11:20-24; 12:31-37; 13:11-15, 37-43, 47-50; 15:13ff.; 16:24-27; 18:3-9, 34ff.; 19:16-29; 22:1-14; 24:45—25:46; cf. John 3:14-21; 5:14-29).

The joyful hope of either being with Christ upon leaving this world or of seeing him return to welcome his people into a renewed order of things pervades the entire apostolic witness. Basic to New Testament ethics is the belief that Christians should live on earth in the light of heaven, should make decisions in the present with their eyes on the future, and should avoid behaving here in a way that would jeopardize their hope of glory hereafter. "Store up for yourselves treasures in heaven, where moth and rust do not destroy, and where thieves do not break in and steal," says Jesus (Matt. 6:20). "A man reaps what he sows," says Paul. "The one who sows to please his sinful nature, from that nature will reap destruction; the one who sows to please the Spirit, from the Spirit will reap eternal life. Let us not become weary in doing good, for at the proper time we will reap a harvest if we do not give up" (Gal. 6:7-9).

All the promises that the glorified Christ in his letters to the seven churches holds out to those who "overcome" the world, the flesh, and the devil relate to a future state (see Rev. 2:7, 10ff., 17, 26-28; 3:5, 12,

21). The many passages of this kind in the New Testament make it obvious that one should live in such a way that the ledgers of eternity will declare one rich before God. This is something no old-time Christian would ever doubt.

But in recent times a number of developments coming together have weakened the impact of this truth. Marxists and others have mocked the idea of "pie in the sky when you die" as a pipe dream for spineless sentimentalists who cannot face reality, thereby intimidating some Christians and making them ashamed of their hope. The same critics have suggested that a hope of heaven is bad because it destroys interest in opposing and abolishing evil on earth, and this has added guilt to shame in impressionable Christian hearts.

This criticism is nonsense. As C. S. Lewis points out:

> If you read history you will find that the Christians who did most for the present world were just those who thought most of the next. The apostles themselves, who set on foot the conversion of the Roman Empire, the great men who built up the Middle Ages, the English Evangelicals who abolished the Slave Trade, all left their mark on Earth, precisely because their minds were occupied with Heaven. It is since Christians have largely ceased to think of the other world that they have become so ineffective in this.[4]

Many Christians, however, do not read history and so are unaware how wrong the Marxists are and how right Lewis is at this point.

Then again, those who live in the post-Christian West breathe every day the poison gas (so we may well call it) of materialistic secularism in both its popular form (the media) and its sophisticated form (the arts and higher education). This damages our spiritual eyes, lungs, and heart, destroying both the vision of and the passion for realities beyond the present world order of space and time. The combined force of these factors has made Western Christianity this-worldly in a way that can only be described as a radical distortion.

For today, by and large, Christians no longer live for heaven and, therefore, no longer understand, let alone practice, detachment from the world. Nowadays nonconformity to the world is limited to the means that the world adopts to achieve its goals and rarely touches the goals themselves. Does the world around us seek pleasure, profit, and privilege? So do we. We have no readiness or strength to renounce these objectives, for we have recast Christianity into a mold that stresses happiness above holiness, blessings here above blessedness hereafter, health and wealth as God's best gifts, and death, especially early death, not as thankworthy deliverance from the miseries of a sinful world (the view that the old Anglican prayer book expressed), but as the supreme disaster and a constant challenge to faith in God's goodness.

Is our Christianity now out of shape? Yes, it is, and the basic reason is that we have lost the New Testament's two-world perspective that views the next life as more important than this one and understands life here as essentially preparation and training for life hereafter. And we shall continue out of shape till this proper otherworldliness is recovered. Such otherworldliness does not in any way imply a low view of the wonder and glory and richness that life in this world can have. What otherworldliness implies is that you live your life here, long or short as it may be, seeing everything from the pilgrim perspective immortalized in Bunyan's classic work and making your decisions in terms of being a traveler on the way home.

Peter's first letter spells this out. By God's mercy and through Christ's resurrection, says Peter, believers have a sure hope of glory, for the enjoyment of which God is currently preserving and preparing them (1:3-9). So "set your hope fully on the grace to be given you when Jesus Christ is revealed" (v. 13), "live your lives as strangers here in reverent fear" (v. 17), and "as aliens and strangers in the world, abstain from sinful desires, which war against your soul" (2:11). Endure hostility, human and satanic, without flinching, standing firm in your hope of glory, your loyalty to Christ, and your trust in God the Father, "and the God of all grace, who called you to his eternal glory in Christ . . . will himself restore you and make you strong, firm and steadfast" (5:10). That was, is, and always will be the true Christian path.

Second, love for God and hope in God are life-transforming motivations.

One of the marks of modern Western culture is that we are, as we say, cool cats. We make a show of enthusiasm about this and that, but our feelings are only skin deep. Basically we are blasé, laid back, deeply moved by nothing except our own private concerns. Why is this? It is, in part, a defense mechanism against the sensory overload of hype with which advertisers and publicity people swamp us these days. But it is also, I suspect, a sign that we do not think in the deep and sustained way that our forebears in less complex, fast-moving, and distracting eras used to do. Sustained imaginative reflection is, if I am not mistaken, so rare today that few of us understand its power to motivate and are not ourselves motivated by it. *Meditation* is the historic Christian word for focused thinking that motivates, but how much meditating do we do?

In the New Testament we see God's redeeming love and the Christian's hope of glory decisively controlling believers' lives. Paul is a case in point. Paul was so forceful, passionate, and exuberant in his evangelism and pastoral care that the Corinthians thought he was unbalanced—in a word, crazy; and they ridiculed him for it. Paul was not fazed by this. "If we are out of our mind," he retorted, "it is for the sake of God; if we are in our right mind, it is for you." Then he explained why he behaved the way he did. "For Christ's love compels us . . ." (2 Cor. 5:13ff.). *Compels* ("constrains," "overmasters," "leaves us no choice" in other versions) is a Greek word meaning "put under strong pressure." What Paul means is that his knowledge of Christ's atoning love on the cross had enormous motivating force for him, just as it did for the pioneer missionary C. T. Studd, who declared: "If Jesus Christ be God, and died for me, then no sacrifice is too great for me to make for him."

A few verses earlier Paul had spoken of the sustaining and animating power of hope in his life, keeping him going under the seemingly intolerable strain of illness, isolation, insult, and indifference (see 1:3-10; 6:8-10; 11:23-29). "We are hard pressed on every side, but not crushed; perplexed, but not in despair; persecuted, but not abandoned; struck down, but not destroyed. We always carry around in our body the death of Jesus. . . . It is written: 'I believed: therefore I have spoken.' With that same spirit of faith we also believe and therefore speak, because we know that the one who raised the Lord Jesus from the dead will also raise us with Jesus and present us with you in his presence. . . . Therefore we do not lose heart. Though outwardly we are wasting away, yet inwardly we are being renewed day by day. For our light and momentary troubles are achieving for us an eternal glory that far outweighs them all. So we fix our eyes not on what is seen, but on what is unseen. For what is seen is temporary, but what is unseen is eternal" (4:8-18).

While the source of Paul's inward renewal is the quickening power of the Spirit, agent of the risen Christ who is our life and our hope (see 4:10ff., 12:9ff.; Col. 3:4; 1 Tim. 1:1), the means of it is the hope of glory, consciously entertained. It is plain that Paul could have said, with Bunyan's Mr. Standfast, "The thoughts of what I am going to, and of the Conduct that waits for me on the other side, doth lie as a glowing Coal at my Heart."[5] It was God's love and promise that changed Paul's life and made him the man he was.

About this change John also speaks in categorical and universal terms. "This is love: not that we loved God, but that he loved us and sent his Son as an atoning sacrifice for our sins. . . . We know and rely on the love God has for us. . . . We love because he first loved us" (1 John 4:10, 16, 19). Christians love God responsively, and their fellow Christians gratuitously, on the model of Jesus himself (3:14, 16-18, 23; 4:11, 20ff.); knowledge of Christ's love enables them to love. Furthermore: "How great is the love the Father has lavished on us, that we should be called children of God! And that is what we are! . . . What we will be has not yet been made known. But we know that when he appears, we shall be like him, for we shall see him as he is. Everyone who has this hope in him purifies himself, just as he is pure." (3:1-3). A person whom hope did not motivate in this way and love did not control would have been diagnosed by the apostle John as not really a believer at all.

The apostolic experience and expectation was that the love and hope Godward that the gospel message evokes would radically transform one's life, both behaviorally in one's lifestyle and motivationally in one's heart. God's love would evoke self-sacrificing love for the Lord and for others. God's promise of heaven would trigger resolution in the face of hostility and discouragement. Resistance to sin—that is, to tempting prospects of pleasure, profit, and privilege in this world, never mind about God, such prospects as captured the hearts of Adam and Eve (see Gen. 3:6)—would be strengthened. But did apostles or anyone else ever expect this twin evangelical motivation to transform our lives without being turned over and over in the heart by constant meditation? What Paul and John assumed, both from their own experience and from their God-taught understanding of divine grace, was that the reality of redeeming love and the certainty of heaven would so thrill believers' hearts that they would think about these things all the time, just as newlyweds think joyfully and often about the sweetness of their spouses and the delights of all their future plans. And that is how it ought to be!

Very true; so it ought. But indwelling sin opposes, and the world around distracts. Satan, temptation's ringmaster, is resolved that love and purity shall not blossom if he can help it. Therefore, constant effort has to be made to keep thoughts of love and hope toward God vivid and their motivating effect powerful. The historic Christian name for this special effort, as was said earlier, is meditation.

Meditation, an exercise of directed thinking that has often been compared to a cow chewing the cud, is not well understood today; so I make no apology for appealing to two giants from the Christian past to instruct us in it. Here, first, is Calvin, who in the *Institutes* precedes his treatment, earlier referred to, of the rightness of gratefully enjoying such pleasures as God gives, by a chapter (III.ix) titled "Meditation on the Future Life." He states that our attitude to this world must be one not of *desiderium* (desire for what it has to give, leading us to become its slave), but rather of *contemptus* (recognition that, so far as we are concerned, it has no ultimate worth, so that we become detached from it and are willing to lose it as and when God wills). "It must be grasped, that the mind is never seriously raised to desire and meditate on the future life till it has been imbued with contempt for the present life."[6] Ronald Wallace summarizes Calvin's overall view thus:

> The conditions, then, for a right use of this world are to pass through it as pilgrims should who have their minds fixed on another country to which they are traveling, to offer all that we possess and enjoy here in our open hands as a sacrifice to God

to take from us whenever it pleases Him, to make such tokens of the divine love as we enjoy in the midst of this present creation whet our appetites for the fuller glory that is yet to be—in other words to use this world thankfully as a preparation for that which is to come. Under such circumstances it is right for us to indulge in a real and thankful love of this life. We thus have the paradoxical truth that we are able to love this life truly only when we have truly learned first to despise this life.[7]

How then, according to Calvin, do we meditate on the future life? By deliberately thinking about it (throughout the chapter he calls his readers to "learn," "conclude," "ponder," "reflect," "consider," "judge"—in other words, to use their minds on the subject). But what sort of thoughts about the future life should we form? We must think about it, says Calvin, in terms of its intrinsically greater glory, both because of the closer fellowship with God that it will bring and the limitations from which it will deliver us (sec. 4) and because of the vindication of God, godliness, and the godly to which the manifesting of it will lead (sec. 6). These thoughts will raise us above the world and give us the encouragement we need for patience here on earth until God's time comes to take us to our heavenly home.

Richard Baxter lived a century after Calvin. He was a chronically sick Puritan, tubercular from his teens and suffering constantly from dyspepsia, kidney stones, headaches, toothaches, swollen limbs, intermittent bleeding at his extremities, and other troubles—all before the days of pain-killing drugs. Yet he was always energetic, outgoing, uncomplaining, and utterly healthy-minded, even though sometimes (and who can wonder?) a trifle short-tempered. By 1661, when he was forty-five years old, he had just about evangelized the entire town of Kidderminster (two thousand adults, plus children), besides writing, amid many books, two classics that have been regularly reprinted since his day—*The Saints' Everlasting Rest* and *The Reformed Pastor*. Then during the next thirty years, when as an ejected clergyman he was no longer able to hold a pastoral charge, he wrote so much that he now has a niche in history as the most prolific English theologian of all time.

What kept this frail invalid going so single-mindedly and even spectacularly through the years? In *The Saints' Everlasting Rest* Baxter tells the secret. From his thirtieth year he practiced a habit that he first formed when he thought he was on his deathbed: For something like half an hour each day he would meditate on the life to come, thereby escalating his sense of the glory that awaited him and reinforcing his motivation to use every ounce of energy and zeal that he found within himself to hasten up the path of worship, service, and holiness toward his goal. This cultivation of hope gave him daily doggedness in hard work for God, despite the debilitating effect of his sick body. He stands for all time as proof that there is supernatural strength for God's service that is beyond human explanation.

In one respect he went beyond Calvin: He devoted the fourth part of *The Saints' Everlasting Rest* to a detailed demonstration of how you and I may meditate as he did, and so enter more deeply into the life of redirected love and hope in which he himself was so proficient. No Christian teacher before or since has ever dealt with "heavenly meditation," as Baxter called this discipline, half so fully or half so well. If you want to master this fine and fruitful art, it is to part four of Baxter's treatise that you should go.[8] Is this not something we all need to do?

Today the love of luxury and the pull of pleasure are more intensely felt than at any time in Christendom, except perhaps on the Renaissance princes and the aristocracy of eighteenth-century England and France. The quest for pleasure—intellectual, sensual, aesthetic, gastronomic, alcoholic, narcissistic—is one aspect of that Western decadence that seers such as Solzhenitsyn detect and denounce. This "cult of softness," as it has been called,[9] is fed from the vast smorgasbord of pleasures that our amoral, technically resourceful society makes available to us, and the quest gains rather than loses momentum as the years pass. This phenomenon bodes ill for our culture, just as it dilutes the quality of our Christianity. Observation assures me that only a new quest for heavenly mindedness, a new depth of self-denying love for our Lord and of hope directed toward heaven, can keep us from being swept off our feet by the quest for pleasure that the world prosecutes so zealously all around us. Scripture convinces me that there is no dimension of renewal that we currently need more.

Keeping our heads despite the pull of pleasure is as hard a task as any for the affluent believer. To react by trying to negate pleasure altogether, as if God himself was against it, would be arrogant ingratitude to him, as we have seen; but to retain pleasure in its proper place when all around us seem to have gone pleasure-mad calls for more wisdom than most of us can muster. Let Ecclesiastes, the preacher, instruct us once more. To enjoy simple everyday pleasures and let them refresh your spirit is, he says, part of wisdom. Here are his key statements:

> *I commend the enjoyment of life, because nothing is better for a man under the sun than to eat and drink and be glad. Then joy will accompany him in his work (8:15).*

> *A man can do nothing better than to eat and drink and find satisfaction in his work. This too, I see, is from the hand of God, for without him, who can eat or find enjoyment? (2:24ff.; 3:12ff.; 5:19).*

> *Light is sweet, and it pleases the eyes to see the sun. However many years a man may live, let him enjoy them all (11:7ff.).*

> *Enjoy life with your wife, whom you love, all the days of this meaningless life that God has given you under the sun (9:9).*

The wisdom that thus commends and commands the joys that God providentially provides is not a calculating hedonism. It is a wisdom that offers three imperatives as the answer to the question of how we should live—worship ("fear God"), obedience ("keep his commandments"), and hope. "For God will bring every deed into judgment," rewarding in a future state those believers who have made good, not evil, and obedience, not pleasure-seeking, their aim. (See Eccles. 12:13ff.) This wisdom from Ecclesiastes is the wisdom I mentioned earlier. It is the wisdom that knows that happiness is the spin-off of holiness, the sweet by-product of devotion to God. By taking this wisdom to heart, we may learn how to enjoy the pleasures God gives without lapsing into the love of the world. Thus we shall be able to steer a straight course for heaven amid a culture obsessively preoccupied with earth.

Earlier I quoted Isaac Watts's celebration of the joys of the Christian life. I now close my argument by citing his transcript of the healthy, expectant Christian's state of mind.

> *My thoughts surmount these lower skies,*
> *And look within the veil;*
> *There springs of endless pleasure rise,*
> *The waters never fail.*
>
> *There I behold, with sweet delight,*
> *The blessed Three in One;*
> *And strong affections fix my sight*
> *On God's incarnate Son.*
>
> *His promise stands forever firm,*
> *His grace shall ne'er depart;*
> *He binds my name upon his arm,*
> *And seals it on his heart*
>
> *Light are the pains that nature brings;*
> *How short our sorrows are,*
> *When with eternal future things*
> *The present we compare!*
>
> *I would not be a stranger still*
> *To that celestial place*
> *Where I forever hope to dwell,*
> *And see my Savior's face.*

Blessed are those who thus hope for glory. The mastery of present pleasure, even as they enjoy it, is within their grasp. And this, too, along with mastery of sin and victory over the devil, belongs to the fullness of their life in Christ.

5

A CHRISTIAN STYLE OF LIFE

Managing Our Labor, Leisure, Pleasure, and Treasure

Since the Second World War the West has grown affluent. Society practices and promotes spending rather than saving, self-indulgence rather than self-improvement, and amusement at all costs. (*Amusing Ourselves to Death* is the telling title of Neil Postman's assessment of television;[1] the same phrase might be used to describe the behavior that has led to the AIDS epidemic.) Evangelical Christians have responded by emphasizing work rather than leisure,[2] activity rather than rest, and life commitments rather than lifestyle choices. Thus they have sought to tool themselves up to be salt and light in our dying culture. But on rest, leisure, and lifestyle as such they have had very little to say.

To note this comparative silence is to state a fact—not to offer a criticism. Indeed, criticism would be out of place here. For Christians to be preoccupied with living and working for God is healthy, just as a preoccupation with leisure and luxury is unhealthy. If, as it appears, leisure and luxury are becoming the main interests of the Western world, a deadly decadence has evidently set in, against which Christians ought to be standing with all their might, advocating and modeling something entirely different. Christians must see this decadence as a form of worldliness and invoke against it such Scripture passages as 1 John 2:15-16: "Do not love the world or the things in the world. The love of the Father is not in those who love the world;

for all that is in the world—the desire of the flesh, the desire of the eyes, the pride in riches—comes not from the Father but from the world" (NRSV). God forbid that paying attention to questions about leisure and lifestyle should have the effect of promoting in the church a worldliness like that of the modern West.

Yet if these questions are not discussed, evangelicals will be in trouble another way. All around the world, as capitalist consumerism and the market economy grind on, carrying all before them, leisure and lifestyle are becoming areas of entrapment for Christian people. Failure to see this as a fact, to perceive it as a problem, to think about it in biblical antithesis to the ruling secular notions, and to plan to operate as God's counterculture in these areas would indicate that we were already falling into the traps or (to change the metaphor) being blown up in the minefield. My best hope for this chapter is that it might offer the makings of a mine-detecting survival kit.

We begin with definitions to make sure that we know what we are talking about. *Leisure* and *lifestyle* are the words with which we start. *Leisure,* like *pleasure* and *treasure,* is a familiar word, and focusing its meaning is not a problem. My copy of Webster defines *leisure* thus: "freedom from occupation or business; vacant time; time free from employment; time which may be appropriated to any specific object."

Lifestyle is too recent a coinage for my Webster to take note of, but the contents of a junk mail envelope that arrived recently, with the words "Valuable Coupons Inside—Save on All Your Lifestyle Needs" printed on its front, give us the idea. Inside were coupons offering great deals on ornamental painted plates, the world's greatest perfumes (that is what was claimed, anyway), scenic address labels, items of personal hygiene, carpet shampooing, a course in piano playing that focuses on leading singing at parties, wigs, baseball cards, a doll built for lifetime companionship, family photos, furnace cleaning, a machine for streamlining the female figure, videos featuring the late Victor Borge, the *Encyclopedia Britannica*, skin cream, book club membership, and deodorant.

All one's lifestyle needs? Hardly, but the selection points to the definition. *Lifestyle,* or *style of life,* are evidently umbrella terms used to describe the way of living that we achieve by our choices among the various options that our affluent consumerist society makes available to us—choices of clothes, food, hobbies, vacations, places of residence, cars, clubs, careers, associates, amusements, and (of course) a church of our choice, as well as choices of luxury items such as those listed above.

"Lifestyle" is thus the label for both the ideal existence that our choices aim at and the actual existence that our choices produce. Our concept of our lifestyle hovers between being directional, stating how we want to live, and being descriptive, showing how we do live. In a day of multiple choices with regard to almost everything, we may well say: "By their lifestyle you will know them; by my lifestyle you will know me." Where society sets us free to choose, our choices will show who and what we are, where we want to be, and where we are actually going.

Not all lifestyle choices are leisure choices, as we can see; but, as we can also see, all leisure choices are lifestyle choices, and they will say something about our view of life as a whole.

What sort of problems do we face in connection with leisure and lifestyle? There are three obvious ones, all with far-reaching theological, moral, and devotional implications.

The first problem is *idolatry*, the worship of false gods. The basic biblical insights here are that whatever controls and shapes one's life is in effect the god one worships and that human nature is so constituted that no one can avoid a personal subservience to some god or other. As Bob Dylan sang some years ago, "You've got to serve somebody." Those who do not live to exalt the God of the Bible will inevitably be enslaved to some modern counterpart of the Baals and Molechs of the nature- and nation-worshiping cults that Scripture denounces. Then one's god may be some human individual or group—one's employer, perhaps, whose interests one devotes oneself to advancing; or one will worship and serve self directly, treating the gratifying of one's desires as all that matters and seeing everything as a means to that end—a lifestyle in which one constantly falls victim to "greed, which is idolatry" (Col. 3:5). Greed, the mind-set that reaches out to grab things for oneself, becomes the liturgy of self-worship. In idolizing objects of desire, we idolize ourselves, the desirers; and so idolatry in this twofold sense becomes our life.

Regarding the matter in hand, we see that some people idolize work while others idolize play; some make a god of leisure activities (vacations, sports, hobbies, music, books, gardening, and so on) while others make a god of their bank balance and social position or of power; and others again make a god of their addictions (drink, drugs, sex, or whatever). Motivations and self-perceptions get very tangled here and need a lot of sorting out in particular cases. Yet the bottom line is always the same. To the extent that we are not actively living to God, for God, and in the presence of God, seeking to glorify and enjoy him in and through all we do, we have lapsed into some form of idolatry whereby we worship and serve created things rather than the Creator (cf. Rom. 1:25). But idolatry in all its forms must be avoided.

The second problem is *hedonism,* with which we may join, as its opposite, *anti-hedonism.* What is in question here is the place of pleasure in Christian living, a topic we have already touched. Hedonism means the enthroning of pleasure as life's supreme value and therefore as a goal that one pursues directly. Hedonism says, in effect, that pleasure-seeking is the height of wisdom and virtue and that maximizing pleasure is the highest service we can render. Popular Western culture is largely hedonist, and modern Christians are constantly exposed to its brainwashing influences through the media and the relationships of life that draw them along the hedonist path. That God wants us all to be happy, right now; that total satisfaction is what Jesus offers, right now; that it is a good and godly thing to engage in genital homosexual behavior, if that gives you positive pleasure—all of these notions have become very familiar in the church in recent years. That leisure is entirely for pleasure and that improving one's lifestyle means simply increasing one's pleasures are unchallenged axioms in today's advertising industry and unquestioned assumptions among many professed Christians. There is clearly a major problem here.

Recently the phrase "Christian hedonism" has gained prominence as a tag for the truth that the God who promises his people joy and delight in their relationship with him, both here and hereafter, does in fact fulfill his promise here and now.[3] As a corrective of what we may call "Christian anti-hedonism" (the view that pleasure has no place in godly living, that God will always want us to do what we least want to do, and that the real Christian life on earth will always be, in Churchillian phrase, blood, toil, tears, and sweat—in short, sustained heroic misery), Christian hedonism speaks a word in season.

In itself, however, "Christian hedonism" is not a good phrase for its purpose; for it seems to say that rating pleasure as life's supreme value is something that Christianity itself teaches us to do, and that is not so. Biblical Christianity does not teach that any pleasure or good feelings, or any form of present ease and contentment, should be sought as life's highest good. What it teaches, rather, is that glorifying God by our worship and service is the true human goal, that rejoicing and delighting in God is central to worship, and that the firstfruits of our heritage of pleasures forevermore will be given us as we set ourselves to do this. But should we start to seek pleasure rather than God, we would be in danger of losing both. It is apparent that this is what the exponents of Christian hedonism do themselves think; so my difficulty is limited to their choice of words. But hedonism—real hedonism—must be avoided.

The third problem is *utilitarianism*, the view that the value of anything is to be found in the extent to which it is useful and productive as a means to an end beyond itself. Utilitarian thinking is very widely applied today in the realm of technology and business, but it has a radical built-in shortcoming: It overlooks the fact that what it values as a means to an end may have an intrinsic value, too, for the sake of which it should be promoted and preserved irrespective of how it rates in the means-to-end calculus. Leisure is a case in point. Utilitarianism says that the whole rationale of leisure and recreation is to "re-create" people for more of their productive labor.

Christianly speaking, this is part of the rationale of leisure, no doubt; after the Sabbath rest one goes back to work. But where utilitarianism urges that leisure and rest be kept to a minimum so that productive work may be maximized (hence the fearfully long working hours of the early days of industrialization and of some workers and workaholics today), Christian thinkers find intrinsic value in leisure activity that is, as Leland Ryken puts it, "nonproductive in the sense in which we ordinarily use that term. Leisure does not meet our needs of physical or economic survival. It does not put bread on the table or clothes in the closet. Leisure is a self-enclosed world that carries its own reward. . . . [As Lee W. Gibbs puts it,] 'the purpose of play is in the play itself.'"[4]

The Christian work ethic has sometimes been misrepresented as a sanctified workaholism, but this ignores the biblical celebration of God as the one who "richly provides us with everything for our enjoyment" (1 Tim. 6:17)—a divine generosity that requires leisure for its appreciation, as the exponents of the authentic Christian work ethic well knew. So Christians should value leisure as more than a periodic pit stop before further work, and they should resist the narrowing impact of the money- and manufacture-mesmerized mind-set that marks utilitarian social thinking. High though it rides as a public philosophy today, utilitarianism too must be avoided.

This identification of the three main problem areas in relation to leisure and lifestyle gives parameters for the rest of our study. We should not lapse into idolizing either work or leisure; it is not Christian to be either a workaholic or a drone. Nor should we lapse into hedonism, letting the pursuit of pleasure shape our lives, any more than we should lapse into anti-hedonism, censuring pleasure in Manichean style as a worthless and unhelpful distraction and treating pleasurelessness as an index of virtue. Nor should we lapse into utilitarianism, valuing work or leisure or any aspect of lifestyle purely as a means to an end beyond itself and not at all as a field of creativity or a means of expression or a form of enjoyment. So far, however, all of this has been negative; we have merely noted what we should not do. Now we have to ask, what positive principles of action should be guiding us in shaping the life we live? To answer this question is our next task.

Let us then stand back for a moment and look at the overall ideal of a redeemed sinner's life in Christ, which is the frame into which biblical teaching on leisure and lifestyle fits. The redeemed life is commonly spoken of these days in terms of *wholeness;* fifty years ago it was thought of in terms of *balance;* Thomas Aquinas saw it as life in *proportion;* and John Calvin spoke of it as a life of *moderation*—and indeed it has all of these qualities. It is the life for which Jesus, himself the perfect man, is the model. Thomas's four cardinal virtues—

prudence (wisdom), temperance (self-possession), justice (fairness), and fortitude (stick-to-itiveness, resilience, and what we call guts)—are basic to it. His three theological virtues—faith, hope, and love—are central to it. And the ninefold fruit of the Spirit that Paul lists—love, joy, peace, patience, kindness, goodness, faithfulness, gentleness, and self-control (Gal. 5:22-23)—constitute a character profile of it, just as they do of the Lord Jesus himself. It is a superhuman version of human life; it is our natural life supernaturalized by grace.

On what principles is this redeemed life lived? Four may be briefly mentioned.

First, it is lived as a life of *duty to God,* glorifying him by our obedience out of gratitude for his grace. The phrase derives from the Catechism in Cranmer's first prayer book (1549): "My duty towards God, is to believe in him, to fear him, and to love him . . . to worship him, to give him thanks, to put my whole trust in him, to call upon him, to honour his holy Name and his Word, and to serve him truly all the days of my life."

Second, this redeemed life is lived as a life of *neighbor-love.* "My duty towards my Neighbour," Cranmer's Catechism continues, "is to love him as myself, and do to all men, as I would they should do unto me."[5] Love seeks the well-being and advancement of the loved one in every way that it can; it is a matter of the mind and will more than of the feelings, and of sustained commitment rather than momentary intensities. The duty of love, to one's neighbor as to one's God, calls for discipline of life.

Third, the redeemed life is a life of *freedom* (cf. Gal. 5:1), in four senses: freedom from the need to work for salvation, freedom from the restrictions imposed by the typical enactments of God's Old Testament law, freedom for the use and enjoyment of all created things (1 Tim. 4:4-5; 6:17), and freedom in the sense of fulfillment and contentment in working for God ("whose service is perfect freedom," as Cranmer's prayer book declares).[6]

Finally, the redeemed life is lived as a life of *expectancy,* as we look to receive both God's Word and his gifts—including the providential gifts of leisure and pleasure, which are our special concern at present.

Within this framework I now offer brief reflections to indicate the specific positives that should guide us through our perplexities about these matters. Giving myself the pleasure of tidy titling, I shall arrange my matter under four headings: the call to labor, the role of leisure, the place of pleasure, and the use of treasure.

THE CALL TO LABOR

In this chapter I use *labor* and *work* as synonyms. My concept of work thus includes not only the idea of obligation (work has been defined as whatever you have to do when you would like to be doing something else), but also the idea of effort (for *labor* signifies work that is hard and demanding—laborious, in fact). Work is thus both a strenuous activity, one that exhausts you however much you enjoy doing it, and a required activity, mandated not just by society but by God himself. That people should work is an imperative of the order of creation (before the Fall, Adam was put in charge of the Garden of Eden and the animal kingdom) and also of the order of redemption (see how Paul scallywags nonworkers and thieves in 2 Thess. 3:6-12; Eph. 4:28). The command to labor is the frame within which our reflections on God's gifts of leisure, pleasure, and treasure must be set.

There are many kinds of work in today's world—manual and intellectual, agricultural and manufacturing, productive and distributive, educational and caregiving, managerial and menial, casual and contracted, stipendiary and voluntary, and so on. There is teamwork and solo work, schoolwork and research work, homemaking and breadwinning, the work of artists and craftsmen, the routine of a "hand" (telltale word!) on an assembly line, the labor of communicators and salespeople. The variety is enormous.

There were many different kinds of work in the ancient world, too. But what the Bible teaches about work applies to all of them— namely, that everyone should be involved in some form of productive and beneficial labor; that to be a worker is one facet of the image of God in which mankind was made; that whatever work we choose to do or find ourselves set to do (I think here of slaves, soldiers, and all subordinates who live under orders) should be done with creative concentration and to the best of our ability; that good work of whatever kind glorifies God as well as benefiting others; that our skills are gifts of God, for which we should thank him as we use them; that work itself is a gift of God, without which we would be in a permanent state of discontent and unfulfillment, the nemesis of people with no outlet for their God-given creativity; and that the world of work is a training ground and display ground for Christian character (personal integrity, responsible stewardship of resources, compassionate altruism and fidelity, practice of the Golden Rule, passion for excellence, patient persistence in well-doing, and more). Work, of whatever kind, is more than a means to an end (e.g., survival, money-making, personal or professional advancement). Work is service of God, and it should be offered to him and done in a way that honors him at every point. George Herbert hit the nail on the head when he wrote:

> *Teach me, my God and King,*
> *In all things thee to see;*
> *And what I do in anything*
> *To do it as for thee.*
>
> *All may of thee partake;*
> *Nothing can be so mean*
> *Which, with this tincture, "For thy sake,"*
> *Will not grow bright and clean.*
>
> *A servant with this clause*
> *Makes drudgery divine;*
> *Who sweeps a room, as for thy laws,*
> *Makes that and the action fine.*

Evading work through idleness, laziness, or sloth displeases God and blights one's own life. The world has always been inclined to think that freedom from work is as near heaven on earth as one can get. But the Bible writers knew that, whatever frustrations we may meet as we work in this fallen and twisted world, not to have tasks that we perform creatively as service to God and others is itself a frustrating of our humanity, a condition in which emotional maturity becomes impossible and selfish irresponsibility grows while true human dignity withers. Work that exposes us to boredom, stress, and exploitation is still better than no work at all. If such work yields little satisfaction, being unemployed and idle yields even less, as surely we all know.

Embittering circumstances abound in the world of work today, making it hard to receive what I have just said. Lack of job security, as firms shed their long-term employees and hire part-timers on a contingency basis, meaning no benefits and no guarantee of continuance; forced choices between early retirement and demotion, and sometimes early retirement with no choice; the tyranny of rat-race professionalism, whereby one's time, energy, enthusiasm, attention, and focus are increasingly claimed by the need to maintain one's status and not be passed over or tossed out as insufficiently competent or motivated; demands from above for moral corner-cutting that benefits the firm or institution at the expense of the public; having to accept unacceptable policies as the price of one's career—these are just some of the realities working people today face, and it is no wonder that sometimes they see their work as more of a curse than a calling. To work in a way that honors God in a world like ours is a challenge to faith at every turn. But the call to labor—to work, and work hard, one way or another, for God and for other people—remains, and we must never lose sight of it.

Assuming, then, our acceptance of that call, we now move on to think about the managing of leisure according to the will of God.

THE ROLE OF LEISURE

What is leisure? We have already cited a dictionary definition, but more needs to be said.

Leisure is one of a pair of words, the other of which is *work*. Work, as we have just noted, means not just one's wage-earning employment but everything that one must do as a matter of obligation, whether one enjoys it or not. Jobs and commitments out of the house, jobs that need to be done in the house, necessary studying, fulfilling promises one has made—all of these count as work because of the sense of "having to" that attaches to them. By contrast, leisure means time that is ours to use for our own pleasure on a discretionary basis.

Some leisure time we fill with things we choose to do for their own sake, just because we want to do them; these are the activities of absolute leisure. Some leisure time we spend doing things we both want and ought to do, from joining in public worship and fulfilling volunteer roles at church or in a club to looking after pets and reading to keep informed; these are better called activities of "semi-leisure." All leisure, including semi-leisure, is a gift from God that, when used wisely, "provides rest, relaxation, enjoyment, and physical and psychic health. It allows people to recover the distinctly human values, to build relationships, to strengthen family ties, and to put themselves in touch with the world and nature. Leisure can lead to wholeness, gratitude, self-expression, self-fulfillment, creativity, personal growth, and a sense of achievement."[7] So leisure should be valued and not despised.

What Bible truths bear on our use of leisure? At least the following:

1. *The duty of rest.* In the quasi-liturgical, quasi-poetical, highly stylized narrative of Genesis 1:1—2:3, God the Creator presents himself as setting the world in order in six days, after which he rested on the seventh. Whether the six days should be understood as 144 of our hours, as six vast geological epochs, or as a pictorial projection of the fact (the *what*) of creation that gives no information about the time (the *when*) or the method (the *how*) of creation is an interpretive question that need not concern us now.[8] What matters for us here is that on the basis of this presentation God directs that each seventh day—each Sabbath, that is—be kept as a day of rest from the labors of the previous six (Exod. 20:8-11; 31:12-17). The day is to be kept "holy"—that is, it is a time of semi-leisure, to be used for honoring God the Creator by worship, as well as for refreshing human creatures by the break from otherwise unending toil.

This prescribed rhythm of work and rest is part of the order of creation and should be upheld as such, whether we take the disputed older view of Sunday as the Christian Sabbath or not. (Bible students go both ways on that question.) Human beings are so made that they need this six-plus-one rhythm, and we suffer in one way or another if we do not get it. The leisure, or at least semi-leisure, of a weekly day for worship and rest is a divine ordinance that our work-oriented Western world ignores to the peril of its health. In today's community as Christian faith fades, society's standards fall, and economic competition becomes more cutthroat, the historic function of the Christian day of rest as a bulwark against employers' demands for a seven-day week is being increasingly circumvented, and the outlook is somewhat bleak.

2. *The goodness of pleasure*. This has already been discussed, so here I merely quote the pregnant words of Ecclesiastes 8:15: "I commend the enjoyment of life," and move on.

3. *The rightness of festivity*. The Bible is full of feasts. In Leviticus 23 six "holy convocations," at which work was prohibited, were prescribed for Israel each year; they are called "appointed feasts." In John 2 Jesus is found at a wedding feast, miraculously creating extra wine. The fact that his critics were able to dismiss him as "a glutton and a drunkard" (Matt. 11:19) shows that such festal celebrations were a recurring part of his life. All through the Bible the feast table is the place and the emblem of refreshing, celebratory fellowship—a very proper leisure activity and certainly one to encourage.

4. *The reality of stewardship*. We are stewards of all the time God gives us, of all the abilities and skills that are ours, and of all the opportunities offered to us. We are also stewards of our own bodies and of this earth. Stewardship means responsibility for managing, caring for, and making the most of the resources God commits to our trust, and doing it in a way that squares with his known wishes. That does not in any way diminish our freedom to make use of created things for our enjoyment, but it does mean that in doing so we shall take care not to seem to approve what is immoral and demoralizing, nor to expose others to unhelpful influences, nor to play with fire ourselves. The Puritans closed theaters not because they did not enjoy drama but because the theaters of their day were immoral and demoralizing places.

In a positive sense, recognition of our stewardship—both its privileges and its responsibilities—should incline us to choose the leisure activities that bring us closest to God, to people, to beauty, and to all that ennobles. "Whatever is true, whatever is noble, whatever is right, whatever is pure, whatever is lovely, whatever is admirable—if anything is excellent or praiseworthy—think about such things" (Phil. 4:8). We should not let the mediocre become the enemy of the good in leisure activity any more than we should let the good become the enemy of the best.

THE PLACE OF PLEASURE

A quick review of what was spelled out in the previous chapter is all that is needed at this point in our discussion. What is pleasure? As was noted earlier, Webster defines it as "the gratification of the senses or of the mind; agreeable sensations or emotions; the feeling produced by enjoyment or the expectation of good." Like joy, it is a gift of God, but whereas joy is basically active (one rejoices), pleasure is basically passive (one is pleased). As God himself takes pleasure in being God and in doing what he does,[9] so he means human beings to find pleasure in being his.

God values pleasure, both his and ours, and it is his pleasure to give us pleasure as a fruit of his saving love. In the order of creation, pleasures as such are meant to serve as signposts directing us to God, which is why we must appreciate them rather than renounce them. Being greedy for pleasures is ungodly, but being grateful for pleasures is one aspect of reverence and worship. Calvin and the Puritans, as we saw, were clear and strong in this. It is supremely ironic, and pathetic and tragic too, that after two millennia of Christian culture, the West should now be plunging back into a self-defeating hedonism horribly similar to the barbaric pagan lifestyle of the first century, and that it should be doing so in the belief that the Christian religion is basically anti-human because it does not set up pleasing oneself as life's highest value. But Calvin's wisdom about pleasure remains basic to authentic Christian living in this or any age.

THE USE OF TREASURE

Should I apologize for dignifying our money with the label "treasure," when the word suggests something of enormous value, even though I know firsthand that I—and I suspect most of my readers—do not rate among the world's wealthy? Not necessarily. One does not have to have a lot of money for it to become "my precious," as Gollum constantly calls the fateful ring in J. R. R. Tolkien's epic, and for it to affect one as Jelly-Roll Morton sang that jazz affected him—"The more I have, the more I want, it seems; I page old Doctor Jazz in my dreams."[10] Small sums of money are almost more effective than large ones in grabbing the heart and setting one dreaming and scheming about ways of getting more.

In his wise and searching book, *Money, Possessions and Eternity*, Randy Alcorn quotes Cyprian's description of the affluent of his day: "Their property held them in chains . . . chains which shackled their courage and choked their faith and hampered their judgment and throttled souls. . . . They think of themselves as owners, whereas it is they rather who are owned; enslaved as they are to their own property, they are not the masters of their money but its slaves." Alongside this Alcorn sets the testimony of John Wesley, whose word to his preachers and society members was: "Gain all you can, save all you can, give all you can. . . . Money never stays with me. It would burn me if it did. I throw it out of my hands as soon as possible, lest it find its way into my heart."[11] From these quotations the impossibility that Jesus announced—that of serving both God and mammon (money)—becomes plain (Matt. 6:24). A conscious refusal to serve money is therefore a necessary part of the Christian lifestyle, as the following quotations show:

> *Do not store up for yourselves treasures on earth, where moth and rust destroy, and where thieves break in and steal. But store up for yourselves treasures in heaven, where moth and rust do not destroy, and where thieves do not break in and steal. For where your treasure is, there your heart will be also. (Matt. 6:19-21)*

> *Command those who are rich in this present world not to be arrogant nor to put their hope in wealth, which is so uncertain, but to put their hope in God, who richly provides us with everything for our enjoyment. Command them to do good, to be rich in good deeds, and to be generous and willing to share. In this way they will lay up treasures for themselves as a firm foundation for the coming age, so that they may take hold of the life that is truly life. (1 Tim. 6:17-19)*

The point is plain. Money is for giving, and it is to be used to do good. Since all the money we have is God's gift to us, it is not to be loved and hoarded or laid out for purely selfish purposes. Rather, it is to be stewarded for the service of God and one's neighbor. So generosity linked to frugality, rather than conspicuous consumption, must mark the Christian. If that means that he or she cannot keep up with the world's wealthiest Joneses, well, so be it. There are in any case more important things to do.

COUNTERCULTURAL

In a post-Christian era such as ours in the West, an authentic Christian lifestyle—with its built-in balance of work and leisure, worship and witness, self-denial and self-giving for the glory of God and the good of others—is bound to seem countercultural and implicitly censorious. That is what happened in the pre-Christian world of first-century Graeco-Roman paganism and in the pre-evangelical world of Elizabethan and Jacobean England, where the Puritans sought the conversion of their country and became highly unpopular for doing so. Some unpopularity is inseparable from the practice of consistent Christianity, and we had better brace ourselves to meet it; for as things stand now in the West, it can only increase. But as Jesus has told us, "wisdom is proved right by her actions" (Matt. 11:19). The motto of the first institution at which I taught was "Be right and persist"; that is a word in season for all who would honor their Lord by their lives today.

6

GUIDANCE

How God Leads Us

WISDOM ALONG THE WAY

Evangelicals differ from most Roman Catholics and liberals in that they are constantly uptight about guidance. No other concern commands more interest or arouses more anxiety among them nowadays than discovering the will of God.

It was of evangelicals that Joseph Bayly wrote in 1968: "If there is a serious concern among Christian students today, it is for guidance. Holiness may have been the passion of another generation's Christian young men and women. Or soul-winning. Or evangelizing the world. . . . But not today. Today the theme is getting to know the will of God."[1]

Again it was of evangelicals that Russ Johnston declared in 1971: "I've spoken at many conferences where part of the afternoons are set aside for workshops. . . . If you make one of the workshops 'Knowing the Will of God,' half the people sign up for it even if there are twenty other choices."[2]

And it was of evangelicals that Garry Friesen reported in 1981: "Interest in the subject of guidance is consistently high. The demand for magazine articles and books on the subject continues unabated. People continue to seek guidance on guidance."[3]

My own experience confirms this. The more earnest and sensitive a believer is, the more likely he or she is to be hung up about guidance. And if I am any judge, the evangelical anxiety level on the subject continues to rise.

Why is this? The source of anxiety is that a desire for guidance is linked with uncertainty about how to get it and fear of the consequences of not getting it. Such anxiety has an unhappy way of escalating. Anxious people get allured by any and every form of certainty that offers itself, no matter how irrational. They become vulnerable to strange influences and do zany things. This makes the guidance issue more perplexing than ever before. Over the past 150 years there has been a buildup of tension to a point where it muddles minds, darkens counsel, and obstructs maturity in a way that is Spirit-quenching.

When muscles are hurting, relaxation is the first step toward a cure, and the same is true of anxiety about guidance. The persons most worried are regularly those with least cause for alarm.

First, let it be said that the desire to know God's guidance is a sign of spiritual health. Healthy believers want to please God. Through regeneration they have come to love obedience and to find joy in doing God's will. The very thought of offending him grieves them deeply. They desire to live in a way that shows gratitude to God for his grace. As they grow spiritually, this desire becomes stronger. Naturally, they want clear indications of the will of God.

Reinforcing this desire is bewilderment at the vast range of choices in every field of our civilization. To want help in decision-making is understandable. Some turn for this help to gurus, palmists, astrologers, clairvoyants, Ann Landers, and specialist counselors. Healthy Christians, however, while valuing human advice, look to God also. There are many promises of divine direction in Scripture and many testimonies to its reality. It is wrong for Christians not to seek God's help in making the choices, commitments, and decisions that shape their lives.

Secondly, let it be said that the fear of spiritual ruin through mistaking God's guidance is a sign of unthinking unbelief. I have a particular fear in mind, one that I have met many times in my ministry. It is widespread. It is not the product of any one school of thought. Rather it is the twisting of truth that our fallen minds, with their legalistic bias and their inclination to view God as an ogre, easily fall into.

Satan, who loves to misrepresent God and make him seem ugly, naturally sponsors it!

It may be stated as follows: God's plan for your life is like an itinerary drawn up for you by a travel agent. As long as you are in the right place at the right time to board each plane or train or bus or boat, all is well. But miss one of these preplanned connections, and the itinerary is ruined. A revised plan can only ever be second-best compared with the original.

The assumption is that God lacks either the will or the wisdom to get you back on track. A substandard spiritual life is all that is now open to you. You may not be on the scrap heap, but you are on the shelf, having forfeited much of your usefulness. Your mistake sentences you to live and serve God as a second-rate Christian.

Many Christians run scared, fearing such disaster every time a major decision has to be made. Others trudge along with heavy hearts, believing that this fate is already upon them because of some imprudence long ago. The fruit that so fearful a fancy bears is bitter.

The kernel of truth in the above scenario is that bad decisions have sad consequences from which we cannot expect to be shielded. But beyond that, the fear expresses nothing more than unbelief regarding the goodness, wisdom, and power of God. God can and does restore the years that the locusts have eaten (see Joel 2:25). Scripture shows us a number of saints making great and grievous mistakes about the will of God for them—Jacob fooling his father, Moses murdering the Egyptian, David numbering the people, Peter boycotting Gentile believers—yet none became incurably second class. On the contrary, they were each forgiven and restored. This is how all true saints live.

Misconceiving God's will is less sinful than knowing it and not doing it. If God restored David after his adultery with Bathsheba and murder of Uriah, and Peter after his threefold denial of Christ, we should have no doubt that he can and will restore Christians who err through making honest mistakes about his guidance.

The last phrase paves the way to my third point: Wrong ideas about God's guidance lead to wrong conclusions about the right thing to do. The basic fault here is disregard of a principle that is writ large in Scripture—too large perhaps for some to see. The principle is that the right course is always to choose the wisest means to the noblest end, namely the advancing of God's kingdom and glory. Moral law delimits the area within which the choice must be made (for sin is always out of bounds; the end never justifies the means). God-given wisdom, comparing the short- and long-term effects of alternative courses of action, then leads us within these limits to the best option. That option will always be the greatest good, or in invidious situations where no course of action or inaction is free from regrettable aspects, the least evil.

In making our choice, that which is merely good ("good enough," as we say) must never become the enemy of the best. It is never enough to ask, as the Pharisees did, whether such and such a course of action is free from taint of sin. The question should be: Is it the best I can envisage for the glory of God and the good of souls? God enables us to discern this by prayerfully using our minds—thinking how Scripture applies, comparing alternatives, weighing advice, taking account of our heart's desire, estimating our capabilities. Some call this common sense. The Bible calls it wisdom. It is one of God's most precious gifts.

Is there a personal touch from God in all this? Most certainly. Those whom God wants in the pastorate, in cross-cultural missionary work, or some other specialized ministry are ordinarily made to realize they will never find job satisfaction doing anything else. When God has a particular career in mind for a person, he bestows on that person an interest in that field of expertise. When God plans that two people should marry, he blends their hearts. But God's inclinings of the heart (as distinct from our own self-generated ambitions and longings) are experienced only as meshing in with the judgments of wisdom. Thus interest in an unsuitable person as a life partner or a ministry beyond one's ability should be seen as a temptation rather than a divine call.

Over the past 150 years, however, a different approach to Christian decision-making has established itself, one that plays down the significance of thought and wisdom in the quest to know God's will. A mode of guidance more direct and immediate than the forming of a wise judgment on the matter in hand has come to be desired. Why is this? The desire seems to reflect a mixture of things.

One is the anti-intellectual, feeling-oriented, short-term mentality of today's secular culture, invading and swamping Christian minds.

Another is an admirable humility. Believers do not trust themselves to discern the ideal course of action, and so they want it directly revealed to them.

Another is the false idea that what God wants his children to do is irrational by ordinary standards and not something to which wisdom would direct us.

Another is the fancy that, since each Christian is a special object of God's love, special instructions from God can be expected whenever he or she has to make a significant decision—a fancy that seems to reflect as much of childish egoism as it does of childlike faith.

Another is the presence in Scripture of guidance stories involving direct revelation, stories on which latter-day narratives of guidance are verbally modeled, leaving the impression that guidance is usually given this way.

Some seek guidance by making their minds blank and receiving what then rises into consciousness as a divine directive. This was a daily devotional routine in Frank Buchman's Oxford Group (afterwards Moral Rearmament). It undoubtedly kept people honest with their own consciences, and that was good. But murky urges and self-indulgent dreams as well as pricks from conscience will surface at such times. Those who assume that whatever "vision" fills the blank is from God have no defense against the invasion of obsessive, grandiose, self-serving imaginations spawned by their own conceit.

Others, like the diviners of ancient paganism and the devotees of modern astrology, want to be told facts about the future in light of which they may chart a knowledgeable course in the present. This is what guidance means to them. But Scripture directs us to live by God's precept, rather than by prying into his hidden will or purpose. As Deuteronomy 29:29 says: "The secret things belong to the LORD our God; but the things that are revealed belong to us and to our children forever, that we may follow all the words of this law."

Others, rather than seeking wisdom to do the best and most God-honoring thing in the circumstances, will draw lots or set up situations in which they ask God for signs (a practice loosely based on Gideon's action recorded in Judges 6:36-40, and therefore sometimes called "fleecing"); or they will wait for a "prophecy" or dream or vision or heavenly voice in their inner ear. Sometimes they succeed in inducing the experience they seek, as did covetous Balaam. There are few experiences that cannot be induced if one wants them badly enough. Many have been led in this way to embrace wildcat schemes and immoral follies, believing that God has approved or even instigated such plans.

A similar mistake is to find in Scripture private messages from God that in fact are no more than one's own reading into the text a meaning that cannot be read out of it. My long-time friend and teacher Alan Stibbs, after promising to serve a church in northern England, was invited to an attractive post in South Wales. He read in Isaiah 43:6 (RSV), "I will say to the north, Give up," and got the idea that God was promising him providentially to terminate his prior commitment so as to free him to do what he felt he most wanted to do. When this did not happen, Alan looked again at his text and saw that it goes on: "and to the south, Do not withhold." He then realized that the verse concerns the gathering of God's people from all over following the Exile and that he had been fooling himself with his original fancy.

God is sovereign and gracious to those who humbly seek him. No doubt he has given guidance on occasion by all the means I have mentioned, and no doubt he will do so again. But such cases are exceptions, and to expect them to be the rule is to ask for trouble. What sort of trouble? Either delusion and misdirected zeal, or apathy and lack of motivation as a result of concluding that if guidance has not come in this way, there can be nothing in particular that God wants one to do. Which is worse—fanatical activity or passive idleness? Being a lunatic or being lazy? Each is bad. But a biblical approach to guidance will save us from both kinds of trouble.

How may we formulate such an approach? I offer the following ten checkpoints as a summary:

1. Ask the question: What is the best I can do for my God?

2. Note the instructions of Scripture. The summons to love God and others, the limits set and the obligations established by the law, the insistence on energetic action (Eccles. 8:10; 1 Cor. 15:58), and the

detailed drilling in wisdom (see Proverbs and James especially) enable one to make the best choice among behavioral options.

3. Follow the examples of godliness in Scripture. Imitate the love and humility of Jesus himself. If we do this, we cannot go far wrong.

4. Let wisdom judge the best course of action. Consider not only the wisdom God gives you personally, but the corporate wisdom of your friends and mentors in the Christian community. Don't be a spiritual Lone Ranger. When you think you know God's will, have your perception checked. Draw on the wisdom of those who are wiser than you are. Take advice.

5. Note nudges from God that come your way—special concerns or restlessness of heart might indicate that something needs to be changed.

6. Cherish the divine peace that Paul says "garrisons" (guards, keeps safe and steady) the hearts of those who are in God's will (Phil. 4:7).

7. Observe the limits set by circumstances to what is possible. When it is clear that those limits cannot be changed, accept them as from God.

8. Be prepared for God's guidance to be withheld until the right time comes for a decision. God usually guides one step at a time.

9. Be prepared for God to direct you to something you do not like and teach you to like it!

10. Never forget that if you make a bad decision, it is not the end. God forgives and restores. He is your covenant God and Savior. He will not let you go, however badly you may have slipped. "Rejoice not over me, O my enemy; when I fall, I shall rise; when I sit in darkness, the LORD will be a light to me" (Mic. 7:8 RSV).

Micah's words, just quoted, offer great comfort to all who want to do God's will but find themselves afraid they may have missed it. The Lord is my Shepherd. He leads me. He restores me. He stays with me. I need not be uptight! What a relief!

FANTASY AND REALITY

As we said at the outset, guidance is a very tricky subject for many modern Christians. Most of us have had firsthand experience with guidance problems, either our own or those of others whom we have tried to help. Focus now on these perplexities. Why do so many problems of this sort arise? Where do the difficulties come from? Most of them are of our own making. In our quest for God's guidance we become our own worst enemies. What happens? We go into a twofold tailspin.

On the one hand, we lose theological control, so that erratic superstitions take over. We isolate and narrow the guidance issue to major decisions that involve sizable risks for the future—the choice of a life partner, a vocation or employment, or a place to live. That isolation is bad theology and leads to the further mistake of thinking that guidance on these matters comes "out of the blue," like an oracle reflecting facts about the future that we ourselves do not and cannot know. Those who look for guidance through a prophecy, inner voice, "fleece," or random selection of Bible verses are under the spell of this misconception.

On the other hand, we embrace the romantic fancy that all experiences of true guidance can be reported in terms of the formula: "The Lord told me" thus and so. Such experiences, so we think, produce absolute confidence about the rightness of a specific action. In the absence of any experience that we could describe in this way, we say we have not received guidance as yet. If, however, after prayer we find ourselves with a pressing urge in our minds, we hail it as "my guidance" and defy anyone to talk us out of it. Are we right? Probably not. Yet this idea of guidance is so well established in our thinking that a recent book could call it the "traditional" view.

What shall we say of it? The first thing to say is that this idea of guidance is actually a novelty among orthodox evangelicals. It does not go back further than the last century. Second, it has led people to so much foolish action on the one hand and so much foolish inaction on the other, as well as puzzlement and heartbreak when the "hotline" to God seems to go silent, that it has to be seen as discredited. Third, it must be said that Scripture gives us no more warrant constantly to expect personal "hotline," "voice-from-the-control-tower" guidance than to expect new authoritative revelations to come our way for the guidance of the whole church.

Certainly God's guidance is promised to every believer. Certainly some individuals in Scripture (Gideon, Manoah and his wife, and Philip, for instance) received guidance in "hotline" fashion—just as some biblical characters did receive revelations of universally authoritative truth and just as Gideon's "hotline" guidance, given by theophany, was later confirmed to him by remarkable things that happened to a sheepskin on two successive nights. But, as was said earlier, we must learn to distinguish between the ordinary and the extraordinary, the constant and the occasional, the rule and the exception.

God may reveal himself and give guidance to his servants any way he pleases. It is not for us to set limits on him. But it remains a question as to whether or not we are entitled to expect "hotline" disclosures on a regular basis. The correct answer is no. All the biblical narratives of God's direct communications with men are on the face of it exceptional, and the biblical model of personal guidance is quite different.

Scripture presents guidance as a covenantal blessing promised to each of God's people in the form of instruction on how to live, both in broad policy terms and in making specific decisions. "I will instruct you and teach you the way you should go; I will counsel you with my eye upon you" (Ps. 32:8 RSV). "Good and upright is the LORD; therefore he instructs sinners in his ways. He guides the humble in what is right and teaches them his way" (Ps. 25:8-9). How does God guide? By instructing. How does he instruct? Partly by his shaping of our circumstances and partly by his gift of wisdom to understand the teaching of his Word and apply it to our circumstances. God's regular method of guidance is a combination of providence and instruction. What more he may do in a particular case cannot be anticipated in advance. But wisdom will always be given if we are humble and docile enough to receive it.

God's guidance is more like the marriage guidance, child guidance, or career guidance received from counselors than it is like being "talked down" by the airport controller as one flies blind through the clouds. Seeking God's guidance is not like practicing divination or consulting oracles, astrologers, and clairvoyants for information about the future. Rather, this quest is comparable with everyday thinking through of alternative options in given situations to determine the best course open to us. The inward experience of being divinely guided is not ordinarily one of seeing signs or hearing voices, but rather one of being enabled to work out the best thing to do.

The classic Bible presentation of the guided life and of the reality of the guidance that produces it is Psalm 23, the beloved shepherd psalm. Christians should read it as a declaration of what it means to be a believer led through life by the triune God who is the Father, the Son, and the Holy Spirit, the "he" who is "they." The picture is of the saint as a divinely led sheep. Silly and apt to stray as I am ("prone to wander, Lord, I feel it; prone to leave the God I love,"[4]), my covenant God will not leave me bereft of either security or sustenance. He provides rest ("beside still waters"), refreshment ("he restores my soul"), protection ("through the valley of the shadow of death"), enrichment ("thou preparest a table"), and enjoyment ("goodness and mercy shall follow me"). Guidance is one facet of that total covenant care whereby the King of Love draws me into the destiny of deliverance and delight that he planned for me before the world was made.

Look more closely at verse 3: "He leads me in paths of righteousness for his name's sake." "Paths of righteousness" are behavior patterns that please God because they correspond to his commandments and match his moral nature. Perceptive and prudent vocational decisions are certainly included, but the basic idea is that our holy God calls us to be holy. This is the essence of biblical guidance. "For his name's sake" refers to the furthering of his glory (i.e., our responsive praise for his revealed praiseworthiness) through his demonstration of covenant faithfulness. The Lord is my Shepherd; he is pledged to watch over me, order my travels, stay with me, and bring me safely home. He will not fail in his commitment. Finally, "he leads me" means that by his providential instruction he gives me wisdom to see the right thing—the best, the most fruitful, the purest and noblest, the most Christlike and God-honoring thing—to do in each situation, and he motivates me to that end.

How does God give this discernment? We say it is a matter of wisdom. Where does this wisdom come from? That question may be answered in two ways. Formally and theologically, the answer is: from

God's Word and Spirit. Personally and experientially, the answer is: from being transformed by God's grace. Each answer is part of the other; both go together.

God's teaching in Scripture is our basic guide for living. Bible history and biography illustrate and enforce, both positively and negatively, the divine demand for faith and faithfulness that so many didactic passages spell out. The Holy Spirit who inspired the Scriptures authenticates them to us as the Word of God, making us unable to doubt their authority. He also interprets them to us as we read and meditate on them and hear and read others' expositions of them. Interpretation means precisely seeing how they apply. Commentaries can tell us what the text meant as an expression of the writer's mind to the original audience, but only the Holy Spirit can show us what it means as God's Word of direction for our lives today. Only through the Spirit is guidance from Scripture a reality.

Two points often are overlooked. First, in many situations the general principles of Scripture are all the guidance we either need or get. In military operations the general will give the field commander his orders of the day in the form of objectives (capture this strong point, defend that position, move troops to such and such a place), and leave it to him to devise the ways and means. God often guides us in the same fashion, leaving it to us to use the intelligence he gave us to work out the best way to implement biblical principles and priorities. It is part of the process whereby he matures us in Christ.

Second, the moral law of Scripture, which is the family code for all God's children, leaves us free to make our own choices as to how we use created things—what interests we pursue, what hobbies we have, and so forth. No guidance is to be expected in these areas beyond the general maxims of not letting the good displace the best, not hurting others by the ways in which we enjoy ourselves, and not hurting ourselves by excessive indulgence that diverts us from heaven to earth and from the Giver to his gifts. These are the rules of using liberty responsibly.

On the other hand, inward discernment of the best and holiest thing to do is always a fruit of faith, repentance, consecration, and transformation by the Holy Spirit. We know the opening words of

Romans 12: "I appeal to you therefore, brethren, by the mercies of God, to present your bodies as a living sacrifice, holy and acceptable to God, which is your spiritual worship. Do not be conformed to this world but be transformed by the renewal of your mind . . ." (vv. 1-2 RSV). Less often, however, is stress laid on what comes next: "That you may prove what is the will of God, what is good and acceptable and perfect" (v. 2). *Prove* means "discern by examining alternatives." Paul's point is that there is a moral and spiritual precondition of being able to see in each situation what God wants done. Those whose minds God is currently transforming may still err about specific aspects of God's will in areas where their earthly perspective yet holds sway, but where no work of inward renewal is in progress, no adequate discernment of God's will at any point can be expected. Guidance is God's gift to those who are looking to him—that means precisely, looking to Jesus Christ—to save them from sin. "He leads *the humble* in what is right, and teaches *the humble* his way" (Ps. 25:9 RSV, emphasis added).

We should note here the importance of models. The apostles tell us to imitate Christ and also themselves. What this imitation amounts to is catching the spirit of lowly, costly, self-giving love—love that in its desire to make the other person great spends and is spent up to the limit. Part of discerning God's will is an awareness of the need to maintain this attitude in all relationships and to avoid the ego trips that negate it.

The importance of corporateness in our quest to know the will of God also needs to be stressed. We were neither made nor redeemed for self-sufficient aloneness. We must not expect our private stock of wisdom and discernment to suffice. "In an abundance of counselors there is safety" (Prov. 11:14 RSV). We must never be too proud to take advice from persons wiser and godlier than ourselves. Personal guidance that we believe we have received by an inner nudge from the Lord needs to be checked with believers who are capable of recognizing unrealism, delusion, and folly when they see it. The Holy Spirit regularly uses the fellowship of the body of Christ to deepen our discernment of God's will. It is part of the discipline of divine guidance to be ready for the Spirit to confirm his will for our lives through other believers.

Such, then, is divine guidance according to the Scriptures. It may be more than this. What is certain, however, is that it will never be less. Any supposed guidance that deviates from the Bible, the limits of possibility set by providence, and the discernment of the regenerate heart as to what most honors and pleases our Savior God must be judged phony and delusive.

In this age of shallow, secularized self-confidence pitfalls abound. We need to search our hearts time and again lest we fool ourselves and others by imagining that we have received God's guidance when really our own desires are leading us astray. Yet God remains faithful, and it may still become every Christian's honest and true testimony that "he leads me in paths of righteousness for his name's sake." Praise his holy name!

TRUE GUIDANCE

I have already said that God ordinarily guides his children in their decision-making through Bible-based wisdom. I have dismissed the idea that guidance is usually or essentially an inner voice telling us facts otherwise unknown and prescribing strange modes of action. I have criticized the way some Christians wait passively for guidance and "put out a fleece" when perplexed, rather than prayerfully following wisdom's lead. After all this, I am sure there are mutterings. Some readers may believe that I have played down and thereby dishonored the guiding ministry of the Holy Spirit. One cannot say what I have said in today's steamy Christian atmosphere without provoking that reaction. So there is need now to discuss the Holy Spirit's role in guidance in a direct way.

The last thing I want to do is to dishonor, or lead others to dishonor, the Holy Spirit. But the fact must be faced that not all endeavors that seek to honor the Holy Spirit succeed in their purpose. There is such a thing as fanatical delusion, just as there is such a thing as barren intellectualism. Overheated views of life in the Spirit can be as damaging as "flat tire" versions of Christianity that minimize the Spirit's ministry. This is especially true in relation to guidance.

What does it mean to be "led by the Spirit" in personal decision-making? That phrase, found in Romans 8:14 and Galatians 5:18, speaks of resisting sinful impulses, not of decision-making. However, the question of what it means to be Spirit-led in choosing courses of action is a proper and important one.

The Spirit leads by helping us understand the biblical guidelines within which we must keep, the biblical goals at which we must aim, and the biblical models that we should imitate, as well as the bad examples from which we are meant to take warning.

He leads through prayer and others' advice, giving us wisdom as to how we can best follow biblical teaching.

He leads by giving us the desire for spiritual growth and God's glory. The result is that spiritual priorities become clearer, and our resources of wisdom and experience for making future decisions increase.

He leads, finally, by making us delight in God's will so that we find ourselves wanting to do it because we know it is best. Wisdom's paths will be "ways of pleasantness" (Prov. 3:17). If at first we find we dislike what we see to be God's will for us, God will change our attitude if we let him. God is not a sadist, directing us to do what we do not want to do so that he can see us suffer. He wants joy for us in every course of action to which he leads us, even those from which we shrink at first and that involve outward unpleasantness.

No one, I hope, would dispute what I have said, but some would say that it is only half the story. Part of what being Spirit-led means, they would tell us, is that one receives instruction from the Spirit through prophecies and inward revelations such as repeatedly came to godly people in Bible times (see Gen. 22; 2 Chron. 7:12-22; Jer. 32:19; Acts 8:29; 11:28; 13:4; 21:11; 1 Cor. 14:30). They believe this kind of communication to be the fulfillment of God's promise that "your ears shall hear a word behind you saying, 'This is the way, walk in it,' when you turn to the right or when you turn to the left" (Isa. 30:21 RSV). They are sure that some impressions of this kind should be identified as the Spirit-given "word of knowledge" in 1 Corinthians 12:8. They insist that this is divine guidance in its highest and purest form, which Christians should therefore constantly seek. Those who play it down, they would say, thereby show that they have too limited a view of life in the Spirit.

Here I must come clean. I know that this line of thought is sincerely believed by many people who are, I am sure, better Christians than I am. Yet I think it is wrong and harmful, and I shall now argue against it. I choose my words with care, for some of the arguments made against this view are as bad and damaging as is the view itself. The way of wisdom is like walking a tightrope, from which one can fall by overbalancing either to the left or to the right. As, in Richard Baxter's sharp-sighted phrase, overdoing is undoing, so overreacting is undermining.

The issue here is not whether a person's life in the Spirit is shallow or deep, as if the further one advances spiritually, the more one will seek and find guidance through prophecies and inward revelations. Nor is the issue whether God has so limited himself that he will never communicate directly with present-day Christians as he did with some saints in biblical times. In my view there is no biblical warrant either for correlating spiritual maturity with direct divine guidance or for denying that God may still directly indicate his will to his servants. The real issue is twofold: what we should expect from God in this regard and what we should do with any invading impressions that come our way.

What should Christians do when they feel that God has directly told them to say or do something? They should face up to the following facts:

1. If anyone today receives a direct disclosure from God, it will have no canonical significance. It will not become part of the church's rule of faith and life; nor will the church be under any obligation to acknowledge the disclosure as revelation; nor will anyone merit blame for suspecting that the disclosure was not from God. If the alleged disclosure is a prediction (as when Rees Howells, founder of the Bible College of South Wales, predicted back in 1930 in his book *God Challenges the Dictators* that there would be no Second World War), Moses assures us that there is not even a *prima facie* case for treating it as from God until it has come true (Deut. 18:21ff.). If the alleged disclosure is a directive (as when a leader claims that God told him to found a hospital, university, mission, or crusade of some kind), any who associate themselves with his project should do so because wis-

dom tells them that it is needed, realistic, and God-honoring, not because the leader tells them that God directly commanded him (and by implication them) to attempt it.

People who believe they have received direct indications of what God will do or what they should do should refrain in all situations (worship services, board meetings, gatherings of family or friends, preparation of publications, or whatever) from asking others to agree that direct revelation has been given to them, and Christians should greet any such request with resolute silence.

2. Guidance in this particular form is not promised. For it to occur is, as we have said, extraordinary, exceptional, and anomalous. No Scripture leads us to hope or to look for it. Isaiah 30:21, which may seem to point this way, is actually a promise of wise teaching through wise teachers. No one, therefore, who believes that he received a direct revelation at any time should look for this event to recur. The idea that spiritual persons may expect this sort of guidance often or that such experiences are proof of their holiness or of their call and fitness to lead others should be dismissed out of hand.

3. Direct communications from God take the form of impressions, and impressions can come even to the most devoted and prayerful people from such murky sources as wishful thinking, fear, obsessional neurosis, schizophrenia, hormonal imbalance, depression, side effects of medication, and satanic delusion, as well as from God. Impressions need to be suspected before they are sanctioned and tested before they are trusted. Confidence that one's impressions are God-given is no guarantee that this is really so, even when they persist and grow stronger through long seasons of prayer. Bible-based wisdom must judge them.

Two tragedies of misguided impressions come to mind. Both involved godly men who were greatly used in spiritual ministry. Rees Howells, whom I have already mentioned, informed his Bible college community that through him God was forbidding marriage to those who wished fully to serve the Lord. Havoc resulted from this unscriptural teaching.

Again, some years earlier, the American Frank Sandford had an impression that he should cruise the Atlantic in a yacht to intercede for worldwide revival. When a colleague became ill, he had an impression that they should not put in to port for treatment. The man died. After serving a prison term for his action, Sandford had an impression that he was called to reproduce the hidden life of Elijah prior to the contest at Carmel. So he did, living entirely incognito save to a handful of friends, until his death. These are examples of unjudged impressions and their sad results. To follow impressions, however much they are bound up with the holy concerns of evangelism, intercession, piety, and revival, is not to be Spirit-led.

Following unjudged impressions, particularly when they concern sex, money, and power, makes the Lord's enemies blaspheme and discredits the whole idea of a guided life. In reaction some conclude that no specific impressions are ever given by the Holy Spirit and that every claim to them must be a delusion. But that also is wrong. Impressions—not revelations of information but focusings of concern—belong to Christian living. When we say we have a "vision" or "burden" about something, we are referring to an impression. When our concern is biblically proper, we are right to regard our impression as a nudge from the Holy Spirit.

Nehemiah speaks of what "God had put into my heart to do for Jerusalem" (Neh. 2:12 RSV), and by prayer, persuasion, and push, Nehemiah got the job done. Paul and Silas "attempted to go into Bithynia, but the Spirit of Jesus did not allow them" (Acts 16:7 RSV)—that is, an inner impression restrained them. God, as they soon discovered, was leading them to Greece. Paul's "mind could not rest" while evangelizing Troas, because Titus had not come (2 Cor. 2:13; *mind* is "spirit" in the Greek, meaning a mind enlightened by God's Spirit). So Paul left, construing his restlessness as God prompting him to go in search of Titus rather than continue the Troas mission. These are biblical examples of saints pulled or pressed by God in particular directions. This is an experience that most Christians know.

My point is not that the Spirit of God gives no direct impressions, but rather that impressions must be rigorously tested by biblical wisdom—the corporate wisdom of the believing community as well as personal wisdom. If this is not done, impressions that are rooted in egoism, pride, headstrong unrealism, the fancy that irrationality glorifies God, a sense that some human being is infallible, or similar misconceptions will be allowed to masquerade as Spirit-given. Only impressions verified as biblically appropriate and practically wise should be recognized as from God. People who receive impressions about what they should believe or do should question such impressions until they have been thoroughly tested.

Nor can one be certain even then about one's impressions. Some impressions seem to be instances of clairvoyance, sanctified for restraint or encouragement (as in recorded cases of Christians feeling constrained to leave trains and planes that later crashed or when C. T. Studd saw in the margin of his Bible the words "China, India, Africa," the three parts of the world where he subsequently served as a pioneer missionary). There is no certain way to test such impressions. Sometimes one will not be able to tell whether they are a message from God or a human fancy. The correct conclusion to draw is that as we seek to do what by biblical standards best serves God's glory and the good of others, God will be with us—just that.

The radios of my youth would crackle with atmospherics, making clear reception impossible. All forms of self-centeredness and self-indulgence, from surface-level indiscipline and lawlessness to the subtlety of grandiose elitism or the irreverence of not obeying the guidance one has received already, will act as atmospherics in the heart, making recognition of God's will harder than it should be and one's testing of impressions less thorough and exact. But those who are being "led by the Spirit" into humble holiness will also be "led by the Spirit" in evaluating their impressions, and so they will increasingly be able to distinguish the Spirit's nudges from impure and improper desire. "He . . . teaches the humble his way" (Ps. 25:9 RSV). Blessed, then, we may say, are the pure in heart. They shall know the will of God.

7

JOY

A Neglected Discipline

Homes have kitchens, and kitchens have counters, and on many kitchen counters today stands a plastic container labeled "Joy"— "Lemon Fresh Joy," to be precise. What does it hold? Detergent for the operation that in England is called "washing up" and in America "doing the dishes." (Think about the fact that "wash up" in America means "make yourself clean and comfortable, ready for a meal," and you will see how right Oscar Wilde was to speak of England and America as two great nations separated by a common language.)

Why call a detergent Joy? The question is not hard to answer. *Joy* is a word that has "good vibes." It is a word that makes one feel bright, and when washing dishes, one needs bright feelings. The word has this effect because it connects to the desire of our heart. We want joy. We were made for joy. The value of human beings is sometimes affirmed by quoting, from a black source, the words, "God don't make no junk." In similar fashion, we may affirm the true goal of human life by saying, "God don't make nobody for misery." If we are miserable, it is because we have chosen to say no to joy. The fact remains that God intended joy for us from the start.

JOY IS INTENDED

Let me spell that out. Scripture shows that God creates human beings with their joy in view. "Man's chief end is to glorify God, and [in so doing] to enjoy him for ever" (Westminster Shorter Catechism, answer to question 1). Joy was God's plan for people from the beginning. God's purpose that we should enjoy him, both directly in face-to-face fellowship and indirectly through enjoyment of what he has created, is pictured by the earthly home he gave Adam and Eve—a pleasure-garden (Eden) where he himself walked in the cool of the day. The psalmist regains a spiritual sanity he had almost lost when he declares: "I am always with you; you hold me by my right hand. You guide me with your counsel, and afterward you will take me into glory. Whom have I in heaven but you? And earth has nothing I desire besides you. . . . God is the strength of my heart and my portion for ever. . . . It is good to be near God" (Ps. 73:23-28). The thought is the same as in Psalm 43:4, where God is called "my joy, and my delight."

The New Testament tells us that our redemption and life in Christ reverses our damnation and death in Adam (see Rom. 5:12-19; 1 Cor. 15:21ff.), that God "richly provides us with everything for our enjoyment" (1 Tim. 6:17), and that glorified saints endlessly delight in the God whom they endlessly adore (see Rev. 7:9-17; 21:1-4; 22:1-5). Thus it appears that God's saving activity vindicates, restores, and fulfills his original purpose of joy for man that satanic malice and human sin have thwarted. Joy to the world remains God's goal.

The New Testament takes us a step further in understanding this truth. In John's Gospel the veil is lifted on the mutual love and honor that bind Father, Son, and Holy Spirit together in the unity of the one eternal God (see John 2:16ff.; 4:34; 5:19-30; 6:38-40; 12:27ff.; 13:31ff.; 14:31; 16:13-15). Jesus prays to his Father that his disciples may be "one . . . in us . . . as we are one: I in them and you in me" (John 17:21-23). With that, and in reality as one aspect of it, he states his wish "that they may have the full measure of my joy within them" (v. 13). God's original purpose was that human beings should share the joyful togetherness of the Trinity. The Gospel of Christ, which proclaims deliverance from sin and is backed up by God's providential kindness (see Acts 14:17; Rom. 2:4), is an invitation to enter this joy through penitent and trustful worship. It is in love to the Father and the Son, love that mirrors the Son's love for the Father, that the fullness of joy will be finally found. But sin—self-worship, transgression, unbelief, impenitence—separates us from the joy of God and exposes us to a godless eternity instead (see John 3:16-21; Rom. 1:18—2:16; Rev. 22:11-15). Yet the gospel invitation still stands, and if by embracing sin we miss joy, both present and future, the fault is ours.

Stop now and ask yourself: Do I know joy as a central staple, a constant reality in my life? "Rarely, rarely, comest thou, /Spirit of delight," wrote Shelley. His experience should not surprise us, for he was a stubborn, passionate atheist. The Christian, however, discovers that, though living in this fallen and disordered world is never a "joy ride," it may become a "joy road" through response to the call of God.

JOY IS PRECIOUS

To dwell at length on the preciousness of joy is needless. Joy makes you shout; joy makes you jump; joy turns mere existence into real living. Joy is life with a capital *L*. Joy produces tears, and when you weep for joy, it is not because you are miserable. I remember my son at the age of seven or eight rolling around the floor with his eyes full of tears, saying, "I'm so happy! I'm so happy!" Why was this? For the first time in his life he had beaten his daddy at Ping-Pong, and he couldn't get over it! We talk about the huge joys of childhood, and they are indeed huge, but there is no reason why joy of equal intensity should not be part of adult life. That it can be and should be, this chapter seeks to show.

Salutations in England bear witness to the preciousness of joy. Where Americans greet their friends by saying, "Hi! How're you doing?" it has become common in England to hail friends with the words, "Any joy?" This is a good question. If you are concerned about another person, this is what you want to know. Has anything happened to make them sing, shout, and feel on top of the world? Sometimes the answer has to be no, for the world these days is short on joy. But it is sad when that is the only answer one can give. "Any joy?" is my question to you who read this, and your life will be poor and barren indeed if the facts force you to say no.

Joy is at the heart of satisfied living. It is also at the heart of real and credible Christianity, the Christianity that glorifies God and shakes the world. As joy is, to quote C. S. Lewis, "the serious business of heaven," so it is central to serious godliness on earth. "The king-dom of God is not a matter of eating and drinking, but of righteous-ness, peace and joy in the Holy Spirit" (Rom. 14:17). A joyless Christianity (and joylessness cannot be hidden) will become an obsta-cle to believing Paul's statement and will render the faith repulsive rather than attractive. However, a joyful Christianity is a most arrest-ing advertisement for the transforming power of the Gospel. So all who hope to cut ice as witnesses for Christ will do well to study the art of joy as part of their spiritual preparation.

The joy that gives Christians credibility also gives them energy. When Nehemiah organized a day in Jerusalem for the reading and preaching of the Law, the people were so overwhelmed as they real-ized what they had been missing for so many years that they dissolved in tears. Nehemiah told them to stop weeping and start celebrating: "Go and enjoy choice food and sweet drinks, and send some to those who have nothing prepared. . . . Do not grieve, for the joy of the Lord is your strength" (Neh. 8:12). Back in the 1930s, Hitler lifted the thought "Strength Through Joy" from this passage and made it the motto of the Hitler Youth movement; the secularization was grotesque, but the psychology was sound. In times of persecution it has always been joyful Christians who have proved strong under pres-sure. In times of difficulty it is the joyful Christians who decline to be discouraged and who show most of what America calls stick-to-itive-ness and England stickability. So if we want to prove strong in the Lord, we need to study joy.

Do I arouse eagerness in your heart? Or do I irritate you? There are people who resent the suggestion that joy is for everyone. "Oh," they say, "that may be all right for you, but it's no use for me; it's just mockery as far as I'm concerned." They say that because they are hurt-ing emotionally. If you are hurting, it is hard to believe that there is any possibility of joy for you. You feel bitter and angry when you know that others experience joy and want to pass it on to you. But to read-ers enmeshed amid the four black D's—disappointment, desolation, depression, desperation—or bogged down in any one of the four black F's—frustration, failure, fear, fury—I wish to say two things.

First, Christians are not victims and prisoners of either the past or the present. The powers of forgiveness and new creation are at work in their lives. Before them lies a sure and certain hope of deliverance, transformation, and glory. Joy will someday be theirs in fullest measure, and they should not give way to the dark feeling that life will never be better for them.

Second, Christians have, so to speak, larger souls than other people; for grief and joy, like desolation and hope or pain and peace, can coexist in their lives in a way that non-Christians know nothing about. Grief, desolation, and pain are feelings triggered by present situations, but faith produces joy, hope, and peace at all times. This does not mean that grief, desolation, and pain cease to be felt (that idea is inhuman); it means that something else is experienced alongside the hurt. It becomes possible for Christians today, like Paul long ago, to be "sorrowful, yet always rejoicing" (2 Cor. 6:10). People who sorrow should be told that God offers them joy whatever their circumstances, for this assurance is just as true for them as it is for anyone else.

JOY MODELED

Paul's description of himself as "sorrowful, yet always rejoicing" might sound so paradoxical as to be incredible. Demonstrably, however, it was the sober truth. For the demonstration, one need only look at his letter to the Philippians. Philippians is relaxed and informal as compared with, say, Galatians or Romans or 1 Corinthians. Paul writes it to his converts, who are also his friends, not to settle major matters of faith or practice, but to thank them for a gift, to tell them how he was doing, to encourage them in the Lord, and to announce Timothy's forthcoming visit to them. You and I, writing to our friends, will probably share our troubles more than our joys, but Paul's letter radiates joy from first to last. This is remarkable since he is writing from a Roman prison, probably chained to a guard day and night, and with a capital charge hanging over his head!

Joy and *rejoice* are the key words of Philippians. Paul calls his converts his joy (4:1); he prays for them with joy (1:4); he rejoices in their generosity to him, seeing it as furthering their own spiritual welfare (4:10, 17); he asks them to practice unity, so as to make his joy brimful (2:2); he rejoices that Christ is being preached, even though sometimes from false motives (1:18); he finds joy even in the possibility of his own martyrdom and tells his friends that should it happen, they must rejoice in it too (2:17ff.), though he expects that he will be released "for your progress and joy in the faith, so that through my being with you again your joy in Christ Jesus will overflow" (1:25ff.). At what for the moment he takes to be the end of his letter, he writes: "Finally, my brothers, rejoice in the Lord!" (3:1). Then, after discovering that he has a good deal more to say, and saying it, he comes back with emphasis to the same point: "Rejoice in the Lord always. I will say it again: Rejoice!" (4:4). Note that he does not say "sometimes" but "always!" He does not merely encourage constant joy; he commands it, which is rather breathtaking. Yet when he tells his friends always to rejoice, he is not asking them to do anything more than he does himself.

Two situations that find Paul rejoicing are specially noteworthy. Both might have been expected to cut off rather than produce joy. The first is an experience of personal malice. Cooped up in captivity, Paul cannot be out and about, spreading the Gospel of Christ in the way that his apostolic commission and evangelistic instincts direct, and that is undoubtedly frustrating for him. However, this cloud has a silver lining. Local Christians have been stirred up through knowing that Paul is, as he says, "in chains for Christ" (1:13) to witness in public more boldly than before.

Looking behind actions to motives, as good pastors do, Paul sees that "some preach Christ . . . out of goodwill . . . in love, knowing that I am put here for the defense of the gospel" (1:15ff.). One imagines them sending him messages: "Don't fret, Paul, because you can't come out and preach; we'll preach, you pray, and together we'll advance the Gospel." Such messages would have been most supportive and encouraging.

Others, however, as Paul also sees, "preach Christ out of envy and rivalry . . . out of selfish ambition, not sincerely, supposing that they can stir up trouble for me while I am in chains" (1:15, 17). Malice is motivating these preachers. They want to make Paul feel wretched and miserable, perhaps because they are publicly disagreeing with him on key points, deliberately arousing prejudice against him, usurping his leadership, or simply because he lacks the freedom to preach as they do. It seems unbelievable that men who preached Christ could take pleasure in rubbing salt into the wounds of Paul the great apostle, but such pettiness has recurred constantly in the history of the church, and it is not unknown today.

Note how Paul reacts. It would have been easy, and in a sense natural, for him to slip into the spineless self-pity and nail-biting misery that his rivals were wishing upon him. He knew, however, what every one of us needs to know: We are free not to choose the feelings that others choose for us. So he declines to feel miserable. "What does it matter?" he writes. "The important thing is that . . . Christ is preached. And because of this I rejoice" (1:18).

Magnificent! Yes—and a model for us. How do we react when meanness and malice link arms to create misery? How do we cope when we become objects of a vendetta, finding ourselves surrounded by people who want to pull us down? How do I, as an author, handle contemptuous reviews of my books? From Paul's example we learn that even at such times joy and peace are possible. We do not have to react as others want us to react. To a greater extent than we may yet have realized, we can choose what to think about (see 4:8). If we focus our mind on joy-inducing facts, we become impervious to those who would plunge us into misery, however great their hostility, however strong their influence, and however little we can do about them at present.

The second triumph of joy in Paul's life that Philippians reveals is yet more amazing. It is joy in the expectation of possible martyrdom. Paul knows that his imprisonment may end in the death sentence. He lives with that uncertainty, hoping that God will bring about his release but not able to be sure (1:19-26). Even so, joy breaks in. He knows that if his life is cut short, he goes to be with the Lord, and that whatever happens is the will of God. He can say, "Even if I am being poured out like a drink offering on the sacrifice and service coming from your faith"—if, in other words, my death accompanies and completes your giving of your lives to God—"I am glad and rejoice with all of you" (2:17). Living under this sword of Damocles, he is still lighthearted enough to talk playfully as if the choice between death and life is really his, and he is finding it hard to make up his mind (1:21-24)! In the power of his joy he faces death as readily and squarely as he faces life. Could you? Could I?

In Britain and America execution for active Christianity is unlikely to come our way, but it is morally certain that some who read this will be called upon one day to glorify God by dying of cancer. What does that thought do to us? Does it strike a chill into our hearts? Cancer is a beast. But it is clear that Paul could have faced cancer and rejoiced, and if we master the secret of his joy, so may we.

JOY COMMANDED

And joy of Paul's kind—holy, strong, supportive, unquenchable—is actually commanded! "Rejoice in the Lord always. I will say it again [for emphasis, as when we ourselves repeat things]: Rejoice!" (Philippians 4:4). This is not an option; it is an order. This is what Paul, as Christ's official spokesman, directs us to do. The command comes from the Lord himself. The *New English Bible's* "I wish you all joy in the Lord," the *Good News Bible's* "May you always be joyful in . . . the Lord," and Goodspeed's "Good-bye, and the Lord be with you always. Again I say, good-bye," miss the point being made here. Paul's words express not just a pious wish but a practical imperative, requiring and obliging us to cultivate joy. (Granted, the Greek allows this watering down—just!—but the earlier use of "rejoice" in its full sense, plus the flow of thought in the context, makes the pious-wish exegesis most unlikely.) The practice of joy, then, is an art that we are required to learn.

JOY DEFINED

The first task is to discern what Christian joy actually is, and the first step toward that is to focus our ideas about the nature of joy. Many seem to stumble here, so I start with some negative statements to clear the ground.

Negation number one: Joy is not the same thing as fun and games. Many people "have fun," as we say, seeking and finding pleasure without finding joy. You can "enjoy yourself" and remain joyless.

The restless, relentless pursuit of pleasure (sex, drugs, drink, gadgets, entertainments, travels) is very much a mark of our time, at least in the affluent West. This quest clearly indicates a lack of joy. Christians who know the joy of the Lord find that a great deal of fun comes with it, but joy is one thing and fun is another. By contrast, Paul in prison had no fun (that seems a safe statement). Yet he had much joy. You can have joy without fun, just as you can have fun without joy. There is no necessary connection between the two.

Negation number two: Joy is not the same thing as jollity—that is, the cheerful exuberance of the person who is always the life of the party. This person can be relied on for jokes and general effervescence, and there's never a dull moment when he (or she) is around. Some Christians are like that; others are not and never will be, but this is a matter of temperament that has nothing to do with joy. One may have a bouncy temperament and yet miss joy, or one may be a low-key person with a melancholic streak, whom no one would ever call "jolly," and yet have joy in abundance. That is good news, for if joy depended on having a jolly temperament, half my readers, and I with them, would have to conclude ourselves debarred from joy forever. But the truth is that however our temperaments differ, the life of "joy in the Lord" is available to us all.

I remember as a young Christian hearing a venerable pulpiteer insist with great emphasis that good Christians have teapot faces rather than coffeepot faces. Standard English teapots are spherical, and the teapot face is round with a big, broad beam and four-inch smile. Standard English coffeepots, by contrast, are long and thin, and the coffeepot face is the same—grave and somber. Much impressed by this, I was considerably depressed when next I looked in the mirror! But I reflected that what the preacher had been talking about was bone structure, and bone structure will not be changed till God gives us our new bodies. So, willy-nilly, my coffeepot face would be mine for life.

Did that mean that I could not experience or express Christian joy? Not at all! The preacher's point, that every Christian should radiate joy, was right, but he had made it in the wrong way. (Perhaps he was betrayed by having a chubby teapot face himself—who can say?) Anyhow, the point is that though some people will never be jolly and whoop it up in the way that other people do, both the exuberant ones and the quiet ones may know the joy that is the gift of God.

Negation number three: Joy is not the same thing as being carefree. Advertisements that picture nubile young adults sprawling all over the Bahamas seek to persuade us that "getting away from it all" on vacation is the recipe for joy. Many people agree. But if that is so, as soon as the vacation ends, and you return to the responsibilities and burdens and abrasiveness of life—the depressing workplace, the uncongenial company, the repeated disappointments—joy will end. Joy, on this view, will only be available to us during our two- or three-week vacation each year! This is the escapist idea of joy; we should be thankful that it is not true.

On the evening of his betrayal and arrest, perhaps twelve hours before his crucifixion, Jesus, who had already indicated that he knew what was facing him, said to his disciples: "I have told you this [i.e., that obedience will keep you in my love] so that my joy may be in you and that your joy may be complete" (John 15:11). These words tell us that joy was his at that moment, though he was not carefree. Similarly, Paul in prison, living with the possibility of summary execution, was not carefree. Yet he had joy in abundance. Joy despite killing pressure was reality for Jesus and Paul, has been reality for tens of thousands of Christians since, and can be reality for us also.

What is joy? We have seen what it is not. A positive definition is now overdue. Though spiritual joy is our special interest in this study, we shall understand it better if first we focus on joy in its generic form. Here is my definition. Joy is a happiness of the heart, linked with good feelings of one sort or another. The word *joy* covers the entire spectrum of what may be called the rapturous, ranging from the extreme ache of ecstasy to the quiet thrill of contentment. Webster defines joy thus: "Excitement of pleasurable feeling caused by the acquisition or expectation of good; delight; exultation; exhilaration of spirits." Joy is a condition that is experienced, but it is more than a feeling; it is, primarily, a state of mind. Joy, we might say, is a state of the whole man in which thought and feeling combine to produce total euphoria. The preciousness of joy, the integral place of joy in the ideal life, and the pitifulness of joylessness are apparent from the definition.

Sources of Joy

Still thinking in generic terms, we now ask: Where does joy come from? What causes it? What are the perceptions in which it is rooted? If we consulted a professional counselor on this point, we could expect to be told that joy springs from four sources.

First, joy flows from awareness of being loved. No one has joy who does not know that there is someone who values, accepts, and cares for him (or her). To feel that as a person I count for nothing in people's eyes, that I do not matter to anyone, and that what happens to me is not going to bother a single person is a great joy-killer. It makes impossible any sense of personal worth or well-being. The Western world is full of lonely people who never taste joy for this reason. The experience of being loved is a fountainhead of joy.

Second, joy flows from accepting one's situation as good. As morphine kills pain, so discontent kills joy. People who are always fretting about the way things are, wishing they were different, and longing for things to happen that are not likely to happen thoroughly disqualify themselves from joy.

Third, joy flows from having something worthwhile. We speak of our spouses, our children, our homes, our books, our hobbies as our joys. This, that, or the other, we say, is "a joy to me," "a real joy," "a great joy." What we mean is that in these relationships and activities we have something that is precious and makes life worth living. If nothing you have seems worthwhile, you will not have joy.

Fourth, joy flows from giving something worth giving. Our self-centered age can hardly grasp that giving might be a way of joy, but it is. Every normal mother knows that giving is a way of joy; she works tirelessly to give her children a home and a life they will enjoy, and when they are happy, she is happy, too. There are, broadly speaking, two sorts of human beings: those who are constantly giving and those who are constantly taking—acquiring, manipulating, exploiting, draining other people dry in their own insatiable self-absorption. There is no question about which category knows the most joy. Many go through life without ever learning that joy is like jam, sticking to you as you spread it, but that is the truth all the same.

CHRISTIAN JOY

I have been generalizing about joy in all its many modes and forms, both secular and sacred. But Paul in Philippians is exemplifying and prescribing Christian joy—joy "in the Lord," joy that flows from one's relationship to Jesus Christ. This will be our specific theme from now on. Any who have not yet committed themselves to the risen Christ as their Savior and Master will find themselves left behind. For now we are to see, in terms of our four-source formula, how the knowledge of one's saving relationship to Christ can bring unquenchable joy into believing hearts. Only Christians can understand this joy. "Rejoice in the Lord" means rejoice in being Christ's, in having Christ's Father as your Father, in being right with God the Father and an heir of his glory through Christ's mediation, in possessing salvation and eternal life as Christ's gift. We are to let joy flow from this source. How will that happen? Through the fulfilling of the four-source formula, as stated above.

The first source of joy is the awareness that one is loved. Christians know themselves loved in a way that no one else does, for they know that God the Father so loved them as to give his only Son to die on the cross in shame and agony so that they might have eternal life. "God demonstrates his own love for us in this: While we were still sinners, Christ died for us" (Rom. 5:8). "He who did not spare his own Son but gave him up for us all—how will he not also, along with him, graciously give us all things? . . . I am convinced that neither death nor life, neither angels nor demons, neither the present nor the future, nor . . . anything else in all creation, will be able to separate us from the love of God that is in Christ Jesus our Lord" (Rom. 8:32, 38-39). In this love that paid so great a price to save sinners, the Father and the Son were at one, for "Christ loved the church and gave himself up for her to make her holy" (Eph. 5:25ff.). Every Christian should follow Paul in drawing out the personal implication—"the Son of God . . . loved me and gave himself for me" (Gal. 2:20).

> Amazing love! How can it be
> That thou, my God, should'st die for me?

The measure of love, human and divine, is how much it gives. By this standard the love of God is immeasurable, because both the greatness of the gift and the cost of giving it are beyond our power to grasp. All human parallels fall short; all comparisons are inadequate.

> *Never was love, dear King,*
> *Never was grief like thine.*

Humbled and awed, Christians should bask daily in the awareness of God's overwhelming, incomparable love.

The second source of joy is the acceptance of one's situation as good. Christians can do this everywhere and always because they know that circumstances and experiences, pleasant and unpleasant alike, are planned out for them by their loving heavenly Father as part of their preparation for glory. "We know that in all things God works for the good of those who love him, who have been called according to his purpose" (Rom. 8:28). God's *purpose* is that those whom he calls should be remade so that they become like their Savior, the incarnate Son Jesus Christ. Their *good* is the fulfilling of this divine purpose for them, and God *works* unceasingly in and through everything that happens so that it becomes in one way or another a means of bringing them closer to the goal.

It is a mistake, as we saw earlier, to imagine that the good for which God works is our unbroken ease and comfort. God's goal is, rather, our sanctification and Christlikeness, the true holiness that is the highway to happiness. Constant ease and comfort, therefore, are not to be expected. Yet Christians may nonetheless derive constant contentment from their knowledge that God is making everything that happens to them a means of furthering and realizing their glorious destiny. "Whatever is good for God's children, they shall have it," wrote Richard Sibbes the Puritan, "for all is theirs to further them to heaven. If crosses be good, they shall have them; if disgrace be good, they shall have it, for all is ours, to serve our main good." To understand this statement is to have the secret of abiding contentment in one's grasp.

Paul exemplifies such contentment, telling the Philippians: "I have learned to be content whatever the circumstances. I know what it is to be in need, and I know what it is to have plenty. I have learned the secret of being content in any and every situation, whether well fed or hungry, whether living in plenty or in want. I can do everything"—everything, that is, that the ongoing flow of my God-governed life requires of me—"through him who gives me strength" (Phil. 4:11ff.). This contentment is the soil in which Paul's joy is rooted and grows.

A single lady of about fifty, a career woman of some eminence in her profession, came to a conference in a condition bordering on nervous collapse. Her parents, who were both still living, had never treated her as anything other than their little girl whom they expected to dance attendance on them. (The story of unimaginative parents failing to adjust to the fact that their children have become adults is unfortunately not uncommon.) Her resentment of her parents' attitude had built up to such a pitch of intensity that it was tearing her to pieces.

During the conference, however, another woman showed her Christian love and care and helped her to understand how Romans 8:28 applied to her home situation. The single woman learned to see her circumstances as shaped by the Lord for her good. She went home rejoicing in the certainty that if she continued faithful in honoring her parents and ministering to them in Christian love, God would give her peace and further his work of grace in her life.

Rarely have I seen so complete a transformation in so short a time. The secret was that she accepted her circumstances from the Lord as sent for her good. This is not always an easy lesson; it was not easy for her. But it is a basic lesson that all who would know Christian joy must learn.

Joy's third source is possession of something worth possessing. Here, too, the Christian is supremely well placed, as we see from Paul's further words about himself. In Philippians 3 we find him celebrating the incomparable worth of the saving relationship with Christ that he now possesses—or rather that now possesses him. "I consider everything a loss compared to the surpassing greatness of knowing Christ Jesus my Lord, for whose sake I have lost all things" (v. 8). (So he had; he was an up-and-coming rabbi, a top-class Pharisee, a man marked out for distinction as a leader in Judaism. When he became a Christian, he forfeited his status and all prospects of advancement and found himself having to cope constantly with Jewish plots against his liberty and his life.) "I consider them [i.e., all the things I have lost] rubbish" (literally, dung—worthless stuff that can be jettisoned cheerfully), "that I may gain Christ and be found in him, not having a righteousness of my own that comes from the law, but that which is through faith in Christ—the righteousness that comes from God and is by faith" (vv. 8-9). (*Righteousness* is a salvation-word in Scripture, meaning a relationship with God that is right and as it should be, having been reestablished and set right after prior disruption. Righteousness is never a human achievement brought about through law-keeping, as the Pharisees supposed, but is always a gift of God's free grace, received *in Christ, through faith in Christ*—that is, by means of union and communion with the living Savior. In that fellowship Christ's own perfect righteousness, both active [law-keeping] and passive [sin-bearing], is imputed to us—that is, is accounted ours in the sense that God the Father now pardons and accepts us fully for Jesus' sake. Paul is celebrating this righteousness that the Father gives in and with and through Christ, glorying in it as his present and permanent possession.)

"I want to know Christ" (that is, to keep extending my knowledge of him, ever coming to know him better than I knew him before); "I press on toward the goal to win the prize for which God has called me heavenward in Christ Jesus" (Phil. 3:10, 14). That prize is essentially more of the precious relationship itself.

To paraphrase Paul: "I have lost a great deal, but I have gained more. What I have gained is something supremely worth having, something that is glorious and that will grow, broaden, deepen, and become richer to all eternity—namely, an ongoing love relationship with Jesus Christ the Savior, and through him with God the Father. The more I have of it, the more I want of it; thus it establishes itself as the best and most valued thing in my life." This is Paul's emphasis, and his words will find an echo in every healthy Christian heart.

In courtship the goal for both parties is lifelong togetherness in mutual love, honor, and enjoyment of each other. They see their relationship as an end in itself; they intend to keep seeing it that way through marriage, parenthood, and whatever the future holds. They expect it to continue to be what it already is to them—a source of supreme delight and joy.

The situation is similar when a sinner has come to know Jesus Christ as Savior. Christ is the great lover and giver whose welcome of us who believe guarantees that for all eternity we shall be beneficiaries of his goodwill and generosity. Gratitude for this amazing grace prompts the Christian to say, with Paul: "I have Christ. I know Christ. I love Christ. He is the pearl of great price. He is all I want. I am the happiest of human beings, for I am his, and he is mine forever, and I will cheerfully let anything go in order to hold on to him and enjoy the full fruits of his love." These thoughts are a third source of joy.

The fourth source of joy is to give something worth giving. This also is an element of Christian experience in a special and unique way. Christ sends believers into the world to be his witnesses. When they share their knowledge of Christ with others, they know they are giving people the one thing supremely worth giving and also desperately needed. Paul found joy in the privilege of being put in trust with the Gospel. So should Christians today rejoice in this task, even when for the moment the Good News is unappreciated, and those to whom one is trying to bring it are rude and offensive in rejecting it.

As was said earlier, Christians can experience both joy and sadness at the same time. There is joy in making known the Word of Life, even when sorrow is also being felt because the gift has been spurned. But what joy there is when someone to whom one has witnessed comes to faith in Christ! Christians sometimes find themselves wondering whether their life is worthwhile, whether they are doing anything that is worth doing. They are sometimes concerned about frittering away precious time and opportunities, wondering whether the serious concerns of adult existence in Christ's service have not slipped through their fingers. Sometimes these feelings are justified; Christians sometimes really are wasting their lives, and there is no joy in that. But Christians who invest time, effort, ingenuity, initiative, and prayer in spreading the Gospel and helping build the faith of others do not feel this self-doubt. They have no reason to do so. In a dying world, surrounded by fascinating fellow mortals who because of their sins face a lost eternity, nothing is so well worth doing as sharing the good news about Jesus and the salvation he gives. No form of love to our neighbor is so appropriate and, indeed, so urgent as evangelism. Christians who see this and are consciously, wholeheartedly committed to this good work, as Paul was before them, find joy in it, just as he did.

CHOOSING JOY

Paul, as we have seen, not only testifies to joy in his own prison experience, but he commands his Philippian friends to practice joy as a constant discipline of life. "Rejoice in the Lord always," he writes, and repeats himself for emphasis. It is as if he should say: You must pray, worship, love each other, keep the commandments, bear one another's burdens, set your moral sights by the Sermon on the Mount, witness, avoid all forms of sin, be Spirit-filled to do battle with Satan and temptation when they assault you, pursue good works, and seek to display the fruit of the Spirit constantly—and along with all that, as a matter of special importance, you are to rejoice in your relationship to Jesus Christ all the time! Joy is to be yours always and everywhere.

Joy is, in fact, one aspect of the fruit of the Spirit. But the habit of rejoicing in the Lord, as the appointed means whereby joy becomes a reality, is as much a matter of divine command and Christian duty as is the doing of any other things mentioned. It is true that joy, both natural and spiritual, will periodically come upon us as a gust or glow of unsought exhilaration, an unexpected kiss from heaven as it were, for which we should be grateful every time. But we are not on that account to think of joy as essentially a mood of euphoria for which we ask and then sit down to wait. Joy is a habit of the heart, induced and sustained as an abiding quality of one's life through the discipline of rejoicing. Joy is not an accident of temperament or an unpredictable providence; joy is a matter of choice. Paul is directing his readers to choose to rejoice, because it is in and through the activity of rejoicing that joy becomes a personal reality.

We have seen this truth demonstrated by Paul. He prays for the Philippians "with joy" because of their partnership in the Gospel (1:5) and calls them his "joy" (4:1), as he does the Thessalonians, too

(1 Thess. 2:19ff.; 3:9). What he means is that when he thinks about them, dwelling on God's grace in their lives, joy flows into his heart. Thus he rejoices in them, or rather rejoices in the Lord because of them, as for instance in Philippians 4:10: "I rejoice greatly in the Lord that at last you have renewed your concern for me."

As we also saw, Paul can choose to rejoice in one aspect of a situation of which other aspects are calculated to depress. He rejoices that Christ is being preached and refuses to brood on the bad motives of the preachers or to indulge in self-pity because he is not able to do what they are doing (1:15-18). This attitude, more than anything else, makes it clear that joy is a choice; one chooses to focus on facts that call forth joy. Such is the secret of "rejoicing in the Lord always," namely, to choose what you think about. It is as simple—and as difficult!—as that.

Can we really choose what we are going to think about? In these days when we are endlessly overstimulated from outside and the ever-present TV encourages the passive mind-set that makes us wait to be entertained, the idea of regularly choosing themes for our thoughts seems strange to the point of freakiness. But Paul has no doubt that thought-control is possible. He actually commands it. "Finally, brethren, whatever is true, whatever is honorable, whatever is just, whatever is pure, whatever is lovely, whatever is gracious, if there is any excellence, if there is anything worthy of praise, think about these things" (Phil. 4:8 RSV). Controlling and directing one's thoughts is a habit, and the more one practices it, the better one becomes at it.

Motivation, of course, helps, and Christians have a strong motivation—a deep-rooted urge, instinctive to them as regenerate persons—to center their thoughts on God's grace and glory at all times. As a person in love thinks loving thoughts of the beloved one spontaneously and constantly, so does the regenerate Christian think loving thoughts of God the Savior. And as it is common today for travelers to turn on their Walkman and let their attention be absorbed by the music, so it has always been common for Christians to let their thoughts be drawn up to God, magnet as he is to the regenerate mind, and to meditate—that is, talk to themselves and to God silently or aloud—concerning God's nature, works, and ways. Such meditation prompts praise and adoration and brings endless delight to the heart. Paul's instruction in what to think about simply gives focus and direction to this regenerate instinct, so as to ensure that our meditation will profit us as much as possible.

But what in particular are the true, honorable, just, pure, lovely, gracious, excellent, and praiseworthy things on which we are to center our thoughts? They are the doings of God and the fruit of those doings in human lives. They certainly include the fourfold awareness that we have discussed: first, that God loves me infinitely and eternally; second, that everything comes to me from God, at least with his permission and always under his protection, to further my eternal good; third, that my saving knowledge of the Lord Jesus, which will eternally increase, is something supremely worth having; fourth, that the gospel message of salvation that I seek to pass on to others is something supremely worth giving. These thoughts will always prime the pump of joy in our hearts and produce a steady flow of joy, peace (see 4:7, 9), and delight. Try it and see!

The secret of joy for believers lies in the fine art of Christian thinking. It is by this means that the Holy Spirit, over and above his occasional visitations in special moments of joy, regularly sustains in us the joy that marks us out as Christ's. Our Lord Jesus wants our joy to be full. Certainly he has made abundant provision for our joy. And if we focus our minds on the facts from which joy flows, springs of joy will well up in our hearts every day of our lives. This upwelling of joy will turn our ongoing pilgrimage through this world into an experience of contentment and exaltation of which the world knows nothing. From this experience will come strength for service. Joy—that is, rejoicing in the Lord—is thus a basic discipline of the Christian life, essential to spiritual health and vitality. Few Christians seem to understand this, and fewer still seem to practice the discipline with diligence. But what a difference it makes when we do!

Sixty years ago I was close to a certain Christian family. Spiritually I owe more to them than I think they ever realized. Life was not easy for them. The father died young, after being immobilized for years by heart disease. The daughter never grew normally and died in her teens of rheumatic fever. One son was so retarded mentally that he had to be institutionalized. The mother remarried but died of cancer in middle age. Thereafter her second husband lived alone for some years, totally housebound with crippling arthritis.

When I visited him, his gentle, sunny joyfulness in Christ, free from all complaint and self-pity, was a tonic from which my memory still draws nourishment. It is of him that I think when I hear Balaam's words: "Let me die the death of the righteous, and may my end be like theirs!" (Num. 23:10). I saw in him the power of joy, and it was a revelation. Now I celebrate the power of joy as part of the Gospel. Beethoven wrote on the score of his *Missa Solemnis,* "From the heart; may it in turn go to the heart." I could have put the same words at the beginning of this chapter. God grant that my readers will get the message. I close with two Scriptures for you all who have followed me thus far.

"May the God of hope fill you with all joy and peace as you trust in him, so that you may overflow with hope by the power of the Holy Spirit" (Rom. 15:13).

"To him who is able to keep you from falling and to present you before his glorious presence without fault and with great joy—to the only God our Savior be glory, majesty, power and authority, through Jesus Christ our Lord, before all ages, now and for evermore! Amen" (Jude 24-25).

8

SCRIPTURE AND SANCTIFICATION

How the Bible Helps Us to Holiness

"Sanctify them by the truth," prays Jesus, adding adoringly, "your word is truth" (John 17:17). *Truth* here bears a theological sense: It is a declaration and disclosure of reality as God knows it. Since all Holy Scripture is God's Word of truth, we are right to infer from Jesus' words that biblical teaching is the means of the sanctification for which he prayed. Since he was praying not just for those who had already become his followers but "also for those who will believe in me through their message" (v. 20), his prayer was as much for us as it was for Peter, John, Augustine, Bunyan, Spurgeon, or whomever. Though his heavenly intercession (Rom. 8:34; Heb. 7:25) would seem to be more a matter of active intervention on our behalf than of continual supplication before the Father, we may be sure that the sanctification of his people remains his constant concern. And the means whereby it takes place is the Word of God.

What is sanctification? The root meaning of the word is relational, or as some say, positional: To sanctify, or consecrate, is to set something or someone apart for God, either in general and inclusive terms or for some specific purpose, and to have it, or him, or her, accepted by God for the end in view. So in the high-priestly prayer from which we have just quoted, Jesus says: "For them I sanctify myself, that they too may be truly sanctified" (v. 19). Jesus' self-sanctification was the specific setting apart of himself to be the sacrifice for his disciples' sins; their sanctification and ours is the inclusive setting apart of ourselves to be God's holy people in every aspect, department, activity, and relationship of our lives.

But whereas Jesus' self-sanctification is his own act, he speaks of our sanctification as a work of God upon us and in us. This points us to the further truth that when God sets fallen human beings like ourselves apart for himself to be his servants and worshipers and to live in fellowship with him, his action is transformational in its character and effects. Why so? Because those whom God sets apart for himself must be Godlike. If they are not already so, they must be made so.

Accordingly, we find that while some New Testament passages speak of God's sanctification of us in the past tense, as an event, a milestone, something already done (Acts 26:18; Heb. 10:10, 14, 29), others speak of it as something present and future (1 Thess. 4:3-4; 5:23), in other words as a process that goes on. The former texts refer to the relational aspect of sanctification, which becomes real upon our believing, as do justification and adoption, and is momentary. The latter texts refer to the transformational process that is lifelong and that is spoken of elsewhere as growth in grace, growing up into Christ, and being changed from glory to glory by the Holy Spirit (2 Pet. 3:18; Eph. 4:15; 2 Cor. 3:18; cf. Rom. 12:2). It is to this progressive transformation that the word *sanctification* regularly refers in Christian theology, whether Protestant, Roman Catholic, or Eastern Orthodox.

We are talking about God's work of character change in Christians, about the life of God in the soul of man, about the fruit of the Spirit, about the outworking in our behavior of our new supernatural life that is hid in Christ with God. We are talking about God working in us to make us will and act for his good pleasure. We are talking about the family likeness that God the Father wants to see in all his adopted children—the family likeness that is Christlikeness, displaying the love, humility, and righteousness that constitute the moral image of the Son who is himself the image of the holy Father. We are talking about God supernaturalizing our lives and causing us to behave in ways in which, left to our own resources, we never could have behaved. We are talking about an ongoing spiritual mystery.

If regeneration is a work of new creation, sanctification is a work of new formation. If regeneration is a new birth, sanctification is a new growth. If regeneration means our Adamic nature nailed to the cross and Christ's risen life implanted, sanctification means our Adamic nature dying and Christ's life within us flowing. "Those he justified, he also glorified," said Paul (Rom. 8:30). If regeneration is glorification in the seed, sanctification is glorification in the bud, and glorification in heaven is the full flower. Such is the frame of reference within which what Walter Marshall, the Puritan, called "the gospel mystery of sanctification" has to be studied.

In 1984 in my book *Keep in Step with the Spirit,* I expressed some convictions relating to sanctification that I would like to summarize at this point. I see sanctification as a neglected priority in today's church everywhere and a fading glory in the evangelical world in particular. In the past Roman Catholics and Protestants alike emphasized the reality of God's call to holiness and spoke with deep insight about God's provision for holiness. English-speaking preachers in the Reformation tradition (Puritans and eighteenth-century evangelicals in particular) constantly expounded what God's holiness requires of us, what our holiness involves for us, and what the Holy Spirit does in us. They pointed out by what means and through what disciplines he works this momentous change in us and how holiness increases our assurance, joy, and usefulness to God.

Today there are many ministers who believe that their effectiveness depends on their mastery of professional skills, but Robert Murray McCheyne, Presbyterian revivalist in Dundee, Scotland, in the 1830s, was surely right when he declared: "My people's greatest need is my personal holiness." Today the concern for holiness that was once so striking a mark of evangelical people is largely a thing of the past. We rarely handle the issue in a direct way, and when we do, our touch is tentative and insecure. Our situation reminds me of some lines of a poem by Rudyard Kipling titled "The Way Through the Woods."

> *They shut the road through the woods*
> *Seventy years ago.*
> *Weather and rain have undone it again,*
> *And now you would never know*
> *There was once a road through the woods.*

That seems to me to be exactly our story with regard to sanctification. To listen to the sermons and read the books we publish today, you would never know that once the highway of holiness was clearly marked out for Bible-believers and that ministers and people knew it well and spoke of it with authority and confidence. "Weather and rain have undone it again," and now we have to rebuild and reopen the road, starting from scratch.

What has caused this sad state of affairs? Several factors, I think, coming together and reinforcing each other. There is first the factor of preoccupation. Controversy to defend orthodoxy in an age when orthodoxy is being attacked and eroded; inquiry into the breadth of Christian liberty and the propriety of Christian involvement in cultural and social concerns; fixity on the quest for satisfaction, self-fulfillment, and success in one's Christian life—these things have come to possess our minds and have crowded out all study of the matter, manner, motivation, and means of what Scripture calls "good works."

Then there is the factor of confusion. The doctrine of sanctification has in the past been a battle area. Though today the combatants have mostly backed off from each other, rival positions are still being affirmed within their own constituencies. Some preach the victorious life, in which handing over all moral and spiritual issues to Jesus is the secret of tranquil righteousness (this was taught by such as Handley C. G. Moule and F. B. Meyer). Some proclaim a "second blessing," called entire sanctification, that purifies the heart and raises life to a new level of love to God and men (this was taught by such as John Wesley and Oswald Chambers). Some modify "second blessing" teaching into a doctrine of Spirit-baptism or Spirit-filling, in which deliverance from sins and inhibitions is seen as central. Spiritual intuitions as distinct from rational reflections now become the guide of life (this was taught by, for instance, Watchman Nee). Some see sanctification as an ongoing struggle with sin, in which humility, self-distrust, and adoration of God's grace are the notes of spiritual health (this was taught by such as J. C. Ryle and C. H. Spurgeon). In a Christian world where all these views of sanctification jostle side by side, it is no wonder that people become confused and give up.

Then, finally, there is the factor of reaction. Christians today are reacting against the emphasis of an earlier era on separation from the world, which, we think, led not only to avoidance of the world's sins but also to an impoverishing of believers' moral awareness. Also we are reacting against the moral maturity that was expressed by the stiffly sensitive "Victorian conscience." We are much more interested in something called "emotional maturity," which encourages moral tolerance with no emphasis on behavioral standards. In our passion for intimacy with God and our boldness in treating him as a pal, we are reacting against the stress on his holiness and his demand that those who seek his face be holy, too, which emphasis we meet in the writings of our evangelical forebears.

These are the main factors that have for a generation distracted us from taking sanctification seriously as an issue of universal importance. But it is precisely as such that I want you to see it now.

How should we think of sanctification? Following are some basic definitions that will function as reference points and grids for the mind. Here first are two statements from a joint Anglican and Presbyterian source, the Westminster Assembly.

> They, who are once effectually called and regenerated, having a new heart, and a new spirit created in them, are further sanctified, really and personally, through the virtue of Christ's death and resurrection, by his Word and Spirit dwelling in them: the dominion of the whole body of sin is destroyed, and the several lusts thereof are more and more weakened and mortified; and they are more and more quickened and strengthened in all saving graces, to the practice of true holiness, without which no man shall see the Lord. (Westminster Confession, XIII.i.)
>
> Q. What is sanctification?
>
> A. Sanctification is the work of God's free grace, whereby we are renewed in the whole man after the image of God, and are enabled more and more to die unto sin, and live unto righteousness. (Westminster Shorter Catechism, Q. 35)

Next here are comparable definitions of sanctification and holiness from an almost contemporary source, the Congregational Puritan John Owen.

Sanctification is an immediate work of the Spirit of God on the souls of believers, purifying and cleansing of their natures from the pollution and uncleanness of sin, renewing in them the image of God, and thereby enabling them, from a spiritual and habitual principle of grace, to yield obedience unto God, according unto the tenor and terms of the new covenant, by virtue of the life and death of Jesus Christ. . . . Hence it follows that our holiness, which is the fruit and effect of this work, the work as terminated in us, as it compriseth the renewed principle or image of God wrought in us, so it consists in a holy obedience unto God by Jesus Christ, according to the terms of the covenant of grace, from the principle of a new nature.[1]

As for Baptists, it appears that down the centuries most of them have lined up with Westminster and Owen. Here, for instance, are some thoughts from the chapter titled "Sanctification" in the *Abstract of Systematic Theology,* published in 1887 by James P. Boyce,[2] founder and first theology professor of Southern Seminary, which is now located at Louisville, Kentucky.

What now, we may inquire, is the nature of the sanctification which is wrought out in the believer?

It is a personal sanctification . . . a real sanctification . . . of the whole nature, both body and soul.

It is not a sanctification to be completed in this life. The work goes on through the lifetime of the believer, nor is it completed before death. . . . Paul constantly speaks of himself as still struggling against the power of sin, as not counting himself to have attained, as buffeting his body and bringing it into bondage lest he should be rejected, and thus he gives us, in his descriptions of his own experience, a pattern of what has been almost universally acknowledged as that of every other Christian. . . .

(But) the partial sanctification of this life is also progressive . . . it is a growth from the seed planted in regeneration, which is constantly bringing forth new leaves and new fruit; it grows with increased intellectual knowledge of God's truth, with a clearer perception of human sinfulness and corruption, with stronger faith and brighter hope, and more confident assurance of personal acceptance with God, with a more heartfelt conception of the sacrificing love of Christ, and with a more realizing belief in his constant presence and knowledge of what we do. It even increases from its own acquired strength and through the suffering and doing in which it is developed. . . . Temptations and struggles enter into that progress, and not only they, but even the sins and falls which mar the Christian life. The process of sanctification is like the ascent of a mountain. One is always going forward, though not always upward, yet the final end of the progressive movement of whatever kind is the attainment of the summit. Sometimes, because of difficulties, the road itself descends, only more easily to ascend again. . . . Often it is feared that there has been no higher attainment, often that it has been a continual descent, until, perchance, some point of view is gained from which to look down upon the plain where the journey was begun and behold the height which has already been overcome. Often, with wearied feet and desponding heart, the traveler is ready to despair, because of his own feebleness and the difficulties which surround. But he earnestly presses forward and the journey is completed, the ascent is made, the end is attained.

The understanding of sanctification that these passages from the Westminster standards, from Owen, and from Boyce set before us has been characteristic of Protestantism since Protestantism first began. It was the view of Luther and Calvin; it was rooted in the teaching of Augustine, and behind him (so I am persuaded) in the teaching of the New Testament. It was unanimous in Protestantism until Wesley brought in his idea that through faith sin may be conquered here and now, so that we come in this life into that state of perfect motivational purity and love that will mark us in glory. All forms of "second-blessing" teaching about Christian holiness, without exception, have stemmed from Wesley's doctrine, modified more or less by this or that teacher. I believe the older teaching is better, and in *Keep in Step with the Spirit* I argue in detail for my view. In that book I also affirm or imply the following points:

1. The context of sanctification is justification by faith through Christ. The sanctified are justified sinners, saved by grace and living every day only by being continually forgiven their faults.

2. The basis of sanctification is union with Christ in his death and resurrection. The holy life is the Christ-life in us, not the fruit of any natural potential or resources that we have for godly living.

3. The agent of sanctification is the Holy Spirit, who enables us habitually and actively to will and work for God's pleasure and for his praise. It is we who work—there is no psychological passivity here, but rather intense moral effort on our part. Yet we work, not self-reliantly, but in dependence on Christ and in expectation of help from the Spirit. By leading us to form the habits of holiness, the Spirit changes us into Christ's moral likeness.

4. The form that sanctification takes is conflict with the indwelling sin that constantly assaults us. The conflict, which is life-long, involves both resistance to sin's assaults and the counterattack of mortification, whereby we seek to drain the life out of this trouble-some enemy.

5. The rule of our holiness is God's law. The heart of our holiness is the love of our heart in gratitude and goodwill toward God and toward others for his sake. The expression of our holiness is our Jesus-likeness, that is, our manifesting the fruit of the Spirit (Gal. 5:22-24), which is the moral and spiritual profile of Jesus in his disciples.

I take these five positions to be basic and noncontroversial among evangelicals, and therefore spend no time here expounding them in detail; rather, I shall build on them.

How, then, does the authority of Scripture operate in relation to sanctification? First, Holy Scripture shows us the nature of sanctification as a work of God, a "gospel mystery." This we have already reviewed. Sanctification is not natural morality, but supernatural conformity to the moral and spiritual likeness of Jesus Christ. Sanctification is not mystical passivity, as our use of the slogan "let go and let God" has too often implied, but it is active moral effort energized by prayerful and expectant faith. We look for help in practicing righteousness, and we receive it. Nor is sanctification a solitary achievement. Rather, it is to be worked out and expressed in the close and demanding relationships of the Christian church, primarily the local congregation, and also of the family and of the wider worlds of work and citizenship and social concern (see Rom. 12:1—15:13; Col.

3:1—4:6; Eph. 4:1—6:20; 1 Pet. 1:22—4:6). Scripture is emphatic that sanctification is a matter of not serving sin (Rom. 6) and that holiness means (to use the old words) being upright and virtuous, "bearing fruit in every good work" (Col. 1:10) and being "kept blameless" in the eyes of God and men (1 Thess. 5:23; Phil. 2:14; 2 Pet. 3:14).

"When people talk," wrote Bishop J. C. Ryle in 1879, "of having received 'such a blessing' and of having found 'the higher life,' after hearing some earnest advocate of 'holiness by faith and self-consecration,' while their families and friends see no improvement and no increased sanctity in their daily tempers and behavior, immense harm is done to the cause of Christ."[3] That, you must agree, is a scriptural point of view.

Second, Holy Scripture displays to us the standard of sanctification, namely the moral law of God set forth in the Decalogue and summed up in Christ's two great commandments and incarnated (surely we may say this) in the love and humility and self-giving service that we see in our Lord Jesus Christ himself. This is the "third use of the law" that Calvin stressed, after Luther had laid it down that God's law serves first as a standard of civil righteousness in the Christian state and second as a source of conviction of sin.

There is also a third way, urged Calvin, in which God means his law to function, namely as a spur to Christians to stimulate and encourage them in the practice of righteousness. The thought here is that the law is the family code for God's royal children. In this world, royal children live under the public eye, with much expected of them. If they lapse morally, it is noticed. We look to them to live up to their privileged position.

The same is true of God's children. The world watches them and notices if they fall from grace. Then God is dishonored, and the credibility of the Christian claim that God renews us in righteousness is diminished. This makes it vital that we live by God's standard, obeying his law and imitating our master, Christ. Though we are not under the law as a system of salvation, we are divinely directed to keep it, according to Christ's exposition of it, as the rule for our lives (1 Cor. 9:21; Gal. 6:2).

Third, Holy Scripture teaches us the necessity of sanctification.

This has been denied by various sorts of Antinomians who have made the claim that God sees no sin in true believers, and is unconcerned about their immoralities (the precise claim, be it noted, that John is explicitly refuting in 1 John 1:6-10 and Peter in 2 Peter 2). In reality, the witness of Scripture is: "without holiness no one will see the Lord" (Heb. 12:14). There is no heaven without holiness of life.

This conclusion follows first from the revealed nature of God and from his basic command to his people, in which his nature is invoked as being itself the reason why the command must be issued and observed. "Be holy because I, the LORD your God, am holy" (Lev. 19:2). "I am the LORD . . . your God; therefore be holy, because I am holy" (Lev. 11:45). "Just as he who called you is holy, so be holy in all you do; for it is written, 'Be holy, because I am holy. . .'" (1 Pet. 1:15-16).

The same conclusion follows from the revealed plan of grace. The New Testament tells us that we were chosen, redeemed, and called to be holy. The Father "chose us in him [Christ] before the creation of the world to be holy and blameless in his sight" (Eph. 1:4). "Christ loved the church and gave himself up for her to make her holy . . . to present her to himself as a radiant church, without stain or wrinkle or any other blemish, but holy and blameless" (Eph. 5:25-27). "It is God's will that you should be holy. . . . God did not call us to be impure, but to live a holy life" (1 Thess. 4:3, 7). Sanctification is not an option, but an integral part of the salvation package, just as the repentance and consecration that lead into the pursuit of holiness are integral to the response for which the Gospel calls. God's plan is to save us from sin, not in sin; therefore, the need for holiness must be acknowledged and accepted.

The necessity of holiness follows also from the revealed nature of man. There is no happiness without holiness. Human nature is so made that its fulfillment, contentment, and freedom become realities only as we learn to love, worship, and serve our Maker. Psalm 16 shows that the man who finds fullness of joy in God's presence here and hereafter is the one who has chosen the Lord as his portion, who loves righteousness ("the path of life") and delights in the saints. This fact about ourselves needs highlighting in these hedonistic days: Only holiness brings full joy.

Finally, the necessity of holiness follows from the revealed conditions of assurance. People have no right to believe that they are partakers of God's salvation unless they walk the path of conscious, purposeful obedience and service to God. In 2 Peter 1:3-11 we learn that progress in sanctification is the only way to make one's calling and election sure (that is, to make certain of it). Passages such as 1 Corinthians 6:9-11, Galatians 6:7-8, and Ephesians 5:5-6 tell us bluntly that any unholy persons who lay claim to assurance are self-deceived, for the path they are on leads only to wrath and exclusion from God's kingdom. If we value assurance (and Romans 8, which is an ecstatic exposition of the content of Christian assurance, must surely convince us that a valid assurance is of infinite worth), we must seek it by obeying the teaching which has been entrusted to us, thus reaping the fruit that consists of holiness, as Paul puts it in Romans 6:17 and 22.

Feelings of confidence about our salvation need to be tested before they are trusted. First John gives the tests: Those who are born of God practice righteousness, do not habitually sin, honor the Christ who was truly incarnate and truly died for their sins, and love their fellow believers (1 John 2:29; 3:6, 9; 5:1 with 4:1-6 and 5:4-12, 18). True faith in Christ and perceptible sanctification are the conditions of sound and trustworthy assurance among those who have been Christians for any length of time. (The gracious way in which God may fulfill Romans 5:5 and 8:15-16 at the time of a person's conversion is not what I am discussing here, any more than Paul was when he dictated those verses. In both passages, the Spirit's witness in our consciousness to God's love to us and our sonship to him is presented in connection with our actual living of the life of righteousness and patient endurance, and that is always the proper context in which to consider it.)

From all these different standpoints, then, Scripture shows us both the necessity of holiness and the means by which God's work of sanctifying us is carried out. I must say something more about these matters.

On the means of sanctification, John 17:17, with which we began, is the basic text. Citing it, Boyce writes: "The primary means which the Spirit uses for our sanctification is the truth of God. . . . 'Growth in the grace' is inseparably connected with growth 'in the knowledge of our Lord and Savior Jesus Christ' (1 Pet. 3:18)." Boyce shows that this concept is further taught in Scripture by passages that:

- connect spiritual life with truth (see John 6:63; 8:32);
- ascribe quickening power to the Word of God (see Ps. 119:50, 93);
- teach that truth promotes obedience (see Ps. 119:34, 43-44);
- declare its usefulness in preventing sin (see Ps. 119:11);
- associate it with cleansing from sin (see Ps. 119:9; 1 Pet. 1:22);
- state that it produces hatred of sin (see Ps. 119:104);
- assert its power to lead to salvation (see 2 Tim. 3:15-17);
- say that "all things that pertain unto life and godliness" have been given through the knowledge of God and Christ (see 2 Pet. 1:2-3);
- imply that growth in grace is due to greater knowledge (see Heb. 5:12-13);
- announce that all the ministerial gifts bestowed by Christ are "for the perfecting of the saints, unto the work of ministering, unto the building up of the body of Christ; till we all attain unto the unity of the faith, and of the knowledge of the Son of God, unto a full grown man, unto the measure of the stature of the fullness of Christ" (Eph. 4:11-16).[4]

As Boyce goes on to explain, providences, prayer, Christian fellowship, and church worship are means of sanctification only "as they convey truth, or as they suggest truth, or as they are employed in recognition [we would say, celebration] of some truth." This seems to me to be illuminating and right.

On the way of holiness—that is, the way in which what Scripture calls "good works" are performed—what needs to be said is the following. "Good works" must be good not only in their content, but also in the manner in which they are done and the motive with which we do them. The legalistic formalism of the Pharisees concentrated on matter but ignored manner and motive. True holiness requires that the motive be twofold—the glory of God through the expressing of gratitude for grace and the good of our fellowmen through the service of their needs. Holiness requires also that the manner should be appropriate to the matter; in other words, we should do each thing, as we say, "properly."

Our awareness of this need for pure motives should make us realize that we can never hope to do anything right, never expect to perform a work that is truly good, unless God works within us to make us will and act for his good pleasure. Realizing this will make us depend constantly on our indwelling Lord—which is the heart of what is meant by abiding in Christ.

Our living should accordingly be made up of sequences having the following shape. We begin by considering what we have to do or need to do. Recognizing that without divine help we can do nothing as we should (see John 15:5), we confess to the Lord our inability and ask for help. Then, confident that prayer has been heard and help will be given, we go to work. And, having done what we could, we thank God for the ability to do as much as we did and take to ourselves the discredit for whatever was still imperfect and inadequate, asking forgiveness for our shortcomings and begging for power to do better next time. In this sequence there is room neither for passivity nor for self-reliance. On the contrary, we first trust God and then on that basis work as hard as we can. When we do so, we repeatedly find ourselves enabled to do what we know we could not have done by ourselves. That happens through the enabling power of the Holy Spirit, which is the wellspring and taproot of all holy and Christlike action. Such is the inside story of all the Christian's authentically good works.

There is a reciprocal relation between good works and the ongoing moral character change that the Holy Spirit is working in us. The desire to work in a way that will please God springs from the renewed disposition of our regenerate hearts, and each good work helps to form habits of single-minded, joyful, trustful obedience, which then become firm elements in our character.

Disciplined self-examination before God, in order to learn what one's weaknesses, blind spots, and deepest needs are, is an ongoing necessity. In this we need divine help. We need to pray with the psalmist: "Search me, O God . . . test me . . . see if there is any offensive way in me, and lead me in the way everlasting" (Ps. 139:23-24). Self-examination brings the self-knowledge that spiritual realism requires.

In Romans 7:21-23 Paul, wishing to show the connection between the law and sin, gives us a cross-section of his own inner experience as his self-examination showed it to him. He does not say "I *feel*" but "I *find*" and "I *see*." "I *find* this law at work: When I want to do good, evil is right there with me. For in my inner being I delight in God's law; but I *see* another law at work, waging war against the law of my mind and making me a prisoner," he writes. "Find" and "see" show that he is talking, not about his feelings past or present, but about what he had achieved in those moments of action when he set himself to do the best he could. Self-examination reveals to him that his reach had exceeded his grasp, that his desire to serve God had not resulted in perfect service. Once again the hidden hand of sin had held him back, knocked him off course, and dragged him down.

Jonathan Edwards, some twenty years after his conversion, wrote: "I have affecting views of my own sinfulness and vileness, very frequently to such a degree as to hold me in a kind of loud weeping . . . so that I have been often obliged to shut myself up. I have had a vastly greater sense of my own wickedness and the badness of my heart than ever I had before my conversion. . . . It is affecting to think how ignorant I was, when a young Christian, of the bottomless, infinite depths of wickedness, pride, hypocrisy and deceit left in my heart."[5]

Such is the fruit of self-examination. The closer we are to God, the more we see the sin that remains in us (for the light of God shows it up), and the lower we go in our estimate of ourselves. It is not too much to say that sanctification and realistic humility go hand in hand. We see, therefore, why what Puritan Robert Bolton called "The Saint's Self-Enriching Examination" is so important in our Christian lives. "They shut the road through the wood seventy years ago." It is ironic that in this twenty-first century, in which the human sciences have studied human nature so assiduously from their own points of view and piled up such a mountain of knowledge about the human individual, the knowledge of God's way in human sanctification has been so largely and comprehensively lost in the churches; but so it has been.

To recover it, one has to go back to men like Boyce and Spurgeon and the Anglican J. C. Ryle, in his great book *Holiness,* and behind them to Edwards and the Puritans, especially the English Puritans. To be sure, the majestic printed sermons of the late Dr. Martyn Lloyd-

Jones on Romans and Ephesians (Banner of Truth) contain this teaching, although in a rather diffuse form, and two superb small books by Jerry Bridges dealing with it, *The Pursuit of Holiness* and *The Practice of Godliness* (both NavPress), shine like good deeds in a naughty world. But unless you are fortunate enough to come across material of this kind, "now you would never know/There was once a road through the woods."

We evangelicals today do not impress the world with the quality of our humility, humanity, conscientiousness, or compassion. We desperately need a reopening of that closed road first and foremost in our own lives. May we be given grace to hear what the Spirit is saying to the churches about sanctification, that is, about the way in which our Lord's prayer for us in John 17:17 might be answered. The above chapter is nothing like the last word on this subject, but could it function as the first word? I echo Paul: "I speak to sensible people; judge for yourselves what I say" (1 Cor. 10:15).

9

THE TRANSFORMATION TRACK

What It Means to Follow Christ

A half-truth treated as the whole truth soon becomes a whole false-hood; so we who proclaim the good news of God's grace must not set-tle for only half the story. But we do! While we celebrate the *relational* change that Christ brings—justification, forgiveness, and adoption in place of condemnation, wrath, and rejection—we pass over the *real* change, the change of outlook and character, that grace is supposed to work. When quizzed, we have to admit that we know very little about it. Spiritual disciplines, spiritual warfare, spiritual-mindedness, self-denial, self-examination, and mortification of sin are themes on which we are out of our depth. We know that *sanctification* is the umbrella label for this field of concern and that some in the past paid much attention to it, but that is as far as we get.

In his 1879 book *Holiness*, J. C. Ryle quoted largely from the Puritans of the seventeenth century, "an age when, I am obliged to say, experimental religion was more deeply studied and far better under-stood than it is now."[1] What Ryle would say were he here with us today hardly bears thinking about. It is high time we tried to fill in some of these blanks.

The place to start is by recognizing that sanctification means con-secration and repentance lived out in the power of the Holy Spirit, and that *transformation* is the word for what happens when we set our-selves to do that. "Do not conform any longer to the pattern of this world, but be *transformed* by the renewing of your mind," wrote Paul to the Christians at Rome (Rom. 12:2); and to the Corinthians he declared that "we, who with unveiled faces all reflect the Lord's glory, are being *transformed* into his likeness with ever-increasing glory, which comes from the Lord, who is the Spirit" (2 Cor. 3:18). A process of personal change that is the start of our promised glorification is what Paul is talking about, as is Peter when he speaks of Christians being sharers in "the divine nature" (2 Pet. 1:4). While our transformation into a state of bodily Christlikeness remains future (1 Cor. 15:51-53; Phil. 3:21), God's work of changing us into moral Christlikeness is under way already. The new behavior patterns that Paul identifies as the fruit of the Spirit—love, joy, peace, patience, kindness, goodness, faithfulness, gentleness, and self-control—are its result (Gal. 5:22-23).

What are these qualities? They are the character profile of our Lord and Savior Jesus Christ as we watch Him in action in the gospel stories. Now this character profile is being reproduced in Christians: Christ, to use Paul's word, is being "formed" in them (Gal. 4:19). What that means is that acting out the nine virtues mentioned becomes their habit, and it is out of character for them as Christians to do anything else.

To be sure, living this way is not as easy as it might sound. Changing the self-serving habits natural to us into Christlike ways of acting and reacting means a reconstructing of our inner lives that, like any reconstruction job in this world, creates confusion by disrupting existing patterns and generates strains that otherwise would not be there. A blind, anti-God energy that Paul calls "the flesh" and "indwelling sin" pulls against the process in all sorts of ways, distracting, opposing, deceiving, and dragging us down, so that failure to be fully Christlike, despite our best intentions, is part of every believer's personal story. Yet the sovereign Holy Spirit, the divine change agent, continues his work, and the sanctifying transformation goes forward despite the lapses into apathy, indifference, and downright wrongdoing.

We need to be clear that the heart is where the transformation begins. *Heart* here means, of course, not the pump that sends blood through the body, but the central core of the person out of which come the motives, purposes, attitudes, desires, and concerns that shape our living. The milestone that we call conversion or regeneration (with the Puritans I use these words as synonyms for that initial turning to God that is God turning us to himself) is, says Paul, an event literally of new creation (2 Cor. 5:17; Gal. 6:15). In it God renovates our hearts by actually uniting us to Jesus Christ in his death and resurrection so that we start living a new life that is a sharing in his risen life. We all can and must say with Paul: "I have been crucified with Christ and I no longer live, but Christ lives in me. The life I live in the body, I live by faith in the Son of God, who loved me and gave himself for me" (Gal. 2:20). And each of us must acknowledge that hereby our heart has been changed.

What does the change amount to? Why, this: that whereas previously our heart's ruling desire was to please and enjoy ourselves in all we did, now our ruling desire is to please and enjoy God in all we do— to love, honor, obey, exalt, praise, adore, glorify, and delight in him. At its deepest motivational level, our heart is now, as Charles Wesley put it, a copy of our Savior's, as his was when he walked on earth and as it is now while he reigns in glory. This regenerated, new-created, divinely energized heart, sustained by the Holy Spirit who now indwells it, is the direct source of the fruit of the Spirit in Christians' lives.

In our temperament and our mental and emotional makeup, as in our personal history, we are all different. This fact, coupled with God's discretionary variety of action (truly, he loves variation), means that conversion experiences, viewed psychologically as phases of thought and feeling, differ widely from person to person. But the heart transformation outlined above is essentially the same in every case. The Gospel, says Paul, calls on us to "be made new in the attitude of your minds; and to put on the new self, created to be like God in true righteousness and holiness" (Eph. 4:23-24). God works this in us as we come to Christ. So henceforth we live in him, with him, through him, and for him. "To me, to live is Christ" (Phil. 1:21). "Christ . . . is your life" (Col. 3:4).

If now you ask whether one is the same person after conversion as before, the answer is yes and no. Yes, because there is an ongoing personal identity; no, because transformation of the heart has radically redirected the life. C. S. Lewis has people say of the young Narnia visitant Eustace, whom Aslan *undragoned* (read all about it in *The Voyage of the Dawn Treader*), that you would hardly know he was the same boy; that is how converts to Christ get spoken of by reason of the huge motivational change that marks them.

To be sure, not all regenerate persons can tell you when and how they were converted. But where people show a heart for God, hostility to sin, and reverent loyalty to Jesus as mediator and master, you know what has happened to them. They are now truly in a converted condition.

Those thus changed are called to walk the road of further transformation. How do they do that? By being natural in living out what is now the driving desire of their hearts; by resolutely saying no each day to sin's allurements; and by cultivating Jesus' company—indeed, his friendship, for he calls his disciples friends (John 15:15). Being friends with the Son and the Father through the Spirit is in truth as good a description of holy living as I know.

More specifically, *living in faith and hope* furthers transformation. Faith weans us from all forms of self-sufficiency, self-reliance, and self-absorption. Faith is eyes that see, ears that hear, hands that embrace, and feet that move—all directed Christward for unifying communion. Faith trusts God's promises in Scripture, God's wisdom in events, and God's Son as Savior and Shepherd always and everywhere. Faith begets hope, the certainty that the God of grace is leading us home to glory and that "our light and momentary troubles are achieving for us an eternal glory that far outweighs them all" (2 Cor. 4:17). Hope sustains confidence and drives out all forms of apathy and desperation. Living in faith and hope will bring our outlook increasingly into line with Christ's own outlook when he was on earth.

Living in repentance and obedience furthers transformation. Repentance is the humbling honesty that turns with sorrow and shame from doing what one admits to be wrong to do henceforth what one knows to be right. Obedience is the conscientious endeavor to live by God's revealed will for us, without making exceptions in our own favor. A Puritan, asked why he was so precise in his religion (Puritans were called "precisians" in those days), unforgettably replied, "O sir, I serve a precise God." We need to remember that so do we.

Repentance and obedience are less than abundant in our churches today—self-satisfaction and bonhomie having replaced them—but the desire of the renewed heart to please God will prompt Christians to practice both and to watch and pray very seriously against influences of whatever sort that would lead them to be neglectful here. Living in repentance and obedience will make us increasingly single-minded and quick to resist temptation, like Christ when he walked here on earth. (See on this Luke 4:1-13; 22:28; Heb. 4:15; 5:7-8.)

Living in dependence and expectation furthers transformation. The harder we lean on God, the more Christlike we are. Our life each day should be an endless sequence of four repeated steps—identifying what calls to be done, asking God to help us in it, tackling it in expectation of receiving the help we asked for and finding that this happens, and looking back with thanks to God for help given before moving on to the next task. This is how we should implement Paul's admonition to "work out [put into action, *New Living Translation*] your salvation with fear and trembling" (Phil. 2:12). Living in dependence and expectation keeps us looking to Jesus as our model and source of help, and increasingly we will become like what we look at.

Living in submission and steadiness furthers transformation. What we may call the baptismal pattern of going down into what feels like death, out of which God raises us to a new quality of life, recurs by divine appointment again and again in all our lives. Submitting to this process is part of the discipline of discipleship. At such times steady endurance of the pain and grief while they last is required, and by God's help, as he responds to our prayers, steady endurance will be maintained. Jesus himself submissively endured in this way (Heb. 12:2-3; 1 Pet. 2:21-23), and the pain-and-grief element of experience, accepted as from God, will leave us more like Jesus than we were before.

Living in doxology and devotion furthers transformation. The temper of a Christian's life should be a praising temper, and the goal of the Christian's actions should always be that God will be praised as a result of them. This is what Paul means when he says, "Whether you eat or drink or whatever you do, do it all for the glory of God" (1 Cor. 10:31). *Glory* here expresses the idea of praise for praiseworthiness. Paul's thought is that everything we say and do should express the praiseworthiness of God one way or another. That is what doxology means. Doxological purpose is central to all true devotion: We pray and meditate and read and sing first and foremost to honor and exalt God. To pray, "Hallowed [magnified and revered as holy] be thy name," and to mean it, induces Christlikeness at the deepest level, for honoring the Father was and is the focus of the Son's life.

Living in fellowship and service furthers transformation also. There is nothing Christlike or godly about isolating oneself from other Christians, failing to share one's story and life with them when doing so would help them. Strengthening the muscles of our love by seeking others' good no matter what is a central activity in the consecrated life.

Growing into Christ's likeness is a mysterious process, if only because all we see in ourselves throughout is weakness, inadequacy, and shortcomings of one sort or another. Seeking to graduate in the school of transformation is, however, the true Christian life. As we let Christ himself urge us by his Spirit into the paths sketched out above and confirm to our hearts the rightness of what we are doing as we follow him along them, we shall, as Calvin matter-of-factly put it, be making progress. Frankly, this is progress I long to make. Don't you, too? May God help us all!

10

POOR HEALTH
Physical Cures and Healing

Poor health has been a fact of life since the Fall. Had there been no sin, there would be no sickness. As it is, both are universal, the latter being a penal result of the former. So Scripture implies. So, too, did yesterday's Christians view the matter. They did not find poor health and chronic discomforts an obstacle to faith in God's goodness. Rather, they expected illness and accepted it uncomplainingly as they looked forward to the health of heaven.

But today, dazzled by the marvels of modern medicine, the world dreams of abolishing poor health entirely. We have grown health conscious in a way that is itself rather sick and certainly has no precedent—not even in ancient Sparta where physical culture was everything.

Why do we diet and jog and pursue health-raising and health-sustaining things so passionately? Why are we so absorbed with physical health? We are chasing a dream, the dream of never being ill. We are coming to regard a pain-free, disability-free existence as one of man's natural rights.

It is no wonder that Christians nowadays are so interested in divine healing. They long for the touch of God, as direct and powerful as possible, on their lives (and so they should). They are preoccupied with physical health, to which they feel they have a right. (How much there is of worldliness in this preoccupation is a question worth asking, but it is not one we will consider here.) With these two concerns dominating their minds, it is not surprising that today many claim that all sick believers may find physical healing through faith, whether through doctors or apart from them. A cynic would say the wish has been father to the thought.

But is that fair? That it was natural for such a thought to emerge in our times does not make it either true or false. It regularly presents itself as a rediscovery of what the church once knew and never should have forgotten about the power of faith to channel the power of Christ. It claims to be biblical, and we must take that claim seriously.

This teaching uses three arguments from Scripture.

First, Jesus Christ, who healed so abundantly while on earth, has not changed. He has not lost his power. Whatever he did then he can do now.

Second, salvation in Scripture is a holistic reality, embracing both soul and body. Thoughts of salvation for the soul only without, or apart from, the body are unbiblical.

Third, blessing is missed where faith is lacking and where God's gifts are not sought. "You do not have, because you do not ask," says James. "Ask and it will be given you," says Jesus. But Matthew tells us that in Nazareth where Jesus was brought up, he could not do many mighty works because of their unbelief.

All of this is true. So does Jesus still heal miraculously? Yes, I think that on occasion he does. I do not deny healing miracles today. There is much contemporary evidence of healing taking place in faith contexts in ways that have baffled the doctors. B. B. Warfield, whose wife was an invalid throughout their marriage, testily denied that God ever heals supernaturally today. But it looks as if he was wrong.

However, what often is claimed is that healing through prayer, plus perhaps the ministrations of someone with a healing gift, is always available for sick believers, and that if Christian invalids fail to find it, something is lacking in their faith.

It is here that I demur. This reasoning is wrong—cruelly and destructively wrong—as anyone who has sought miraculous healing on this basis and failed to find it or who has had to pick up the pieces in the lives of others who have had that kind of experience knows all too well. To be told that longed-for healing was denied because of some defect in your faith when you had labored and strained every way you knew to devote yourself to God and to "believe for blessing" is to be pitch-forked into distress, despair, and a sense of being abandoned by God. This is as bitter a feeling as any this side of hell—particularly if, like most invalids, your sensitivity is already up and your spirits down. Nor does Scripture permit us to break anyone in pieces with words (Job's phrase, it fits) in this way.

What, then, of those three arguments? Look at them again. There is more to be said about each one.

It is true that Christ's power is still what it was. However, the healings he performed when he was on earth had a special significance. Besides being works of mercy, they were signs of his messianic identity. This comes out in the message he sent to John the Baptist: "Go and tell John what you hear and see. . . . Blessed is he who takes no offense at me" (Matt. 11:4, 6 RSV). In other words, Jesus was saying, "Let John match up my miracles with what God promised for the day of salvation." (See Isaiah 35:5ff.) "He should then be in no doubt that I am the Messiah, whatever there is about me that he does not yet understand."

Anyone today who asks for miracles as an aid to faith should be referred to this passage in Matthew and told that if he will not believe in the face of the miracles recorded in the Gospels, then he would not believe if he saw a miracle in his own backyard. Jesus' miracles are decisive evidence for all time of who he is and what power he has.

But in that case, supernatural healings in equal abundance to those worked in the days of Jesus' flesh may not be his will today. The question concerns not his power but his purpose. We cannot guarantee that because he healed the sick brought to him then, he will do the same now.

It is also true that salvation embraces both body and soul. And there is indeed, as some put it, healing for the body in the atonement. But perfect physical health is not promised for this life. It is promised for heaven as part of the resurrection glory that awaits us in the day when Christ "will change our lowly body to be like his glorious body, by the power that enables him even to subject all things to himself." Full physical well-being is presented as a future blessing of salvation rather than a present one. What God has promised and when he will give it are separate questions.

The wife of a pastor friend bore a "miracle baby" after physicians had declared pregnancy impossible. But the child was malformed and died within a week. Preaching the following Sunday, my friend applied to this bereavement the truth that Christ's death secured bodily healing: "God healed Joy Anne," he said, "by taking her to heaven." Exactly.

Further, it is true that blessing is missed where faith is lacking. But even in New Testament times, among leaders who cannot be accused of lacking faith, healing was not universal. We know from Acts that the apostle Paul was sometimes Christ's agent in miraculous healing, and he was himself once miraculously healed of snakebite. Yet he advises Timothy to "use a little wine for the sake of your stomach and your frequent ailments" (1 Tim. 5:23 RSV) and informs him that he left Trophimus "ill at Miletus" (2 Tim. 4:20). He also tells the Philippians that their messenger Epaphroditus was so sick that he "nearly died for the work of Christ" and we see how grieved Paul himself had been at the prospect of losing him (Phil. 2:25-27). Plainly, had Paul or anyone else sought power to heal these cases miraculously, he would have been disappointed.

Moreover, Paul himself lived with "a thorn in the flesh" that went unhealed. In 2 Corinthians 12:7-9, he tells us that in three solemn seasons of prayer he had asked Christ, the Lord and the Healer, to take it from him. But the hoped-for healing did not occur. The passage merits close attention.

"Thorn" pictures a source of pain, and "flesh" locates it in Paul's physical or psychological system, thus ruling out the idea, suggested by some, that he might be referring to a difficult colleague. But beyond this, Paul is unspecific, probably deliberately. Guesses about his thorn range from recurring painful illnesses, such as inflamed eyes (see Gal. 4:13-15), migraine, or malaria, to chronic temptation. The former view seems more natural, but nobody can be sure. All we can say is that it was a distressing disability from which Paul could have been delivered on the spot, had Christ so willed.

So Paul lived with pain. And the thorn, given him under God's providence, operated as "a messenger of Satan, to harass me" (2 Cor. 12:7 RSV) because it tempted him to think hard thoughts about the God who let him suffer and in resentment to cut back his ministry. How could he be expected to go on traveling, preaching, working day and night, praying, caring, weeping over folk with this pain constantly dragging him down? Such thoughts were "flaming darts of the evil one" (Eph. 6:16 RSV) with which he had to contend constantly, for the thorn remained unhealed.

Some Christians today live with epilepsy, homosexual cravings, ulcers, and cyclical depressions that plunge them into deep waters of this kind. Philip Hughes is surely correct when, commenting on this passage, he writes: "Is there a single servant of Christ who cannot point to some 'thorn in the flesh,' visible or private, physical or psychological, from which he has prayed to be released, but that has been given him by God to keep him humble, and therefore fruitful? . . . Paul's 'thorn in the flesh' is, by its very lack of definition, a type of every Christian's 'thorn in the flesh.'"[1]

Paul perceived, however, that the thorn was given him not for punishment but for protection. Physical weakness guarded him against spiritual sickness. The worst diseases are those of the spirit—pride, conceit, arrogance, bitterness, self-seeking. They are far more damaging than physical malfunctioning. In 2 Corinthians 12 Paul described the thorn as a sort of prophylactic against pride when he said it was "to keep me from being too elated by the abundance of revelations" (v. 7 RSV). He could accept it as a wise provision on the part of his Lord. It was not for want of prayer that the thorn went unhealed. Paul explained to the Corinthians what Christ's response was as he prayed about it. "He said to me, 'My grace is sufficient for you, for my power is made perfect in weakness'" (v. 9). It was as if the Savior was saying, "I can demonstrate my power better by not eliminating your problem. It is better for you, Paul, and for my glory in your life that I show my strength by keeping you going though the thorn remains."

So Paul embraced his continuing disability as a kind of privilege. "I will all the more gladly boast of my weaknesses, that the power of Christ may rest upon me" (v. 9). The Corinthians, in typical Greek fashion, despised him as a weakling. They did not consider him an elegant speaker or an impressive personality. Paul went even further, telling them that he was weaker than they thought, for he lived with his thorn in the flesh. But Paul learned to glory in his weakness, "for when I am weak, then I am strong" (v. 10). And he wanted the Corinthians to learn to praise God for his weakness, too!

One virtuous commentary doubts whether the thorn could be illness in view of Paul's "extraordinary stamina" throughout his ministry. How obtuse! Extraordinary stamina was precisely what Paul was promised. Similarly obtuse was the reviewer who described Joni Eareckson Tada's books as a testimony to "human courage." Courage, yes—but very much more than human! The age of miraculous blessing is not past, thank God, though such blessing does not always take the form of healing. But then neither did it do so in Paul's day.

Three conclusions issue from what we have seen.

The first concerns miraculous healing. Christ and the apostles only healed miraculously when they were specifically prompted to do so—when, in other words, they knew that to do so was the Father's will. That is why their attempts at healing succeeded. Still, miraculous healing for Christians was not universal then, so there is no warrant for maintaining that it should be so now.

The second conclusion concerns sanctifying providence. God uses chronic pain and weakness, along with other afflictions, as his chisel for sculpting our lives. Felt weakness deepens dependence on Christ for strength each day. The weaker we feel, the harder we lean. And the harder we lean, the stronger we grow spiritually, even while our bodies waste away. To live with your "thorn" uncomplainingly, sweet, patient, and free in heart to love and help others, even though every day you feel weak, is true sanctification. It is true healing for the spirit. It is a supreme victory of grace. The healing of your sinful person thus goes forward even though the healing of your mortal body does not. And the healing of persons is the name of the game so far as God is concerned.

The third conclusion concerns behavior when ill. We should certainly go to the doctor, use medication, and thank God for both. But it is equally certain that we should go the Lord (Doctor Jesus, as some call him) and ask what challenge, rebuke, or encouragement he might have for us regarding our sickness. Maybe we shall receive healing in the form in which Paul asked for it. Maybe, however, we shall receive it in the form in which Paul received it. We have to be open to both.

I thank God that I have known more than forty years of excellent health, and I feel well as I write this. But it will not always be that way. My body is wearing out. Ecclesiastes 12, if nothing worse, awaits me. May I be given grace to recall and apply to myself the things I have written here when my own day of physical weakness comes, whether in the form of pain, paralysis, prostration, or whatever. And may the same blessing be yours also in your hour of need.

11

DISAPPOINTMENT, DESPAIR, DEPRESSION

How the Great Physician Touches Troubled Minds

Sometimes a light surprises
The Christian while he sings;
It is the Lord, who rises
With healing in his wings.

So wrote William Cowper, and he was right. When we praise the Savior, he draws near. As you tell him how much you love him, he will make you more vividly aware of how much he loves you. But what about Christians who are not singing because they can find nothing to sing about or give thanks for? What about those who are swamped for whatever reason by bitter feelings and sour, despairing thoughts? The good news is that not even despair puts them beyond the reach of Jesus' love.

On Friday afternoon they took Jesus down from the cross, as dead as a man can be. On Sunday afternoon he walked most of the seven miles from Jerusalem to Emmaus with two of his disciples. He had broken through the death barrier and was alive and well once more on planet Earth. For forty days before ascending to heaven where he now lives and reigns, he appeared to those who had been his followers and friends. Why? First, because he loved them and wanted them to see him alive. Second, he still needed to explain to them his saving achievement and their role as witnesses to him. Last, but not least, some of them were in emotional and spiritual distress and needed the therapy that was uniquely his. All this is reflected in the Emmaus Road story (Luke 24:13-35). (If you do not know this story, I urge you to read it now before you get into my comments on it.)

Who were the patients to whom the Great Physician ministered on that occasion? One was Cleopas (v. 18). The other, not named by Luke, lived with Cleopas, and it is natural to guess (though not possible to prove) that it was Mary, wife of "Clopas" (John 19:25) and mother of James (Mark 15:40), who was at the cross when Jesus died. (In that case, Cleopas was Alphaeus, James's father.) I shall assume this was so and that it was husband and wife trudging home that day. They walked slowly; most people do on a long walk, and they were sharing their perplexity and pain at Jesus' death. Their spirits were very low. They thought they had lost their beloved Master forever; they felt that the bottom had fallen out of their world. They were in the shock of a bereavement experience, hurting badly.

Now picture the scene. Up from behind comes a stranger, walking faster, and falls into step beside them. Naturally they stop discussing their private misery, and there is silence. The stranger breaks the silence by asking them in a way that shows friendly interest what they have been talking about. The question stops them in their tracks: "they stood still, their faces downcast"—or, as older versions of verse 17 put it, "looking sad." Because the couple is in the midst of great grief, it is an effort for them to talk to a third party. They have no interest in this stranger. No doubt they wish with all their hearts that he were not there. Neither of them is even looking at him. This probably is partly to communicate that he is intruding and partly to shield themselves from the stranger's gaze.

When we know grief is written all over our faces, we avoid looking at other people because we do not want anyone to see the signs of our sorrow. So I can imagine this couple swiveling their heads away or gazing stonily at the ground in front of them, not facing their traveling companion at all. Certainly, "their eyes were kept from recognizing him" (v. 16). Had anyone at that moment asked them, "Is Jesus with you?" the reply would have been, "Don't be silly, he's dead, we've lost him. We hoped he was the one to redeem Israel, but clearly he wasn't; we shan't see him again—and nothing makes sense anymore."

Stop! Look! Listen! Here is a perfect instance of a kind of spiritual perplexity that (I dare to affirm) every child of God experiences sooner or later. Be warned: It can be appallingly painful, and if you are not prepared to meet it, it can embitter you, maim you emotionally, and to a great extent destroy you—which is Satan's goal in it every time. You find yourself feeling that God plays cat and mouse with you. Having lifted you up by giving you hope, he now seems to throw you down by destroying it. What he gave you to lean on he suddenly takes away, and down you go. Your feelings say that he is mocking you, taking pleasure in frustrating you and making you miserable. He must be a heartless, malicious ogre after all. So you feel broken in pieces, and no wonder.

Examples are easy to find. Here is a Christian worker, maybe a layperson, maybe a minister, who takes on a task (pastoring a church, leading a class, starting a new work, or whatever), confident that God has called and who expects therefore to see blessing and fruit. But all that comes is disappointment and frustration. Things go wrong, people act perversely, opposition grows, one is let down by colleagues, the field of ministry becomes a disaster area. Or here are a couple who marry in the Lord to serve him together, who dedicate their home, wealth, and in due course children to him. Yet they find nothing but trouble—health trouble, money trouble, trouble with relatives and in-laws, and maybe (the most bitter of all) trouble with their own offspring. What hurts Christian parents more than seeing the children they tried to raise for God give up Christianity? But do not say that these things never happen to truly faithful folk; you know perfectly well they do. And when they do, the pain is increased by the feeling that God has turned against them and is actively destroying the hopes that he himself once gave them.

Some forty-plus years ago a clergyman's daughter was attracted to a young man. She was a Christian; he was not. She did as Christian girls should do at such times—she held back and prayed. He was converted, and they married. Soon the man, who was at that time a prosperous farmer, felt called to sell out and train for the pastorate. Hardly had his ministry begun, however, when he died painfully of cancer, leaving his widow with a small son and no money. Today she has a ministry to individuals that, without that experience, she never would have had. Yet over and over she has had to fight feelings that say, "God played games with me; he gave me hopes and dashed them; he's cruel; he's vile." I expect she will be fighting that battle till she dies. These things happen, and they hurt.

See it in Scripture. Teenager Joseph, youngest in the family, is given dreams of being head of the clan. Furious, his brothers sell him into slavery to make sure it never happens. Joseph is doing well in Egypt as the right-hand man of a leading soldier-politician. The lady of the house, perhaps feeling neglected by her husband as wives of soldiers and politicians sometimes do, wants to take Joseph to bed with her. Joseph says no, and this put-down from a mere slave turns the lady's lust to hate (never a hard transition). She lies about him, and suddenly he finds himself languishing in prison, discredited and forgotten. There he stays for some years, a model convict we are told, but with no prospects and with nothing to think about save the dreams of greatness that God once gave him. "Until what [God] had said came to pass the word of the LORD tested him" (Ps. 105:19 RSV). "Tested him"—yes, and how! Can we doubt that Joseph in prison had constantly to fight the feeling that the God who gave him hopes was now hard at work destroying them? Can we suppose that he found it easy to trust God and stay calm and sweet?

The heartbreaking perplexity of God-given hopes apparently wrecked by God-ordained circumstances is a reality for many Christians today and will be the experience of more tomorrow—just as it was for Joseph and for the Emmaus disciples. Back to their story now to watch the Great Physician at work with them.

Good physicians show their quality by skill in diagnosis. They do not just palliate symptoms, but go to the root of the trouble and deal with that. What did Jesus see as the root cause of this couple's distress? His dealing with them shows that his diagnosis was of *unbelief* caused by two things.

First, they were *too upset*—too upset, that is, to think straight. It was beyond them to put two and two together. They had slid down the slippery slope from disappointment to distress, through distress to despair, and through despair into what we call depression, that commonest of modern diseases. One in every four North Americans has to be treated medically for depression at some point in life. If you have ever experienced depression or sought to help its victims, you will know that these sufferers are marvelously resourceful in finding reasons for not taking comfort, encouragement, or hope from anything you say to them. They know you mean well, but they defy your efforts; they twist everything into further reasons why they should be gloomy and hopeless ("it's all right for you, but it's different for me," and so on). They are resolved to hear everything as bad news. That is exactly what we find here in Cleopas's narrative concerning the empty tomb. (It has to be Cleopas at this point; Mary would not be talking to a strange man, and the story is told in a very male manner.)

"It is now the third day since this happened," says Cleopas. "Moreover, some women of our company amazed us. They were at the tomb early in the morning and did not find his body; and they came back saying that they had even seen a vision of angels, who said that he was alive. Some of those who were with us went to the tomb, and [surprise! surprise!] found it just as the women had said, but him they did not see" (vv. 22-24 RSV). (Implication: There's nothing in this wild talk of him being alive; someone must have desecrated the tomb and stolen the body so as to deny it decent burial.) Thus Cleopas announces the empty tomb as more bad news.

Yet over and over before his Passion Jesus had foretold not only his death but his rising on the third day (Luke 9:22; 18:33; Matt. 16:21; 17:23; 20:19). Straight thinking about the empty tomb in the light of these predictions would have made their hearts leap. "He said he would rise; now the tomb's empty; he's done it, he's done it, he's done it!" But both were too upset to think straight.

This was due to the root cause of their unbelief, which Jesus also diagnosed: They were *too ignorant*—too ignorant, that is, of Scripture. "O foolish ones"—Jesus' tone is compassionate, not contemptuous: "O you dear silly souls" would get the nuance—"and slow of heart to believe all that the prophets have spoken! Was it not necessary that the Christ should suffer these things and [so] enter into his glory?" (vv. 25-26). Jesus then spent maybe two hours showing them from Scripture (memorized) that it was in fact necessary as God's way of accomplishing redemption and establishing his kingdom. His action shows how he saw their fundamental need.

As ignorance of Scripture was the basic trouble on the Emmaus Road, so it often is with us. Christians who do not know their Bible get needlessly perplexed and hurt because they do not know how to make scriptural sense of what happens to them. These two disciples could not make sense of Jesus' cross. Many do not know the Bible well enough to make sense of their own cross. The result is a degree of bewilderment and consequent distress that might have been avoided.

Diagnosing them thus, Jesus did three things to heal this couple's souls. First, he did what all counselors must do: He *asked questions,* got them to talk, established a relationship, and so made them receptive to what he had to say. His opening gambit ("Tell me, what were you talking about?" v. 17) drew from Cleopas only rudeness ("Don't tell me you don't know!" v. 18). Hurting folk often act that way, externalizing their misery by biting your head off. But Jesus was unruffled; he knew what was going on inside Cleopas and persisted with his question ("Do I know? You tell me anyway; let me hear it from your own lips"). Had they declined to share their trouble, Jesus could not have helped them. But when they poured out their hearts to him, healing began.

Then, second, Jesus *explained Scripture*—"opened" it, to use their word (v. 32)—as it bore on their perplexity and pain. He showed them that what had been puzzling them, the death of the one they thought would redeem them in the sense of ending the Roman occupation, had actually been prophesied centuries before as God's way of redeeming in the much profounder sense of ending the burden and bondage of sin. He must have gone over Isaiah 53 where the servant who dies for sins in verses 1-9 appears alive, triumphant, and reigning in verses 10-12; he must have produced many other passages that picture God's Messiah traveling to the crown via the cross; certainly he kept them in a state of dawning comprehension and mounting excitement (their hearts "burned," v. 32) till they reached home. Thus healing proceeded.

The principle here is that the most healing thing in the world to a troubled soul is to find that the heartbreak that produces feelings of isolation, hopelessness, and hatred of all cheerful cackle is actually dealt with in the Bible. The heartbreak makes sense after all in terms of a loving divine purpose. And you can be quite certain that the Bible, God's handbook for living, has something to say about every life problem involving God's ways that we shall ever meet. So if you are hurting because of what you feel God has done to you, and you do not find Scripture speaking to your condition, it is not that the Bible now fails you but only that, like these disciples, you do not know it well enough. Ask wiser Christians to open Scripture to you in relation to your pain, and I guarantee that you will find that to be so. (To borrow a phrase from the early Ellery Queen—challenge to the reader!)

Finally, Jesus *revealed his presence.* "Stay with us," they had said to him on reaching Emmaus. (What a blessing for them that they were given to hospitality! What they would have missed had they not been!) At the table they asked him to give thanks, and as he did so and handed them bread, "their eyes were opened and they recognized him" (v. 31). Whether recognition was triggered by seeing nail prints in his hands or by remembering the identical voice and action at the feeding of the five thousand or four thousand, as some have wondered, we do not know; nor does it matter. Now, as then, Jesus' ways of making his presence known are mysteries of divine illumination. You can rarely say more than that as something was said, seen, read, or remembered—it happened. So it was here; and thus healing was completed.

To be sure, the moment they recognized him, he vanished. Yet plainly they knew that he was with them still. Otherwise, would they have risen from the table in their weariness and hurried back to Jerusalem through the night to share their news? Sensible Palestinians did not walk lonely country roads at night, fearing thugs and muggers (that was why Cleopas and Mary urged the stranger to stay with them in the first place). But it is evident that they counted on their Lord's protecting presence as they went about his business.

"Stay with us," they had said, and inwardly they knew he was doing just that. Thus their broken hearts were mended, and their sorrow was replaced by joy.

Jesus Christ, our risen Lord, is the same today as yesterday, and it belongs to true Easter faith to take to our own hurts the healing of the Emmaus Road. How? First, by telling Jesus our trouble, as he invites us to do each day. He remains a good listener, with what the hymn calls "a fellow-feeling for our pains"; only as we lay aside prayerless resentment and self-pity and open our hearts to him will we know his help. Second, we receive his healing by letting him minister to us from Scripture, relating that which gives us pain to God's purpose of saving love. This will regularly mean looking to the Lord's human agents in ministry, as well as to private Bible study. Third, we ask him to assure us that as we go through what feels like fire and floods, he goes with us and will stay with us till the road ends. That prayer he will always answer.

"We do not have a high priest who is unable to sympathize with our weaknesses, but we have one who has been tempted in every way, just as we are—yet was without sin. Let us then approach the throne of grace with confidence, so that we may receive mercy and find grace to help us in our time of need" (Heb. 4:15-16). So wrote an apostolic man long ago to ill-treated, distracted, and depressed believers. The Emmaus Road story urges us to do as he says—and it shows us how.

A NOTE ON DEPRESSION

I hope that using the word *depression* in the chapter title did not give anyone the idea that I was offering a full account of the causes and cures of depression in Christians. What I wanted to illustrate is simply that, even among believers, disappointment can lead to despair that can cause depression. Depression is a complex psychophysical condition, and many factors—temperamental, physical, circumstantial, and spiritual—can go into the making of it. It is a lapse into miserable hopelessness that is regularly linked with an upset, temporary or long-term, of body chemistry. Often it is impossible to be sure which factors contributed the most to the condition.

Helping someone who is depressed may call for a wide range of specialists—medical, psychological, sociological, and spiritual. Physicians and psychiatrists must not ignore the spiritual dimensions of depression, just as pastors must not ignore the medical dimensions. Partnership is the proper path here.

Among those depressions that have predominantly mental causes are the ones produced directly by spiritual factors, such as the pressure of deficiency in one's relationship with God or of felt emptiness through the lack of any such relationship. In these cases, trusting God's promises and looking for the presence of the Lord Jesus Christ are major factors in finding a cure.

Books that I have found helpful in charting the spiritual factors of depression are *Spiritual Depression* by D. Martyn Lloyd-Jones; *The Masks of Melancholy* by John White; *The Roots of Sorrow* by Richard Winter; and the Puritan classic, "A Child of Light Walking in Darkness," in volume 3 of the *Works* of Thomas Goodwin.

12

KNOW YOURSELF

Identity and Self-Image

"Know yourself" was a tag phrase among Greek philosophers who saw self-knowledge as the beginning of wisdom. And certainly there is no real wisdom without it. We see why self-knowledge is something that most serious people today, with most serious people in every age, do in fact desire and seek. You will constantly be unsure of yourself if you know you do not know who and what you are.

The late Peter Sellers, comedian and character actor, was asked to tape the Bible. He said no and in a moment of honesty explained why: "For a job like that," he said, "you have to know who you are, and I don't know who I am." All of us find ourselves interesting and puzzling (the self-centeredness and lack of integration that flow from original sin ensure that), and as a result self-exploration fascinates us. That is why books of popular psychology sell so well.

I recall how long ago we sixth-formers (twelfth-graders, that is) devoured a programmed-learning paperback titled *Know Yourself As You Really Are*. (Sample of contents: do you like your baths hot or lukewarm? If the former, turn to page so-and-so. If the latter, go to page whatnot and answer the questions there.) Myers-Briggs and similar personality-testing routines are today's counterpart, though they focus more on how one acts than on who and what one is. Also in my teens I read Freud and Jung and got into palmistry. (Left hand shows what you were born with; right hand reveals what you are making of yourself; reverse the formula for left-handers.) Then a phrenologist read my bumps and told me I needed to increase my word power 100 percent. What was I after in all of this? Self-knowledge. Was I odd to want it? I do not think so.

But now, after more than half a century as a Christian, I judge that very little of the self-knowledge we need comes to us from secular sources, despite the psychological preoccupations that perhaps did more to shape twentieth-century minds than any other cultural factor. Yet it would be wrong to say that modern psychology has not taught us anything that matters. On the contrary, it has shown us a great deal about our relationships and how behaviorally they make or mar us. In that connection, it has also highlighted for us the fact that we all carry inside us an idea or image of ourselves (as hero, victim, rebel, helper, or whatever) that more or less self-consciously we live out, feeling that this is our identity.

Coaches in sports always knew this, perceiving that those who see themselves as winners do better than those who expect to lose. The coach considers passionate pep talks of the "you-can-do-it" sort as vital to the success of the trainees. Is he right? Yes. Counseling pundits confirm that in all departments of life our view of ourselves programs our behavior, so that our ideas of what we can and can't do become self-fulfilling prophecies. How true that is!

A bright person I know suffered ten years of academic disaster through internalizing the assurance, dumped on him in grade two, that he was a no-good at schoolwork. His image of himself as a klutz kept him from trying because it told him he would fail and drove him to develop a new identity as the one who played the fool. This kind of thing quite often happens.

Embedded in our self-image is our sense of *worth*. The psychologists have brought this into focus and thereby helped us all to understand each other better. As in some communities it is said that if you're not Dutch, you're not much, so, as we now realize, the world is full of emotional cripples, some of them Dutch, who deep down feel they are "not much," despite being brainy, competent, and by worldly standards successful. In my youth we spoke of them as having an inferiority complex; now we say they have a low self-image.

Children starved of affirmation and affection at home regularly take into adult life a low self-image—a sense of lacking value, being a nobody, counting for nothing. Parents and schoolteachers, the prime authority figures in most children's lives, can do them enormous harm by denying them praise, encouragement, interest, and help forward, the four strands of love in the sense that is relevant here. In the absence of such love, criticism of children for not coming up to expectations or family standards turns the knife in the wound, and the stronger the child's imagination and capacity for fantasizing, the more bitter and more alienating the experience will be. All parents, in particular, need the deep wisdom of the apostle Paul in Colossians 3:21: "do not provoke your children, lest they become discouraged." Nagging one's spouse, children, and friends is a sure-fire strategy for damaging both the relationship and the other person—two ventures in destruction for the price of one.

Low self-image, and the feeling of worthlessness that goes with it, is not a rational judgment, but an emotionally charged attitude that functions like dark-tinted spectacles through which one's mind gazes as one thinks about oneself in relation to others. A Peanuts cartoon I saw tried to laugh it off. ("You look dreadful." "Well, I feel inferior." "Don't worry, lots of people have that feeling." "What, that they're inferior?" "No, that you're inferior." No prizes for guessing which of the above are Lucy's lines.) But those who have such feelings cannot laugh them off like that. The feelings come to stay; they express the pain and compensatory strategies of woundedness, and they do us harm in two ways.

First, a low self-image spawns inhibited, compulsive, and obsessive behavior of many sorts. Insecurity, instability, lack of self-respect, spinelessness, quarrelsomeness, cynicism, pushiness and bluster, isolation and withdrawal, hatred of those—races, classes, or individuals—who remind us of those who we feel failed and hurt us, power trips and power plays, passive and predatory relationships, drug-dependence and addictions, and promiscuity, both heterosexual and homosexual, may all result directly. Some take crazy risks in relationships because they still crave at any cost the affection once denied them; others handle relationships savagely and contemptuously because they no longer hope for genuine affection from anyone and so resent as would-be exploiters any who offer it. And while a low self-image is fairly easily diagnosed from the behavior it breeds, it is in essence an inner lameness that counselors can do little about.

Second, a low self-image puts obstacles in the way of full-hearted receiving of the gospel message. Hostile feelings toward authority figures get extended to God and make it harder to believe what the Bible says about his love. Self-pity caused by inner hurt reinforces the sinful self-centeredness that marks us all and makes it harder to develop a God-centered outlook and live a God-centered life. The ache to be sympathized with and, as we say, stroked prompts a shrugging off of all witness to our being faultier and guiltier and more offensive to God than ever we dreamed, and so makes it harder to take sin seriously. As on the horizontal plane of human relationships, so on the vertical plane of our relationship to God, the heart-pathology of the low self-image is fairly easily diagnosed from the deficiencies described, but to heal it is beyond the counselor's power.

But as I say this, I run ahead of my own argument. For all genuine knowledge of ourselves as God sees and knows us is a supernatural divine gift. It is not the counselor's or preacher's skill that gives it, any more than it is just to those with a low self-image that it is given. Here we must face up to the basic Christian axioms of the double source and the double knowledge.

The doctrine of the double source is that it is through the Word and the Spirit together—the Bible truth, that is, illuminated to the mind and applied to the heart by the Holy Spirit—that understanding of divine things comes about. Without the Word, the facts about Christ and God's promises of salvation through him would not be known; without the Spirit, the reality of Christ calling us to himself, and the acuteness of our need of him as our Savior, Lord, and Friend would not be known either.

The doctrine of double knowledge is that we only begin to know ourselves truly as the sinners and hopeless, helpless cases that God knows us to be as we become aware of how holy and good, how great and gracious, how just and at the same time how kind God himself is. The more we know of God's graciousness, the more we shall be aware of our neediness, and the more we sense his greatness, the more we shall know our smallness. John Calvin gave us classic statements of both principles in his *Institutes* (see I.i. and I.vi-ix).

In a nutshell, then, there is no self-knowledge without some knowledge of God, and there is no knowledge of God apart from Bible truth (the Word) sealed on mind and heart by the Counselor-Helper-Teacher whom God sends (the Spirit). All of us, whatever our self-image and sense of identity may be, are in the same boat at this point.

What do we learn when, through the Word and the Spirit, we begin truly to know God and truly to know ourselves?

First, we learn *how Christ changes for the better our ruined relationship to his Father.* Throughout the New Testament the apostolic message centers on this. The New Testament Gospel announces the reality of divine love to sinners and shows us that love expressed and embodied in the most literal and direct sense in the ministry of Jesus Christ. It tells us, to start with, that Jesus Christ is God—God the Son incarnate, who died, rose, lives, and reigns to save us. It teaches us to see him as the mediator—the one and only peacemaker and reconciler—between God the Father and the human race. It sets him before us as the one with whom his disciples share fellowship now, as they will continue to do forever in heaven; as the one through whose atoning death our guilt is washed out, and we ourselves are adopted into the Father's family when we believe; and as the one in whom by a unique, mysterious, permanent, unitive incorporation into his life as the risen Lord, we are bonded to him and to the Father and to the Holy Spirit in a way that transforms us. The Gospel proclaims Christ's solitary glory as the only Savior, in this breath-taking sense, that the world ever has seen or will see.

Shot through with a drumbeat emphasis on the holiness of the Trinity and the certainty of judgment to come for everyone, and warning that all without Christ face disaster on judgment day, the New Testament Gospel teaches us to measure the love shown in Christ by setting three things together. The Gospel points out how guilty, perverse, and nasty our holy Creator sees us to be; how far the Father went to save us, giving his holy Son to taste the hell we deserve in order to secure our rescue; and how wonderful is the full forgiveness, lasting acceptance, clean slate, and adoption into the divine family that is Christ's free gift in his Father's name to penitent believers. The New Testament Gospel takes us lower in self-abhorrence and despair than inferiority feelings ever do and raises us to an awestruck joy that those with a "good" self-image, left to themselves, would never know. And from this repaired relationship, as is surely very clear, a changed view of ourselves must result.

However unloved and worthless we spiritual Cinderellas may once have felt, and however much self-hate, self-condemnation, and self-pity we may once have nursed, we must now see that by loving us enough to redeem us at the cost of his shame and agony on the cross, Christ the Lord at his Father's will has actually given us value. So we must no longer tell ourselves that we have no value and matter to nobody. We matter to him!

And we must also see that by securing our complete forgiveness, Christ has obligated us to forgive ourselves for whatever haunts us from the past. He has made it sin for us not to do this.

And we must further see that by giving us a destiny of future glory, Christ has made it sin for us to cherish feelings of hopelessness, however powerfully we felt them in the past. It would be irreverence and unbelief to indulge ourselves in feeling hopeless when Christ has given us a hope that is sure, certain, and immeasurable.

So at every point the old way we thought and felt about ourselves must be driven out by a new one that is to last for the rest of our lives. Whether it was self-confidence or self-despair, pride or a low self-image, that shaped our sense of who we are, we are to think of ourselves very differently now that we are "ransomed, healed, restored, forgiven," and adopted children of God. As our habits of behaving will need to be changed, so will our habits of thought.

But before we take that further, there is another point to be made about New Testament teaching, as the Spirit opens it up to Christian hearts.

Second, we learn *how Christ changes for the better our ruined nature as the Father's image-bearers.* This also is a key part of the apostolic message.

Believers, says the Gospel, are new creatures in Christ. Born again, we enter a new kind of life: We have come alive to God. Dying to sin—that is, passing from under its rule—as God changes our hearts, we rise in and with Christ into a Spirit-indwelt state marked by the discovery within ourselves of the inner inclinations of the God-man as we meet him in the Gospels. These inclinations are to love and serve and honor and obey and please and glorify and exalt our heavenly Father, a purpose that in our case embraces God the Son, our Savior, also. The Holy Spirit, who implanted these inclinations by regenerating us (we are "born of the Spirit," John 3:6, 8; "born of God," John 1:13; 1 John 3:9), now indwells us to enable us to fulfill them in daily living. The Spirit is God "who works in you both to will and to work for his good pleasure" (Phil. 2:13). Through the Spirit's ministry Christ himself is mysteriously but really in us (Col. 1:27), living his risen life in our everyday lives. What this means in practice is that we are helped to resist sinful urges that still rise up within us (few bad habits can be quickly broken) as we are moved to show forth the fruit of the Spirit (love, joy, peace, patience, kindness, goodness, faithfulness, gentleness, self-control—Gal. 5:22-23). This fruit is in truth the character of Jesus now being reproduced and growing to maturity in his followers. As he prompts us to such behavior, God the Holy Spirit is transforming us from the inside out, repairing the ruination that sin has effected in our moral being.

Our race, says the Scripture, was made to bear God's image in a dual sense—to be his representatives on earth, his deputy managers as we might say (Gen. 1:26, 28), and to match his moral character in our attitudes, actions, relationships, values, and goals (Col. 3:9-10). But Adam failed, and now we are all born more or less rebellious, disintegrated, and incapable of fulfilling our double destiny. Our reconstruction, however, is in hand. The train stations of England are solid structures of Victorian brick or stone, which one feels might last forever, but today's airports on both sides of the Atlantic undergo constant reconstruction, with new additions, and that illustrates the divine work of which I am speaking.

The miracle of God's saving grace gives us a new identity that our self-image henceforth must express. Our natural self-image is an emotionally charged composite made up of our deepest sense of who and what we are, what we must and must not be, and how we expect to get on in the world of activity and relationships. The seedbed in which it has grown is our sense from the earliest days of other people, other things, and pressures and claims that demand to shape us. Our spiritual self-image, however, will now grow out of what is the biggest reality of life to us, namely our new relationship with God. This new reality is to absorb our natural self-image as a business firm absorbs the company it takes over—that is, by first assimilating and then remolding what was previously there, ending what was not fit to remain and setting something better in its place. The new self-image is to be threefold.

First, in relation to God, we must see ourselves as *inheritors*. In antiquity the childless rich adopted as sons grown males of proven worth to uphold the family name and in due course to receive and manage the family fortune. The Gospel tells us that God in grace not only pardons us sinners, whoever we are and whatever mess we have made of our lives so far, but also adopts us into his family as his sons and heirs, to be glorified in due course alongside Christ himself (see Rom. 8:15-17). ("Sons" there should be understood as part of the picture because in ancient times women did not ordinarily inherit; the New Testament shows that in salvation the distinction between men and women is irrelevant, and both become heirs of the grace of life.) The doxology that opens Peter's first letter focuses on the coming inheritance: "Blessed be the God and Father of our Lord Jesus Christ! According to his great mercy he has caused us to be born again to a living hope through the resurrection of Jesus Christ from the dead, to an inheritance that is imperishable, undefiled, and unfading, kept in heaven for you . . ." (ESV).

Of this inheritance dying Mr. Stand-fast, at the close of Bunyan's *Pilgrim's Progress,* speaks as follows:

> . . . the thoughts of what I am going to, and of the Conduct that waits for me on the other side, doth lie as a glowing Coal at my Heart.
>
> I see myself now at the *end* of my Journey, my *toilsome* Days are ended. I am going now to see *that* Head that was Crowned with Thorns, and *that* Face that was spit upon, for me.

> I have formerly lived by Hear-say and Faith, but now I go
> where I shall live by sight, and shall be with him, in whose
> Company I delight myself.

The first layer in our new self-image should be joy, amazement, anticipation, and a sense of privilege at being a fully instated inheritor of such glory as this.

Second, in relation to this life, we must see ourselves as *travelers*—not permanent residents but pilgrims going home, here to serve but not to settle down. Secular materialism, which surrounds us today, is earthbound, treating this life as all there is and seeking to foist on us a value system based on that assumption. But Christians must resist this pressure, and the first step in doing so is to learn to see ourselves as persons on a journey, who should keep moving because none of the places we pass through is the home where we belong. The two parts of Bunyan's masterpiece (full title, *The Pilgrim's Progress from This World to That Which Is to Come, Delivered Under the Similitude of a Dream, Wherein Is Discovered the Manner of His Setting Out, His Dangerous Journey, and Safe Arrival at the Desired Country*) stand as the all-time classic on this idea of life as a journey. (Have you read it yet?) The second layer in our new self-image should be the traveler's sense of the temporary nature of his stay everywhere he goes and of his enjoyment of each place or condition as he passes through—a sense, in other words, that this world, wonderfully good and enjoyable as it is in so many ways, is not the home that is his destination.

Third, in relation to worldly pulls, sin's promptings, and Satan's prowlings, we must see ourselves as *fighters*. We are soldiers of Christ who cannot hope for a quiet life or an easy passage, but we advance by battling opposition with the armor and weapons that Christ supplies. We make headway across rough terrain by tackling the difficulties head-on. Bunyan's presentation of this truth in the first part of *Pilgrim's Progress* remains as realistic as it is vivid. It is perhaps relevant that twelve years in prison for being an outspoken nonconforming preacher of the Gospel had been part of his preparation in God's providence for writing it. The third layer in our new self-image should be a sense of commitment to unenjoyable but unavoidable conflict with all the different kinds of evil, recognizing that behind them all stands Satan, the devil, Christ's bitterest enemy, malicious, deceitful, and set to ruin all the work of God and destroy all the Christians in the world if he can.

Fourth, in relation to other people, and more particularly to other Christians, we must see ourselves as *carers, bearers, and sharers.* I put those words together not because they rhyme, but because I need all three to express the New Testament idea of how those who live for God must learn to live for others. A life of solitary withdrawal in order to concentrate on one's personal relationship to God is not the godly way. Because uncaring individualism was strong in the first-century Graeco-Roman culture, just as it is in the West today, the New Testament teachers needed to be strong in enforcing neighbor-love in the world, which becomes brotherly love in the church—and strong they certainly were. "By this we know love, that he [Christ] laid down his life for us, and we ought to lay down our lives for the brothers" (1 John 3:16 ESV). "Brothers, if anyone is caught in some transgression, you who are spiritual should restore him in a spirit of gentleness. . . . Bear one another's burdens, and so fulfill the law of Christ . . . as we have opportunity, let us do good to everyone, and especially to those who are of the household of faith" (Gal. 6:1, 2, 10 ESV). "Do not neglect to do good and to share what you have, for such sacrifices are pleasing to God" (Heb. 13:16 ESV).

Passages like this (and there are many such) fully warrant our three rhyming nouns, as do Jesus' own recorded teaching in the Sermon on the Mount, his story of the Good Samaritan, and his farewell discourse (see Matt. 5:38-48; 7:12; Luke 10:25-37; John 13:12-15; 15:12-17). Caring for others and seeking their welfare, bearing their burdens in order to help them, and sharing what we have with them as our practical expression of love for them are a mandated integral part of the Christian way of life. So the fourth layer in our new self-image should be a sense of being bound to spend and be spent in the service of others, in our families, our churches, and our wider communities of whatever kind.

Here, then, is the fourfold matrix of Christian reality out of which our new self-image must crystallize. But how is this to happen? One's self-image, as we saw earlier, is an emotionally charged inner sense of one's identity, potential, and relational prospects. We saw that our image of ourselves is important because it tends to program what actually takes place. A poor self-image inhibits and restricts and produces uncertainty and pessimism and expectations of proving inadequate, so that one dare not hope for worthwhile achievement, and most of the time one runs scared. By contrast, a good self-image yields constant confidence that one can do better, so that in fact one does. What, then, we ask, will turn our knowledge of the vocational quadrilateral, as we may call it, that must shape our identity and behavior into a liberating, motivating, encouraging sense of ourselves—in short, a good self-image by the counselors' standard.

The secret is an open one: It is the same as the secret of joy that we explored earlier in this book. Everything depends on our learning to think in a particular way as a matter of habit. We have to acquire the habit of reminding ourselves over and over of the truths of the quadrilateral, and of telling God over and over in words of worship from our heart how good it is to be living such a life. We have to get into the way of *basking* and *soaking* and *swimming* in the love of the holy Three, of *reckoning up the total* of our wealth in Christ, and of repeatedly *savoring the taste* of the new wine that through the Spirit is our privilege to drink every day. Such meditations will have an effect parallel to that of our regular three meals a day, of which someone wrote:

> *It's a very odd thing,*
> *As odd as can be,*
> *That whatever Miss T. eats*
> *Turns into Miss T.*

As regular meals, duly digested, put flesh on our bones, so the regular digesting of God's grace set forth in the Gospel stamps a Christian self-image on our hearts. Expose yourself to the sun, and your skin tans; expose yourself to God's love, and a godly self-image, cognitively shaped and emotionally charged by the gifts of his love, becomes more and more a part of you. True as it may be that we shall never know fully *who* we are till we get to heaven, we already know in a decisive way *where* we are and where we are going, with our God as our friend and companion. This knowledge determines henceforth how we think and feel about ourselves. The Bible tells us it should, and the Holy Spirit within us ensures that it does. That we should thus know our new identity in Christ, and that a new, good, godly self-image should grow out of it, is one of the best and most brilliant of God's plans for you and me.

One thing more remains to be said. At the heart, not indeed of our self-*image* but of our self-*knowledge*, there remains a profound ignorance. With bated breath, one feels, John wrote: "Beloved, we are God's children now, and what we will be has not yet appeared; but we know that when he appears we will be like him, for we shall see him as he is" (1 John 3:2 ESV). The promise that we shall see our Lord and Savior Jesus Christ as he is offers a wonderful prospect for believers, as any lover who over a period of time has been limited to phone conversations with the loved one will understand. But I would underline as specially significant for us, in light of what I have been saying, John's acknowledgment that "it does not yet appear what we shall be."

There are two reasons why. The first is that we do not know and cannot truly imagine what Jesus' glorified humanity, which we are to see and be conformed to, is like. The second is that, when all is said and done, we know so very little of what we ourselves are now. Due to original sin, despite all the work of grace so far, we remain deeply disintegrated beings. We are largely out of touch with the unconscious, subconscious, preconscious aspects of ourselves that psychoanalysts and analytical psychologists try to dredge up and study, just as we are out of touch with most of the physiological processes that go on in our bodies. As was said at the start of this chapter, we all want to know ourselves thoroughly, and the promise that in heaven we shall "know as we are known" (1 Cor. 13:12 KJV) indicates that one day we shall. As in Christ we shall be fully integrated, as he is, so in Christ shall we be fully self-knowing and self-aware. But we cannot at present imagine what that will be like.

In his letter to Pergamum, our Savior promises: "To the one who conquers I will give some of the hidden manna, and I will give him a white stone, with a new name written on the stone that no one knows except the one who receives it" (Rev. 2:17 ESV). God-given names in Scripture are regularly revelations of the relationship to God and the role in his plans of the person named. So the promise clearly implies that we shall be shown in full exactly where we fitted in to what God was doing in his world. This revelation can hardly come without our being shown also how God knew us and shaped his dealings with us and his use of us in light of what he saw that we were—in other words, in light of our selfhood and makeup and traits and vulnerabilities as he knew them all along. And when I know these things as God knows them, I shall at last know fully who I am. The new name on the white stone will include this knowledge. It also belongs to God's plans for you and me.

So the word of wisdom about our true and full identity in Christ is: Wait—and see! By God's grace I settle for that; I hope you do, too.

13

POWER PATH

Taking the Holy Spirit Seriously

Each December *Time* magazine produces a set of often light-hearted comments on the previous year. At the end of 1987, the editors were isolating the most overworked word of the year, the one most ready for retirement. The word they chose was *power*, as in "power lunch," or "power tie," or "power shopping." I confess that my mind ran to various uses of the word *power* in Christian circles that seemed similarly overwrought, and I rather agreed that there was a strong case for retiring the word.

But then I thought again. Though the word *power* is still overused in society—and I believe often frivolously and unhelpfully used among Christians—it is nevertheless a significant New Testament word. Where would I be if I imposed a self-denying ordinance and declined to use it any longer? Where would the church be if we all acted that way?

THE SPIRIT IN ACTION

During the past two centuries, Christians have been very concerned about power. Have they been wrong in this focus? Not altogether. In the middle and late 1800s, there was great concern to find "the path for power." The path of power meant one's ability to perform set tasks well, starting with truth-telling and maintaining financial integrity, and to overcome temptations, starting with loss of self-control in fits of anger. Was it wrong to seek the power of God for greater self-control and a richer practice of righteousness? Of course not.

At the same time concern focused on being able, through the power of God, to impact others for God through preaching and witness. A great deal was said about the difference between Christians whose witness "had power" and those whose witness did not "have power." Was it right to be concerned that one's witness should have power? Was it right to be anxious lest one's witness should be powerless? Of course it was right. These should be concerns of ours as well.

More recently Christians who have been touched by that movement known variously as Pentecostalism, charismatic renewal, and the third wave have been seeking the ability to channel supernatural demonstrations of God's power in healings of all sorts—healings of the body, inner healing of the heart, and exorcisms where there appears to be something demonic in a person's life. Again I ask myself, is it wrong that Christians are concerned about these things? Though I see various pitfalls of understanding and a great deal of foolishness and unreality here, I cannot find it in my heart to say this is wrong. In my New Testament I read a great deal about such manifestations of the power of God—understood simply as "powers of the coming age" or, in other words, the Holy Spirit in action.

MIRACLES IN ACTION

The coming of Christ the Savior has meant the outpouring of the Spirit on the church and on the world. And the Holy Spirit comes with power. In the New Testament we see this power manifested in all the modes of which I was speaking a moment ago—the ability to perform set tasks and overcome temptation, the ability to impact others through preaching and witness, and the ability to act as a channel for God's power in miracles, healings, and the like. Let us look more closely at all this.

First, in the Gospels we encounter works of power in the physical realm, including miracles of nature and healings of all sorts. The scriptural phrase "signs and wonders" is used for them.

These are, to use C. S. Lewis's apt phrase, "miracles of the new creation," in which the power of God that created the world works again to bring something out of nothing—that is, to bring about a state of affairs for which no explanation can be given in terms of what was there before. Everyone knows you cannot get food for five thousand out of five loaves and two fishes, but food for five thousand was produced nonetheless. Everyone knows you cannot restore life to the dead, but Jesus on three occasions brought the dead back to life— Jairus's daughter, the widow's son at Nain, and Lazarus.

To be sure, these three "raisings from the dead" are not the same as the greater miracle of new creation that occurred when Christ himself was raised from the dead. These were only resuscitations; in each case, the person died again a little further down the line. Jesus, however, rose from the dead never to die again. His resurrection is an even more remarkable miracle of new creation—indeed, it is the normative one: Christ is the first fruits, the beginning of the new creation of God, as the New Testament itself says.

Nevertheless, all these are instances in which the power that created the world out of nothing in the first place produces effects for which no cause can be cited, except that God the Creator has been showing his power again.

WORDS OF POWER

One reads on in the New Testament and finds, second, that words of power in Christian communication are very much a part of the gospel story and of the story of the apostolic church. Luke is particularly interested in the power of God, and there are several texts in Luke that are significant here. Let's look at some of them.

In Luke 4:14 we read that following the wilderness temptation, "Jesus returned to Galilee in the *power* of the Spirit." This text introduces not only his works of power but also the words of power that came from his lips. Then after his resurrection, Jesus told the disciples to wait in Jerusalem until they were endued with "*power* from on high" for the ministry of worldwide evangelism to which he was committing them (see Luke 24:49).

At the beginning of Acts, Luke picks up the same theme. Jesus tells his followers, "You will receive *power* when the Holy Spirit comes on you; and you will be my witnesses . . . to the ends of the earth" (Acts 1:8). Then later we read, "With great *power* the apostles continued to testify to the resurrection of the Lord Jesus, and much grace was upon them all" (Acts 4:33).

EMPOWERED PREACHING

Paul likewise has tremendous things to say about the power of God working through the Gospel and through its messengers. "I am not ashamed of the gospel, because it is the *power* of God for the salvation of everyone who believes" (Romans 1:16). At the end of the lengthy argument that makes up the book of Romans, and speaking of his own ministry, Paul says, "I will not venture to speak of anything except what Christ has accomplished through me in leading the Gentiles to obey God by what I have said and done—by the *power* of signs and miracles, through the *power* of the Spirit" (Rom. 15:18-19).

And again in his first letter to the Corinthians: "For Christ did not send me to baptize, but to preach the gospel—not with words of human wisdom, lest the cross of Christ be emptied of its *power*. For the message of the cross is foolishness to those who are perishing, but to us who are being saved it is the *power* of God" (1 Cor. 1:17-18).

"Words of human wisdom" is a phrase Paul uses to denote a policy and purpose of swapping philosophy with the philosophers. The people in the Greek cities where he went to evangelize expected Paul to parade his own cleverness in this way when he spoke in public. But Paul would not do it. He adopted a style of presentation that at first seemed foolish to those expecting the sort of self-display they got from the other traveling teachers.

"I knew what you wanted," Paul says in the opening chapters of 1 Corinthians, "and I was resolved not to give it to you. You wanted me to show off as a philosopher, with dazzling arguments, but I wouldn't do it. And so you thought me a fool." Rather, Paul says, "My message and my preaching were not with wise and persuasive words, but with a demonstration of the Spirit's *power,* so that your faith might not rest on men's wisdom, but on God's *power*" (1 Cor. 2:4-5).

TRANSFORMED LIVES

The New Testament speaks not only of God's power in the miraculous and in the communication of the Gospel, but also, third, of God's power at work *in us*, enabling us to understand and to do what we otherwise could not.

In Ephesians 1:17-19 Paul tells the Christians what he prays for them: "I keep asking that the God of our Lord Jesus Christ, the glorious Father, may give you the Spirit of wisdom and revelation, so that you may know him better. I pray also that the eyes of your heart may be enlightened in order that you may know the hope to which he has called you, the riches of his glorious inheritance in the saints, and his incomparably great *power* for us [other translations say, "*in* us"] who believe."

It is not just power in the *message* that Paul has in view. It is not just power through the *messenger*. It is power *in and upon those who believe*, making their lives utterly different from what they were before. It is resurrection power—a matter of God raising with Christ those who have become willing to die with Christ. Clearly Paul is expecting tremendous changes in the lives of those who now belong to Christ.

He comes back to this theme at the close of his third chapter: "I pray that out of [God's] glorious riches he may strengthen you with *power* through his Spirit in your inner being, so that Christ may dwell in your hearts through faith. And I pray that you, being rooted and established in love, may have *power,* together with all the saints, to grasp how wide and long and high and deep is the love of Christ, and to know this love that surpasses knowledge—that you may be filled to the measure of all the fullness of God" (Eph. 3:16-19).

Again we see that Paul is talking about something radical in the fullest sense of that word—something that produces a total change. He is praying that through this marvelous inner transformation and enrichment the Ephesians will be utterly different from folk around them—utterly different, indeed, from what they have been so far.

These are samples of the many precious texts in the New Testament about the power of God working through Christ and through the apostles, manifested in works of power in the physical realm, in giving power to Christian communications so that they have a significant impact, and also in enabling Christians to understand and do what otherwise they could neither understand nor do.

HEIGHTENED EXPECTATIONS

Thus, reflecting on the matter in light of the New Testament, I was compelled to correct my initial feeling that *Time* magazine had got it right about retiring the word *power*. Though power is spoken of nowadays in many ways that are hollow and silly, power itself is a theme that Christians must ever hold on to. It is very clear from the New Testament that the power of God is meant to accompany the Gospel and to find expression through its messengers and in the lives of those to whom the message comes.

This conviction leads me to six theses about the manifestation of the power of God among his people today. My aim in sharing them is to make us more disposed to seek the power of God in its various forms.

At the same time, I must frankly say that I think there are unhelpful cross-currents in today's discussions of the power of God in the church of God. Thus I think that some aspects of these six theses are needed for corrective purposes. I trust they will clear the way in our minds and our hearts for right thinking and right practice in relation to the power of God so that this power may be manifested to God's glory in our lives and in our churches.

1. *It is right to bring the supernatural into prominence and to raise Christians' expectations with regard to it.*

Our expectations of seeing the power of God transforming people's lives are not, generally speaking, as high as they should be. It is a fact of history that when the Reformation broke on the church in the sixteenth century, there was a tremendous amount of superstition regarding the saints working miracles. I am not denying that God may well have worked miracles through his saints before and since the Reformation. But the reformers looked around and saw a great deal that seemed to them to be unmistakably superstitious, and they reacted against it.

A truth that abides, however, is that the reaction of man does not work the righteousness of God. If you are walking backward away from something that you think is a mistake, you may be right in supposing it is a mistake, but for you to be walking backward is never right. You know what happens to people who walk backward. Sooner or later they stumble over some obstacle behind them because their mind and their eyes were fixed on what they were trying to get away from. We are meant to walk forward, not backward, and reaction is always a matter of walking backward.

I believe the reformers' reaction against all thought of the supernatural in the lives of God's people in the age of the Holy Spirit was frankly more wrong than right—as have been many subsequent attempts to rule out the present-day reality of the supernatural.

It has been necessary to recover this theme in the twentieth century, and we should thank God that expectations of supernatural healings and answers to prayer have risen during this past thirty or forty years. The thing that I would say here as a caution is not that the recovery is wrong-headed, but that there is a danger going with it of undervaluing the natural and the ordinary. There are people who want every problem to be solved by an immediate miracle, a display of the supernatural, a wonderful providence that will change everything. I think that is a sign of immaturity, and I note that God does not often work that way.

Again and again the Lord leads us into painful and difficult situations, and we pray—as Paul prayed regarding his thorn in the flesh—that the Lord will change the situation. We want a miracle! But instead the Lord chooses to strengthen us to cope, as he did with Paul, making his strength perfect in our continuing weakness.

Think of it in terms of the training of children, and you will see my point at once. If there are never any difficult situations that demand self-denial and discipline, if there are never any sustained pressures to cope with, if there are never any long-term strategies where you have to stick with something for years in order to advance, there will never be any maturity of character. Children who are shielded from these things—coddled, as we would say—will remain spoiled and childish all their lives because everything has been made too easy for them. The Lord does not allow that to happen in the lives of his children.

It is extraordinary how little the New Testament says about God's interest in our success, by comparison with the enormous amount that it says about God's interest in our holiness, our maturity in Christ, and our growth into the fullness of his image. When we start thinking in positive terms about the supernatural in our personal lives, we must also remember it may well please God to leave situations as they are, to decide not to work a miracle, in order to strengthen us so that we can grow personally by working through the difficulty.

EMPOWERED MINISTRY

2. *It is right to aspire to use one's God-given gifts in powerful and useful ministry.*

It is right to want to know what gifts for ministry God has given us. It is right to want to harness them and see them used for the blessing of others as widely as possible.

But there is always a danger that the person who believes that God has given him or her a good sprinkling of gifts will be betrayed by that old enemy, self-importance, for which the classic Christian label is pride. God does not value us according to the number of gifts we have or by their spectacular quality. God does not value us primarily in terms of what we can do—even what we can do in his strength. He values us primarily in terms of what he makes us to be, character-wise, as he conforms us to Christ by his grace.

Jesus was already sounding the warning note when his disciples came back from a preaching tour all gung-ho and excited. "Lord," they cried, "even the demons are subject to us in your name!"

"Very good," says Jesus. "But don't rejoice that the demons are subject to you. That is not the truly important thing. Rejoice, rather, that your names are written in heaven" (see Luke 10:17, 20). That is as if to say: Rejoice in your salvation. Rejoice in what you *are* by the grace of God, rather than in the way God uses you. Rejoice in being his child and in entering upon your destiny of being transformed into Jesus' image. Gifts are secondary. Sanctity is primary. Never let anything divert your mind and heart from holding fast to that truth.

Meeting Needs

3. *It is right to want to be a channel of divine power into other people's lives at their points of need.*

Just be careful, however, lest you become one of those people who suffers from the neurosis of needing to be needed—the state of not feeling that you are anything or anybody unless others are telling you they need you. That is not spiritual health. That is *lack* of spiritual health.

One of the disciplines to which the Lord calls us is the willingness for certain periods of our life *not* to be used in significant ministry. Here, let us say, is a gifted sister, and for quite a long period it may seem that the Lord sidelines her so that her ministry is not being used. What is going on? Is this spiritual failure? It likely is not spiritual failure at all, but the Lord teaching her over again that her Christian fulfillment does not depend on finding that people need her. The source of her joy in life must always be the knowledge of God's love for her—the knowledge that though he didn't need her, he has chosen to love her freely and gloriously so that she may have the eternal joy of fellowship with him.

In the spiritual life, what we are is always prior to what we do. If we lose touch with what we are and with the reality of God's free mercy as the taproot of our spiritual life, the Lord may have to sideline us until we have learned this lesson again.

Empowered Evangelism

4. *It is right to want to see God's power manifested in a way that has a significant evangelistic effect.*

The line of thought I have in mind here is the one that says that evangelism is not evangelism, or at least is not good quality evangelism, until it has a particular kind of miracle attached to it as proof of the presence and power of Christ. Frankly, I think that is a gross overstatement, a real error. The danger here is that those who practice evangelism will think they should devise ways and means of manipulating people and situations to make it look as if wonderful things are happening through the power of God. Dishonesty and deception at this point must prove disastrous.

Nonetheless, it is not wrong to want evangelism to be done in a way that impresses and blesses people, because thus it becomes evident that all this talk about a new life in Christ through the power of God is for real. Moral and spiritual transformation by the Holy Spirit through new birth remains the supreme miracle and should be highlighted in evangelism. Testimonies can be feeble and a great spiritual letdown, but in evangelism there is, I believe, a proper place for them. First-hand witness to Christ doing for lost souls what alcohol and rock music and sex and drugs could not do for them still brings about through the Spirit the most fruitful sort of "power encounter" between other sinners and the Savior.

5. *It is right to want to be divinely empowered for righteousness, for moral victories, for deliverance from bad habits, and for pleasing God.*

The good news is that through the means of grace, all Christians may be so empowered. Through the Spirit, you and I must and may mortify the deeds of the body. Through the Spirit, you and I must and may manifest the new habits, the new Christlike behavior patterns that constitute the fruit of the Spirit. Without holiness, says the writer to the Hebrews, no one will see the Lord (Heb. 12:14). When we realize that real holiness is a real necessity, it is a tremendous encouragement to know also that by the power of the Spirit a holy life is possible even for spiritual weaklings such as we are, and so of course we should want and seek it. I trust that this thesis, like the next one, presents no problem except for the practical one that confronts our will: Now that we know this is how it ought to be, what are we going to do about it?

6. *It is right to want to be divinely empowered for communion with God in a love that answers the knowledge of his love for us.*

Again, this empowering is set before us as our proper goal, and the promise is that, if appropriately sought, it will be found. The last verses of Ephesians 3, some of which I quoted earlier, prove that. Paul's desire is that his readers will come to know "the love of Christ which surpasses knowledge," and so be filled "with all the fullness of God," and his confidence that his prayer for them will be answered as stated appears from the doxology to which he immediately moves: "Now to him who by the *power* at work within us is able to do far more abundantly than all that we ask or think, to him be glory . . ." (vv. 20-21 RSV). So let us pray for this for ourselves and for others. How can we hold up our heads if we do not?

THE POWER PATH

I spoke earlier of what the title of this chapter calls the "power path." Perhaps it will be clearer now what I mean when I say that *the power path is humble dependence on God to become channels of his power.* We are to be the channels, first, through which the power of God flows into the depths of our being as we open ourselves up to our Lord and his grace. Then by God's grace we will find that again and again we are becoming channels of his power into the lives of others.

God's power is *God's* power, and he remains sovereign as he exercises it. He does not give us power as a gift. His power never becomes our possession. The power of God is not something handed over to us for us to use at our discretion. Our relation to the power of God should be one of becoming by his grace means through which his power is exercised. Our attitude toward the power of God must never be such that we seek to possess the power for ourselves so we can use it at our own will. If ever you hear Christians talking about using the power of God, I hope red lights flash in your mind. If, however, you hear Christians talking about finding the place where God's power can use them, I hope you nod your head. Should you seek God's power as a personal possession, you would be off track, perhaps ruinously so, for you would be lining up with Simon the sorcerer! (See Acts 8:9-24.) Don't do that!

WEAKNESS AND STRENGTH

Finally, a few words about what I call "the power scenario." The power scenario is that *God perfects his strength in our weakness.* Therefore, the more conscious we are of that weakness, the better.

Think again of Paul and his thorn in the flesh. We do not know exactly what the "thorn" was. But it was surely something painful, or he wouldn't have called it a thorn, and it was surely something in his own makeup, or he wouldn't have called it a thorn "in his flesh."

Paul went to the Lord Jesus in solemn seasons of prayer three times over. He went to the Lord Jesus because Jesus is the healer, and this was something that needed the healer's touch. He prayed that the thorn might depart from him, but the Lord said no. The Lord said, "I have something better in view for you, Paul." (God always reserves the right to answer our prayers in a better way than we ask them.) "I'll tell you what I'm going to do," the Lord said. "I'm going to make my strength perfect in your continuing weakness so that all the things you fear—the end of your ministry, or at least the diminution and enfeebling and discredit of your ministry—will be avoided. Your ministry will go on in power and in strength as it has done, but it will also go on in weakness. You will carry that thorn in the flesh around with you as long as you live. But my strength will be made perfect in your weakness." (See 2 Cor. 12:7-10.)

This, I believe, is a pattern likely to be worked out again and again in your life and in mine. The Lord first of all makes us conscious of our weakness so that in the face of some particular burden our heart cries out, "I can't cope with this." We go to the Lord, telling him, "I can't handle this. Please take it away!" And the Lord replies, "In my strength you *can* handle this, and in answer to your prayer, I will *strengthen* you to handle it." Thus in the end your testimony, like Paul's, will be, "I can do all things through Christ who strengthens me" (Phil. 4:13 NKJV). That, I believe, is the fullest expression for any of us of the empowered Christian life.

14

MUSINGS ON THE LIFE OF FAITH

Double-Mindedness, Seriousness, Balance, Dying

The musings that follow fill some gaps in the view of the Christian life that has been presented thus far.

THE DOUBLE MIND

I expect that when you hear the phrase "living by faith," you think only of Christians trying to exist with no guaranteed financial support, just as when you hear the word *fundamentalism*, you think only of a version of evangelicalism that seems to you coarse, crass, combative, crude, and best avoided. Thus noble words get narrowed and debased. *Fundamentalism* was actually coined to identify the virtue of faithfulness to Christian fundamentals, and "living by faith" was a Reformational way of characterizing Christian existence. That is why Richard Baxter's treatise *The Life of Faith*, written three centuries ago, is an analysis of the Christian response to all life situations.

What is the life of faith? Well, what is faith? Do not take seriously the legendary child's definition of faith as "believing what you know ain't so," even when (as happens) unbelieving adults embrace it. The human mind cannot believe what seems false; skepticism rots belief as a chinook turns snow to slush. Scripture is clear that faith is the positive response of the whole person to God's total revelation, perceived as such.

While it is true that "the principal acts of saving faith are accepting, receiving, and resting upon Christ alone for justification, sanctification, and eternal life," it is equally true that by faith "a Christian believeth to be true whatsoever is revealed in the Word, for the authority of God himself speaking therein; and acteth differently upon that which each particular passage thereof containeth; yielding obedience to the commands, trembling at the threatenings, and embracing the promises of God for this life, and that which is to come" (Westminster Confession, XIV.2).

Faith, then, is an exercise of mind and heart whereby (1) we learn what God tells us in Scripture about himself and ourselves; (2) we shudder at what is said about our lostness without Christ; (3) we thankfully embrace God's promises of grace to sinners, and the living Christ whom those promises set forth; and (4) we apply to ourselves Bible teaching about God's work, will, and ways, in order to see what attitudes honor God and what actions will please him in each situation. Faith knows that God shapes all situations as a means to our final good. In light of that knowledge faith seeks biblical guidance on what to aim at, pray for, hope for, prepare for, and actually do; on how to handle one's relationship to God and to the rest of creation; and on how to use one's opportunities for glorifying God.

Thus, the life of faith is to be thoughtful, conscientious, and at the same time enterprising. Every Christian's life should reflect, first in private prayer and then in public performance too, Carey's famous maxim: "Attempt great things for God; expect great things from God." Expectation—hope, that is—is a major element in faith. Hebrews 11:1 defines faith as confidence about things hoped for.

It is a sad fact that people who profess faith often come short of its fullness. Sometimes knowledge and belief of God's truth are divorced from personal trust and obedience. That is the "dead" faith of which James speaks in his first and second chapters. Sometimes trust is not guided by truth, so that faith becomes superstition. Sometimes real trust for salvation in the Christ of the Gospel fails to lead us to interpret what God sends by what he says in his Word. That is the vice of "double-mindedness," which ruins both one's prayers and one's walk.

When James says "double-minded" (literally, "two-souled"), he means more than "irresolute," "undecided," and "unable to make up his mind," as various modern versions render the word. He is detecting not temperamental ditheriness, as these translations imply, but unbelief: doubting—that is, mistrusting—the good will of the God whom one relies on for salvation, prays to, and calls Father. The text shows this. Here is the full passage.

> *Count it all joy, my brothers, when you meet trials of various kinds, for you know that the testing of your faith produces steadfastness. And let steadfastness have its full effect, so that you may be perfect and complete, lacking in nothing.*
>
> *If any of you lacks wisdom, let him ask God, who gives generously to all without reproaching, and it will be given him. But let him ask in faith, with no doubting, for the one who doubts is like a wave of the sea that is driven and tossed by the wind. For that person must not suppose that he will receive anything from the Lord; he is a double-minded man, unstable in all his ways. (James 1:2-8 ESV)*

James's style is somewhat abrupt, but the flow of thought is clear.

Welcome trials—meaning "temptations"—says James. Why? Because handling trials produces resilience; strains put on our faith and obedience are God's Outward Bound course, toughening us up spiritually. The maturing that results leads us on to the victor's crown. So anyone under pressure should ask God for the wisdom needed to keep living right through the times of perplexity and upheaval. Will God supply it? Yes. He is a generous giver, always glad to answer this request.

But the two-minded person, while professing faith in Christ as divine Savior and Lord, panics under pressure, thinks with his feelings rather than his brains, and concludes that since God evidently no longer cares for him, his prayers for wisdom and strength cannot expect an answer. Yet God is unchanging in his love and free from any shadow of inconsistency. Don't insult him by indulging such unbelief as your attitude expresses, says James.

What, then, is James's answer to the double-mindedness that juxtaposes trust in God's Word about the hope of salvation with mistrust of his Word about his help under trials? Why, single-mindedness, of course, which means believing all that God says, not just some of it, putting faith in his faithfulness about everything, joyfully trusting his goodness at all times, and seeking to honor him by consistent holiness. That is true purity of heart, and that is the only life of faith worthy of the name. How, I wonder, do we measure up?

ARE WE SERIOUS?

The question whether particular people are *saved* or are *converted* or are *believers* is often heard in evangelical circles. We recognize it as a necessary question because it points to the momentous passage from spiritual death to spiritual life that everyone needs. The question brings up the issue in a way that excludes the sacramentalist fancy that merely being baptized makes you safe forever. Not all, however, are happy with the question in this form, for in the first place it seems to assume that everyone who ever comes to faith will have a dramatic Damascus Road experience to testify to, which is not so. In the second place we find that some who testify volubly to conversion experiences that brought them to faith turn out to be hypocrites and frauds. Does the question as to whether people are spiritually alive or dead have to be asked in these terms?

No, it does not, nor has it always been. For half a century, up till fifty years ago, it was regularly put thus: Do they *love the Lord?* That was a good way of focusing the question, for it zeros in on what people are in the present rather than on what they experienced in the past, and love to the Savior-King who loved us and gave himself for us really is the heart of the Christian life. Before that, in England at the turn of the nineteenth century, Anglican evangelicals used to ask whether people had become *serious.* This also, I think, was a good way of putting the question, once one understood what was implied. Let me spell out the meaning that the question carried.

First, however, a negation, lest we jump to the wrong conclusion at the outset. The question did *not* mean: Have these folks become somber and long-faced? Have they given up cracking jokes and laughing when others crack them? Do they now take themselves terribly seriously? Yesterday's evangelicals knew as well as we do that self-centered seriousness and posturing piosity of that sort is unspiritual and unbalancing, if not actually unbalanced. (Did you know the word *piosity*, by the way? It's British slang, very useful for puncturing the pretentiousness of the pompous. I recommend that you add the term to your vocabulary.)

The truth here is that if you mortify your sense of humor and lose the ability to laugh at yourself, you are actually screwing down one of the safety valves of your sanity. There is nothing godly about doing that. Such action produces people who are profoundly proud, utterly unrealistic, frequently fanatical, and always intolerable to live with. In the hearts of all who are genuinely holy, along with their intensity in adoring the Father and the Son goes a sense of their own silliness, absurdity, and intrinsic unimportance before the Lord, who as they know could get along very well without them. Their refusal to take themselves too seriously, paradoxical as it may sound, is one expression of their evangelical seriousness.

What did those faraway nineteenth-century evangelicals—Wilberforce, Hannah More, and their circle—really mean when they spoke of people becoming *serious?* They meant that these folk had begun to reckon seriously with God, Christ, the Bible, the Gospel, their own sinfulness and guilt, and the issues of eternity, which are settled for good or ill by the choices we make now. Serious writers are those who focus on the long-term, deep-level implications of their themes and point up these implications in what they put out. Serious Christians are those who perceive the eternal implications of the life they live now. They make decisions in light of the eternal realities of God's love and wrath, God's heaven and hell, which will still be there for us after we have left this world and indeed will still be there after this world itself has ceased to be. That is the seriousness we speak of here.

An essay in *Time* dealt with "the *gravitas* factor" (*gravitas* is Latin for seriousness in our sense and was evidently used because the writer did not think any English word can now be trusted to carry his full weight of meaning). The essay distinguished between public figures whose actions showed them to be thoroughly and far-seeingly serious, like Winston Churchill and Margaret Thatcher, as compared with leaders who seemed not to think or care about the long-term effects of what they did, becoming corks tossing around uselessly on the waters of change and crisis, like—well, never mind. Purposeful people like Churchill and Thatcher model for us real Christian seriousness, of which they represent the secular counterpart.

In a narcissistic age like ours, the question of seriousness presses Christians uncomfortably. We can be bright believers, burbling away about our wonderful conversion, and still be living frivolous, unstable, ego-tripping lives. We run from one brief enthusiasm to another, constantly pursuing way-out novelties of belief and behavior and earning for ourselves at home, in church, and in the wider community David Niven's biting comment on Errol Flynn: "At least you knew where you were with him; he *always* let you down." Steady seriousness is one mark of right-living Christians. Am I *serious*? Are you?

BALANCE

When I lived in England, I never got on well with those people, of whom England had many, whose driving motivation seemed to be fear of becoming unbalanced. These cool cats valued poise above passion and middle-class correctness above gestures of enthusiasm. They eschewed exuberance and looked down their noses at lively folk who now and then went over the top emotionally. Some of these blasé balance addicts were evangelical Christians with whom I regularly rubbed shoulders, and their smooth sangfroid, I am afraid, sometimes made me want to spew.

Was that a balanced reaction? Why, no. Balance like theirs was never my thing. If that shows me up as a blurting vulgarian or an inverted snob, so be it, but I was standing for emotional warmth and what is now called relational transparency. Zealous for that, I denounced the desire to be balanced as sinfully self-conscious and Spirit-quenching.

There is, however, another sense in which balance is absolutely necessary for right living, and lack of balance is ruinous. And it is on that other sense that I want to dwell now.

Balance is the secret of successful tightrope walking. It is also one of the secrets of Christian living. Just as there are always two ways in which a tightrope walker can fall, either to his right or to his left, so it is with the believer. At every point where a policy has to be formed or a course of action planned, two extremes of one-sidedness have to be avoided. It is in that sense that we have to learn to keep our balance—and we are not very good at doing it.

We Christians are in fact abysmally bad at avoiding extremes. We are like pendulums, constantly swinging from one extreme to the other. It is the power of reaction, perhaps the strongest negative force in human life, that causes this swing. It works thus: We see, or think we see, something we dislike, and we recoil from it as we would from a snake in the grass. We keep our gaze fixed on it while we put as much distance between it and us as we can. Walking backwards in this way, we soon reach an extreme opposite to that which set us going, though we are likely not to notice its extreme character because we can only think of what we are trying to get away from. So one-sidedness of one sort spawns one-sidedness of an opposite sort. Balance is not sought, nor is it found. The reaction of man thus fails to work the righteousness of God.

One example of this is the pendulum swing of popular evangelical ethics from legalism to antinomianism and from an ethos of separation to one of worldliness during the past half-century. To me, this evangelical flip-flop is a cautionary tale rather than a story of progress, since each extreme is equally unbalanced and unimpressive. If we set them side by side, this will, I think, become plain.

By legalism I mean not justification partly by works (the Galatian heresy), but a living-by-numbers approach to the Christian life that overlays Christian liberty and love with a kind of Christianized Pharisaism. This Pharisaism sees Christian living mainly in terms of outward behavior—things you do and don't do, especially the latter.

So legalism views holiness negatively, emphasizing abstinence from evil rather than doing good; it is elitist in its readiness to censure Christians who are less addicted to its taboos, and it is weak on neighborly love.

By antinomianism I mean not taking God's law seriously as a guide for conduct. Situation ethics, which allows purpose to justify action, is antinomian; so is the mentality that leads folk to make moral exceptions in their own favor on the grounds that diligence in keeping some divine commands excuses one from having to observe others. Antinomians are prone to identify inward impulses as promptings of the Holy Spirit even when they go against the law. They need to see that the moral law of Scripture expresses God's likes and dislikes, so that one can please him only by observing it.

Fifty years ago evangelicals taught Christian living legalistically: "Don't smoke or drink, cheat, lie, or chew/and don't team up with those who do." In those days avoiding the world's defilements was the main concern. This school of thought discounted the idea that Christians are free to enjoy God's creation while they try to change the world for the better. Reaction against that thinking has led now to an opposite extreme. Many Christians have uncritically bought into the self-indulgent lifestyle of the secular world. Biblical condemnation of sexual irregularity and the self-serving quest for wealth, pleasure, and power is ignored, and the behavior patterns of most Christians seem indistinguishable from those of unbelievers. In short, ghetto legalism has given way to antinomian worldliness. Reaction? Yes. Recovery of balance? No.

What should we hope for? What should we aim at? Disgust at Christian moral laxity will probably soon spawn a new legalistic rigorism, but that will be reaction again. Shall we ever achieve Christlike balance and involvement in the world on the basis of being utterly different from it? At least, for now, let us try!

DYING

In today's world death is the great unmentionable, just as physical sex was a hundred years ago. Apart from cynical paradings of a sense of life's triviality (the Grateful Dead; "he who dies with the most toys wins") and egoistic expressions of belief in reincarnation (the New Age; Shirley MacLaine), death is not ordinarily spoken of outside of medical circles. To invite discussion of it, even in the church, is felt to be bad form. It has become conventional to think as if we are all going to live in this world forever and to view every case of bereavement as a reason for doubting the goodness of God. We must all know deep down that this is ridiculous, but we do it all the same. And in doing it, we part company with the Bible, with historic Christianity, and with a basic principle of right living, namely, that only when you know how to die can you know how to live.

There is a great contrast here between past and present. In every century until our own, Christians saw this life as preparation for eternity. Medievals, Puritans, and later evangelicals thought and wrote much about the art of dying well, and they urged that all of life should be seen as preparation for leaving it behind. This was not otiose morbidity, but realistic wisdom, since death really is the one certain fact of life. Acting the ostrich with regard to it is folly to the highest degree.

Why has modern Protestantism so largely lost its grip on this biblical otherworldliness? Several factors have combined to produce the effect.

First, death is no longer our constant companion. Until the twentieth century most children died before they were ten, and adults died at home with the family around them. But nowadays deaths in the family are rarer, and as often as not happen in hospitals, so that we can easily forget the certainty of our own death for years together.

Second, modern materialism, with its corollary that this life is the only life for enjoying anything, has infected Christian minds, producing the feeling that it is a cosmic outrage for anyone to have to leave this world before he or she has tasted all that it has to offer.

Third, Marxist mockery of the Christian hope ("pie in the sky when you die") and the accusation that having a hope of heaven destroys one's zeal for ending evil on earth have given Christians a false conscience that inhibits them about being heavenly-minded.

Fourth, modern Christians are rightly troubled at the cultural barrenness, social unconcern, and seemingly shrunken humanity that have sometimes accompanied professed longings for heaven. We have come to suspect that such longings are escapist and unhealthy.

Fifth, man's natural sense of being made for an eternal destiny, the awareness formerly expressed by the phrase "the greatness of the soul," has largely atrophied amid the hectic artificialities of Western urban life.

How then should Christians think about death—their own death, to start with? Surely as follows:

1. Physical death is the outward sign of that eternal separation from God that is the Creator's judgment on sin. That separation will only become deeper and more painful through the milestone event of dying, unless saving grace intervenes. Unconverted people do well, therefore, to fear death. It is in truth fearsome.

2. For Christians, death's sting is withdrawn. Grace has intervened, and now their death day becomes an appointment with their Savior, who will be there to take them to the rest prepared for them. Though they will be temporarily bodiless, which is not really good, they will be closer to Christ than ever before, "which is better by far" (Phil. 1:23).

3. Since believers do not know when Christ will come for them, readiness to leave this world at any time is vital Christian wisdom. Each day should find us like children looking forward to their holidays, who get packed up and ready to go a long time in advance.

4. The formula for readiness is: "Live each day as if thy last" (Thomas Ken). In other words, "Keep short accounts with God." I once heard Fred Mitchell, Overseas Missionary Fellowship director, enforce this thought shortly before his own instantaneous homecall when the plane in which he was traveling disintegrated in midair. Mitchell lived what he taught, and his biography was justly given as its title the last message radioed by the pilot of the doomed aircraft— *Climbing on Track*. I hope I never forget his words.

5. Dying well is one of the good works to which Christians are

called, and Christ will enable us who serve him to die well, however gruesome the physical process itself. And dying thus, in Christ, through Christ, and with Christ, will be a spiritual blossoming. As being born into this temporal world was our initial birthday, and as being born into God's spiritual kingdom was our second birthday, being born through physical death into the eternal world will be our third birthday.

Dag Hammarskjöld was thinking Christianly when he wrote that no philosophy that cannot make sense of death can make sense of life either. No one's living will be right until these truths about death are anchored in his or her heart.

15

CHURCH REFORMATION
Outward Reordering and Inward Renewal

The word *reformation* is magic to my heart, just as I am sure it is to yours. Say *reformation*, and immediately we think of that heroic sixteenth-century era when so many momentous events that still burn bright in our imaginations took place.

OUR REFORMATION HERITAGE

We think, for instance, of Martin Luther nailing his ninety-five theses to the door of Wittenberg Castle Church, challenging, as it turned out, the whole religious system of his day. We think of Luther at Worms a few years later, facing the Holy Roman Emperor and being told that he must withdraw his challenges to the church and his testimony to justification by faith. His famous response to the emperor, nobles, and ecclesiastical dignitaries of central Europe was this: "Unless you prove to me by Scripture and plain reason that I am mistaken, I cannot and will not recant. My conscience is captive to the Word of God. To go against conscience is neither right nor safe. Here I stand. There is nothing else I can do. God help me. Amen." These magnificent words have echoed down through the centuries, and justly so.

Luther stuck to his guns. He translated the Bible into German, and he preached and wrote tirelessly to spread the evangelical message. He became the pioneer of reformation throughout Germany and northern Europe. His name will surely be honored as long as history lasts.

We think, too, of John Calvin, that shy scholar who wanted nothing more than to be a man of letters, reading and writing books during his entire life. But fierce, red-bearded Guillaume Farel told him he must settle in Geneva to share in the work of the Reformation there, and this he did. Sleeping only four hours a night, he not only preached daily sermons and discharged his full share of pastoral duties, but he also toiled away at his writing, producing among other masterpieces the *Institutes*, that great Christian statement that for many of us still stands in a class by itself. He also wrote commentaries on the greater part of Holy Scripture, setting new and superb standards of faithful exposition. Calvin died at fifty-five, absolutely worn out—another of God's heroes.

We think also of John Knox, obliged to spend years as a galley slave because of his activities as a reformer and then finally rewarded by a few amazing weeks during which virtually the whole of Scotland turned to the Reformation. Almost overnight Scotland became the tenaciously Protestant nation that it has been from that day to this.

We think as well of the English martyrs. First in honor comes William Tyndale, who defied the king by translating the Bible. He was burned eventually in Belgium because Henry VIII sent word to the continent that he must be put to death.

Then there was Thomas Cranmer, Henry's archbishop of Canterbury, who bided his time until it was possible to produce a Reformed confession of faith and a Reformed prayer book for the Church of England. All too soon Edward VI, his royal backer in this enterprise, died, and Mary came to the throne. She resolved to take England back to Rome. She had some 330 English Protestants burned at the stake, including five bishops—and Cranmer was one of them. They threw him into prison where he was put under intolerable pressure—today we would call it brainwashing. Because of this pressure Cranmer recanted his Protestant convictions, signing six documents to that effect a few days before he was to be burned at the stake. He had been told that if he signed, he would be pardoned.

When he found out the next day that he was going to be burned anyway, he sat up all night writing a recanting of his recantation. He read this aloud in St. Mary's Church, Oxford, in the presence of his thunderstruck accusers, who then hurried him off to the fire. He died holding his right hand outstretched into the flames, thus fulfilling a promise from that last speech: "And forasmuch as my hand offended, writing contrary to my heart, my hand shall first be punished therefore; for may I come to the fire, it shall first be burned."

These stories of Christian heroism remain vivid, just as the truths for which these Reformers lived and died remain precious. So when we say *reformation*, we naturally think of these events and thank God for them. The treasures of wisdom enshrined in the theology of these Reformers are more than we have mastered today, and the selfless strength of the Reformers' testimony to the truth is a constant inspiration to us. Theirs is the faith in which I live and by which I hope to die, and I trust that the same is true of you also. Thank God for the Reformation!

THE OVERLOOKED ASPECT OF THE REFORMATION

Now we look at the church of our day and say, "We need another reformation." But do we know what we are saying? As we form our idea of reformation from these historical memories, we are in danger of settling for too narrow a perspective of what reformation is—too narrow a notion of what it was in the past and too narrow a notion of what it will be in the future if God visits us once more. The achievements of the Reformation martyrs that I have mentioned do not tell the full story of this sixteenth-century movement. These are high spots that stick in our minds. But there was more to it than that.

Most of us are children of a tradition for which the historical name is Pietism. Pietism was an answer to deadness in state churches. The pietist movement brought together groups of lively Christians for Bible study, prayer, fellowship, and mutual encouragement. These groups became beacons of light in the dreary darkness of a semi-dead national church in country after country

I am thinking here of Puritan associations in England in the late sixteenth and seventeenth centuries. I am thinking of the "praying societies" in the national church of Scotland and of regular meetings in Holland and Germany in the late seventeenth century. I think, too, of John Wesley's Methodist societies in the days of the evangelical awakening in the eighteenth century and of many other midweek fellowship meetings that were set up in the English parishes that the revival touched. There were also Welsh societies, "experience meetings" as they were sometimes called, that began in the eighteenth century when the evangelical awakening hit Wales, and these continued until the end of the nineteenth century. God blessed these gatherings and made them sources of light and life to many as the years went by.

It is natural for Christians to get together in fellowship meetings to pray, praise God, and encourage each other. And it has happened in this century in parts of the world where little or nothing was known about the Reformation. I think of the revival fellowships that began to emerge in the East African church in the 1930s, mostly though not exclusively Anglican. Seventy years later in the wake of traumatic wars and genocide, the East African revival keeps flaring up in place after place, and fellowship gatherings are still at its heart.

In the days of the Reformation regular small group meetings had already begun. Luther started them, and the Reformer of Strasbourg, Martin Bucer, encouraged the pattern in his churches. He had a Latin name for it: *Ecclesiola in ecclesia* (the little church within the church). These fellowship structures are integral to the Reformation heritage.

Today we tend to follow the majority of Pietists in defining reformation as the outward activity of putting straight the doctrines formally professed by the organized church and the church order that went with them. We think of it as cleaning up superstition and sweeping out errors that have disfigured official religion. But we do not immediately think of reformation as involving an overall renewal of spiritual vitality. As inheritors of what may be called the pietist disjunction, we view the corporate renewal of spiritual life as something distinct from reformation. We believe the former is an inward work of God and should be spoken of in different terms from the latter. These are, we think, two separate realities; they are not necessarily connected. But we are wrong in this—historically and biblically—as I am going to show.

SUBSTANTIAL REFORMATION

The sixteenth-century upheaval that reshaped church doctrine and order was the outward aspect of an inward renewal of faith and devotion. This is a biblical pattern, as we will see. Conversely, whenever God visits his people with spiritual revival, some measure of outward reordering will be involved. That is plain from the scriptural evidence. The point to grasp is that what we are talking about is one work of God viewed from two standpoints, not two works. Reformation and renewal or revival are essentially one.

The Reformers saw themselves as pastors and evangelists no less than as theologians and ecclesiastical statesmen. This was true of Luther, Bucer, Calvin, Zwingli and their colleagues, and of all the British leaders. They saw themselves not only as "washing and cleansing the face" of the church—that is, getting doctrine, church order, and liturgy straight—but also as letting loose the Gospel of God that through the Spirit transforms whole communities and brings new faith, love, and life wherever it is preached.

In the sixteenth century this was what actually happened. Calvin's Geneva took John Knox's breath away. He described it as the most perfect school of Christ the world had seen since the days of the apostles. Godliness and righteousness were everywhere. Calvin's Geneva was not just formally and outwardly right; it was inwardly, substantially, spiritually right—a genuinely godly community.

The same was true of Scotland in John Knox's great days and also of England in ways that most history books overlook. The records of reactions to the preaching of such men as Latimer and Bradford and of the sudden blossoming of Christian philanthropy in England tell their own clear story. The work that God did touched clergy and laypeople with spiritual life and reshaped the organized church into a stance of formal correctness.

When we talk about reformation, then, we should realize that we are talking about a two-sided and yet single vivifying work of God. The Puritans give us the right perspective. They saw the sixteenth-century Reformers as used by God to start reformation by establishing the Gospel in the English church, and themselves as seeking to be used by God to complete the reforming process by converting the English people to a living faith in Christ.

Perhaps you have heard of Richard Baxter, the Puritan evangelist of Kidderminster in the English midlands. In seventeen years he produced a Christian community half the size of Calvin's Geneva, which in moral and spiritual quality was equal or superior to Geneva. There was an amazing transformation of that town under his ministry. Family catechizing, family worship, a public worship pattern full of praise, church discipline, preaching, devotional reading, regular pastoral counseling, and small-group ministry under Baxter's oversight were all part of it, and reformation was Baxter's name for it.

He wrote a classic book on ministerial practice entitled *The Reformed Pastor*. By the word *reformed* Baxter meant spiritually alive and morally in shape, not merely maintaining what we would call Calvinistic doctrine, though he assumes that. His meaning becomes clear when he writes: "If God would but reform the clergy, the people of England would soon be reformed." Kidderminster was a model parish, and Baxter wrote a full account of it because he believed other communities would profit by his experience. He hoped he would see wholesale revival in England in his day. That, to him, would have been reformation finally fulfilled.

But his hopes came to nothing. After the restoration of Charles II, two thousand Puritan clergy were ejected from their pulpits, and the national reaction against godliness lasted for more than half a century. Baxter was heartbroken, for he believed that, given twenty-five more years of the Puritan ministry he had seen and known and been part of countrywide during the Commonwealth decade, the conversion of the English people would have become a reality. Yet the inspiration of his Kidderminster ministry remains, and we do well to take it to heart today. Both Calvin's Geneva and Baxter's Kidderminster show the full dimensions of the revitalizing work of grace that we are examining.

BIBLICAL EXAMPLES OF REFORMATION

The Bible records many striking spiritual movements that the textbooks usually call reformations. In every case this same two-sidedness applies. These movements had an outward aspect; immorality and idolatry were put away. But they also had an inward side; men and women were stirred to seek God and renew their covenant with him.

Joshua 24, for instance, tells how Joshua at the end of his life called the people together and challenged them, saying, "Now fear the LORD and serve him with all faithfulness. Throw away the gods your forefathers worshiped beyond the River and in Egypt, and serve the LORD. But if serving the LORD seems undesirable to you, then choose for yourselves this day whom you will serve" (Josh. 24:14-15).

The people replied, "We too will serve the LORD" (v. 18). Joshua served God; they would do the same.

Joshua continued confrontationally, as preachers sometimes must, for reality's sake. "You are not able to serve the LORD. He is a holy God; he is a jealous God. He will not forgive your rebellion and your sins" (v. 19). The people insisted, however, that they would serve God, and a covenant was made. It seems that for a time there was a true return to God as Joshua commanded.

In 2 Chronicles three striking renewals are recorded, led in each case by a godly king. Chapter 15 tells of reformation under King Asa. "When Asa heard these words and the prophecy of Azariah son of Obed the prophet, he took courage. He removed the detestable idols from the whole land of Judah and Benjamin and from the towns he had captured in the hills of Ephraim. He repaired the altar of the LORD that was in front of the portico of the LORD's temple" (v. 8). This is reformation in our usual narrow sense, a matter of putting right the outward form of things. But in this movement there was more. Asa gathered the people together, and they committed themselves solemnly to the Lord by sacrifice: "They entered into a covenant to seek the LORD, the God of their fathers, with all their heart and soul" (v. 12). It was what so many thousands in Europe did in the sixteenth century: They set themselves to seek the Lord with all their being. "They took an oath to the LORD with loud acclamation, with shouting and with trumpets and horns. All Judah rejoiced about the oath because they had sworn it wholeheartedly. They sought God eagerly, and he was found by them. So the LORD gave them rest on every side" (vv. 14-15).

In 2 Chronicles 29-31 we hear of Hezekiah's reformation. Chapter 29 records how Hezekiah systematically rooted out idolatry, and then chapter 30 tells in detail how Hezekiah brought the people together to keep a solemn passover to God and to renew their commitment.

The week of the passover became such a momentous time to them spiritually that they lengthened it. We read, "The whole assembly then agreed to celebrate the festival seven more days; so for another seven days they celebrated joyfully" (30:23). They were saying, "This time in the Lord's presence has been so good, so enriching, so momentous in our experience that we will extend it." And they did. Verse 26 says, "There was great joy in Jerusalem." New closeness to God always brings joy, and new closeness was the reason why joy was great in Jerusalem in those days.

In 2 Chronicles 34-35 we read of reformation under Josiah. (There is a parallel and supplementary account in 2 Kings 22-23.) Israel was surrounded by nations that worshiped nature gods represented by idols, and idolatry kept flowing over the borders to corrupt successive generations of Israelites, just as nowadays in this era of swift communication the so-called wisdom of the East comes flooding into North America in the New Age movement. In the seventh century B.C. the effect of Hezekiah's reformation in the previous century wore off, paganism took over, and once more purging had to take place. Chapter 34 tells how Josiah stamped out idolatry. Then in 2 Chronicles 35 we read about the other side of the renewal—passover worship and praise.

There was a similar movement under Ezra, recorded in chapters 9-10 of his book. Ezra 9 documents the outward aspects of revival in the ceremonial putting away of pagan wives who, contrary to the will of God, had been taken in marriage by Israelites. The people repented. Then Ezra prayed for forgiveness, and there was a new commitment to God by those who had sinned. This was the inward reality of reformation—that is, spiritual renewal.

In Nehemiah 8-10 the outward form of reformation was a return to Scripture, as explained by Ezra and a team of preachers. The people were moved to tears, and a great national recommitment followed. Reformation? Yes. But it had both an inward aspect and an outward aspect, as the tears and subsequent rejoicing show.

What these Old Testament stories make plain to us is that reformation of the church is a work of God that revitalizes faith and worship, as well as leading to doctrinal and liturgical corrections.

Complementing these stories and confirming this perspective is the New Testament narrative of Pentecost in Acts 2. At Pentecost renewal came through movement out of the old covenant into a new order of things in the Spirit. We would ordinarily call it a movement of revival rather than of reformation. But notice how from the start the body of believers "devoted themselves to the apostles' teaching and to the fellowship, to the breaking of bread and to prayer" (Acts 2:42). This was a new corporate lifestyle. "Every day they continued to meet together in the temple courts. They broke bread in their homes and ate together with glad and sincere hearts, praising God and enjoying the favor of all the people" (v. 46). The inward aspect came from faith in Christ; it expressed itself in joy. But it had as its outward aspect worship, regular prayer, and celebration of the Lord's Supper—a genuinely reformed order for church life. Inward and outward went together, as in the Old Testament visitations from God.

In Revelation 2-3 the same two-sidedness appears. The Savior rebukes the churches, telling them to put away their sins and return to him. But for what? For the outward reordering of their corporate lives? Yes, certainly, but for much more than that—for true spiritual renewal in every department of their personal lives as well.

Spiritual movements vary in what they exhibit, but in them there is always some element of outward purging, reshaping, and reforming, and some element of the inner renewing of faith and communion with God. The late Max Warren helpfully linked revival with reformation by picturing revival as the re-forming—that is, the fresh forming up, briefing, and refitting—of troops for battle so that the army may go forward to fight again. This is a good image to have in mind as we reflect on the outward and inward dimensions of God's quickening visitations. Whether we call them works of renewal, revival, or reformation is not important so long as we are clear on the broad scope of what God actually does when he visits.

THE ELEMENTS IN TRUE REFORMATION

What would a work of divine reformation in our churches today look like? I must be careful here. Different churches have different prob-

lems and needs, so generalizations could easily misfire. Current movements professing to bring new life to churches might suspect me of
implying negative judgments about them, which is not my purpose.
My best course is to try to answer the question by listing some of the
realities that any coming of God to reform his people would produce
anywhere at any time.

First, there would be a sense of biblical authority—that is, an
awareness that biblical teaching is divine truth and that the invitations
and admonitions, threats and warnings, promises and assurances of
Scripture still express the mind of God toward mankind. The Bible
would be honored again as the Word of God, and the perverse pluralism of liberal theology, which still addles the brains and blinds the
hearts of many, would wither and die. The root of this pluralism is that
teachers feel free to ignore some of the things the Bible teaches and to
pull others out of context; the fruit of it is that God's people are led
astray into dry places, and the Holy Spirit of God is comprehensively
quenched. Reformation always begins as a call from God to "come out
of the wilderness" of subjective speculation and spiritual impotence
and learn again in humility the true teaching of the written Word
about grace and godliness, knowing that the secret of power for living lies here. Thus, unhappily, reformation always leads to controversy, for some resist the message.

Second, there would be a spirit of seriousness about eternal issues.
Heaven and hell would be preached about, thought about, and talked
about once again. Life in this world would once again be lived in the
light of the world to come, and the Philippian jailer's question, "What
must I do to be saved?" would be seen as life's basic question once
more. For most of this century the church, liberal and conservative,
in all denominations, has been so occupied with this world that hearts
tuned to eternity have been the exception rather than the rule.
Sociopolitical, cultural, sporting, and money-making interests have
dominated Christian minds rather than the laying up of treasure in
heaven. A work of reformation would change that, not by withdraw-
ing Christians from these fields of action, but by radically altering their
perspective on what they are doing, so that God's glory and eternal values would become the chief concerns.

Third, there would be a passion for God transcending any interest in religion or cultivation of religiosity. One's relationship to God would be seen as the most important thing in the world, and a Bible-based awareness of the greatness and awesomeness of God the eternal Savior-Judge, in whose hands we ever are, would displace all cheap thoughts of God as just a useful pal.

Fourth, there would be a love of holiness, growing out of deep conviction of sin, deep repentance, deep gratitude for forgiveness and cleansing through the blood of Jesus Christ, and with that a deep desire to please God. Casualness about righteousness, cutting moral corners, areas of blatant self-indulgence, love of luxury, and broken commitments of all kinds have disfigured modern Christianity at all levels. This would change, as indeed it needs to, for moral standards among Christian people, as in the world around them, seem to be getting worse rather than better. It is frightening to see how little believers nowadays seem to be bothered about personal sin.

Fifth, there would be a concern for the church. Christians would catch the biblical perspective in which the church is the center and focal point of God's plan and the display ground of his saving and sanctifying wisdom (see Eph. 3:1-12). They would be deeply concerned about the image that the church presents to the world, and any form of unfaithfulness, carnality, false doctrine, formalism, disorder, or wrongheadedness in the church would cause them distress and send them to their knees. God should be honored, not dishonored, in his church, and the church should show itself strong in standing against the world and testifying to its Savior. These are universal Christian concerns at reformation times, and saints at such times will endure and risk anything in order to see the church move in the right direction.

Sixth, there would be a willingness to change—whether from sin to righteousness, or from lassitude to zeal, or from traditional patterns to new procedures, or from passivity to activity, or any other form of change needed. Believers would come together to praise, pray, encourage each other, and see what they could do together to advance the cause of Christ. It would be as if they had awakened after a long sleep. They would wonder how they were able to be somnolent, apathetic, and inactive for so long. What new things they would find themselves doing cannot be specified in advance beyond this general formula, but should God work in reformation, it is safe to say that newness of discipleship and change of ways in some shape or form would be the experience of us all.

THE NATURE OF TRUE REFORMATION

What I have to say about the work of God itself can now be summarized in five points.

1. *Reformation is a divine visitation.* This is Zechariah's message. Visions of renewal and restoration that fill the first few chapters of his prophecy prompted Calvin more than four hundred years ago to say, "This doctrine may be fully applied to our age"; we may equally apply it to our own century. Zechariah wrote, "Therefore, this is what the LORD says, 'I will return to Jerusalem with mercy, and there my house will be rebuilt. . . .' Proclaim further: This is what the LORD Almighty says: 'My towns will again overflow with prosperity, and the LORD will again comfort Zion and choose Jerusalem'" (Zech. 1:16-17). This is reformation in its outward aspect, and it is of God. But with it, says Zechariah, the Lord brings the inward reality too. "'Shout and be glad, O Daughter of Zion. For I am coming, and I will live among you,' declares the LORD" (Zech. 2:10). Such divine visitation is the inmost heart of any truly significant change in the condition of the church.

2. *Reformation is a work of Jesus Christ.* In Revelation 2-3 renewal is pictured as Jesus coming down from his throne by the Spirit and drawing near to rebuke, reorder, and revitalize his people and enable them to overcome pressures currently overwhelming them. This is needed today. Sin and worldliness, error and folly have crept in, as we all know only too well. Churches are corrupted. Purging is needed. Spiritual light burns dim. The secular community goes downhill like the Gadarene swine rushing toward the edge of the cliff; the church has lost its influence and cannot stop the decline. How different from the sixteenth century! The Lord Jesus again and again must come to us to raise up a standard against the evil that comes in like a flood.

3. *Reformation is a constant task for God's people.* We cannot restore

spiritual life, but there is something we can do to prepare the way for Christ's coming to reform his church: We can turn away from error and sin, and thereby prepare the way of the Lord, removing roadblocks and making straight a highway for God into our lives. Undoubtedly this is what is meant by that famous slogan, which I am sure we have heard but have never perhaps thought about as we should: *Ecclesia reformata semper reformanda* (the church that has been reformed needs always to be reformed). That tag has to do, not simply with outward order, but with renewal of inward spiritual life.

4. *Reformation has a constant evangelistic overflow.* Zechariah's vision of restoration ends thus: "In those days ten men from all languages and nations will take firm hold of one Jew by the hem of his robe and say, 'Let us go with you, because we have heard that God is with you'" (8:23; see vv. 20-22). What this points to is that new life from God in a group becomes an attractive force.

The word *evangelistic*, no doubt, suggests to modern Christians special efforts at outreach (crusades, rallies, designated meetings of all sorts), as if evangelism were an activity detached from regular church life. That idea reflects the highlighting of these special activities during the past century when most, if not all, churches were very far from their best. But when in reformation the church comes alive, persons from outside find themselves wanting to share what is going on, and this drawing power is continuous and considerable.

When Augustine declared that God made us for himself and our hearts are restless till they find rest in him, he stated a universal truth. One of God's ways of drawing the restless into his fellowship of life and peace through Christ is to allure them by what they see in others. Acts 2:43-47 shows this happening in the apostolic church right after Pentecost, and the pattern is permanently valid.

5. *Reformation always begins with repentance,* seeking God in new ways and putting away wrong things. This is clear from Christ's words to his people in the letters of the book of Revelation, just as it is clear from the stories of spiritual movements in Old Testament times.

Revelation 3:18-20 answers the question: What can we do to bring about reformation? This passage tells us that the people of God must do three things. First, perceive—perceive, that is, the grim reality of their current situation, just as our Lord called on the Laodiceans to perceive the depths of their own spiritual need. They said they were rich, but they did not realize that they were "wretched, pitiful, poor, blind and naked." Jesus said, "Those whom I love I rebuke and discipline" (vv. 17, 19). We must leave behind unrealism and stop pretending all is well when it is not well and face the guilt of our own unfaithfulness and halfheartedness.

Second, pray. We can talk to Jesus about our need and beg him to draw near to us and in mercy deal with our lukewarmness. The great men of the sixteenth-century Reformation were praying men. They knew that without prayer nothing can be expected to go right, and they acted accordingly. Luther confessed, with startling spiritual realism, "I am too busy to spend less than three hours a day in prayer." It was said that Mary Queen of Scots feared the prayers of John Knox more than she feared the armies of England. The Lord calls us to become men and women of prayer: "I counsel you to buy from me gold refined in the fire, so you can become rich; and white clothes to wear, so you can cover your shameful nakedness; and salve to put on your eyes, so you can see" (Rev. 3:18). Jesus tells us to take note of his rebuke and respond in prayer.

Third, prepare. We may prepare the way of the Lord in the sense suggested by Isaiah 40:3-4, where it is said, "'In the desert prepare the way for the LORD; make straight in the wilderness a highway for our God.'" That means clear the road, throw out the stones, get rid of the roadblocks. Sins embraced are roadblocks. We must forsake them. Ask God to search your heart. "Search me, O God, and know my heart; test me and know my anxious thoughts. See if there is any offensive way in me, and lead me in the way everlasting" (Ps. 139:23-24). Pray the psalmist's prayer and ask God to show you what stones need to be put away. Isaiah says that "every valley shall be raised up, every mountain and hill made low; the rough ground shall become level, the rugged places a plain. And the glory of the LORD will be revealed" (40:4-5). This will happen in part through the work of God's people preparing and clearing the road.

We can ask the Lord to search us right now. We can ask him to save us from that desensitizing complacency that has made us lukewarm, halfhearted Christians, living with perfect orthodoxy (I expect) in our heads and yet like those in a dream—with no spiritual vitality in our hearts.

That is what we are summoned to do in Revelation 3:20. This was not written as an evangelistic text, though it has often been used that way. It was written to backsliding believers. So when Jesus says, "Here I am! I stand at the door and knock. If anyone hears my voice and opens the door, I will come in and eat with him, and he with me," he is calling for repentance and promising a renewal of fellowship and strength to those who heed his call. Will you hear Jesus as he speaks to you? Will you open the door? Will you enthrone him at the center of your personal and church life?

Scripture teaches us not simply to think but also to act with regard to reformation. We cannot precipitate it, but we can put ourselves in the way where it is found. What we can do, we should do. That we, his people, should seek church reformation in this holistic sense is part of his plan for us. May God give us ears to hear, eyes to see, hearts to respond, and wills to act. As he speaks to us in these days, may we realize that it is he himself drawing near to us and that he is on his throne to renew us, sustain us, reform us, and finally bring us to glory. Praise to him forever! Amen.

NOTES

CHAPTER FOUR:
HOT TUB RELIGION

1. *Evangelical Dictionary of Theology*, ed. Walter A. Elwell (Grand Rapids: Baker Book House, 1984), p. 588, emphasis added.

2. *The Screwtape Letters* (London: Geoffrey Bles, 1942), p. 112.

3. Calvin, *Institutes of the Christian Religion*, III.x.

4. *Mere Christianity* (London: Collins, Fontana Books, 1955), p. 116.

5. *The Pilgrim's Progress* (London: Oxford University Press, O.S.A. series, 1945), p. 370.

6. *Institutes of the Christian Religion*, III.ix.1.

7. *Calvin's Doctrine of the Christian Life* (Edinburgh: Oliver & Boyd, 1959), p. 130.

8. Reprints of *The Saints' Everlasting Rest* (drastically abridged) were published by Baker Book House (Grand Rapids, 1978) and by The Billy Graham Center in 1994. The full text is in volume 3 of Baxter's *Practical Works* (Morgan, Penn.: Soli Deo Gloria, 1990).

9. Title of a study of latter-day British culture by Garth Lean (London: Blandford Press, 1965).

CHAPTER FIVE:
A CHRISTIAN STYLE OF LIFE

1. Neil Postman, *Amusing Ourselves to Death: Public Discourse in the Age of Show Business* (New York: Viking Press, 1985).

2. On the Christian view of work, see Carl F. H. Henry, *Aspects of Christian Ethics* (Grand Rapids: Eerdmans, 1964), pp. 37-71; Leland Ryken, *Work and Leisure in Christian Perspective* (Portland, Ore.: Multnomah, 1987).

3. See John Piper, *Desiring God: Meditations of a Christian Hedonist* (Portland, Ore.: Multnomah, 1986); Ryken, *Work and Leisure*, pp. 191ff.

4. Ryken, *Work and Leisure*, p. 187, citing Gibbs, "Ritual, Play and Transcendent Mystery," paper presented to the American Academy of Religion, Midwestern Sectional Meeting, Chicago, Illinois, 17 February 1973, p. 4. Ryken's book, along with R. K. Johnston's *The Christian at Play* (Grand Rapids: Eerdmans, 1983), Johan Huizinga's *Homo Ludens: A Study of the Play-element in Culture*

(1950; repr. Boston: Beacon Press, 1955), and Josef Pieper's *Leisure, the Basis of Culture*, trans. Alexander Dru (New York: Pantheon Books, 1952) are basic for the Christian study of leisure.

5. Cranmer's wording is retained in the catechism in the statutory *Book of Common Prayer* of the Church of England; I am quoting here from the 1962 Canadian revision, *Book of Common Prayer* (Toronto: Anglican Book Center, 1962), p. 548.

6. "Morning Prayer," in the *Book of Common Prayer*, p. 11.

7. Ryken, *Work and Leisure*, p. 38.

8. See Henri Blocher, *In the Beginning*, trans. David G. Preston (Downers Grove, Ill.: InterVarsity, 1984), for an orientation to this question and a compelling argument for the third of these alternatives.

9. See John Piper, *The Pleasures of God: Meditations on God's Delight in Being God* (Portland, Ore.: Multnomah, 1991).

10. "Doctor Jazz," by Jelly-Roll Morton and his Red Hot Peppers (Victor Records, 1926; various reissues).

11. Randy Alcorn, *Money, Possessions and Eternity* (Wheaton, Ill.: Tyndale House, 1989), pp. 402-403.

CHAPTER SIX:
GUIDANCE

1. Joseph Bayly et al., *Essays on Guidance* (Downers Grove, Ill.: InterVarsity, 1968), Preface.

2. Russ Johnston, *How to Know the Will of God* (Colorado Springs: NavPress, 1971), p. 5.

3. Garry Friesen, *Decision Making and the Will of God* (Portland, Ore.: Multnomah, 1981), p. 18.

4. From "Come Thou Fount of Every Blessing," by Robert Robinson.

CHAPTER EIGHT:
SCRIPTURE AND SANCTIFICATION

1. John Owen, *Works*, ed. W. Goold (London: Banner of Truth, 1966), III, p. 386.

2. James P. Boyce, "Sanctification," in the *Abstract of Systematic Theology* (1887, repr. by E. C. Reisinger, n.d.), pp. 412-415.

3. J. C. Ryle, *Holiness* (Ipswich, UK: William Hunt, 1879), p. xv.

4. Boyce, *Abstract*, pp. 418ff.

5. Jonathan Edwards, *Religious Affections*, ed. J. M. Houston (Portland, Ore.: Multnomah, 1984), p. xxxii.

CHAPTER NINE:
THE TRANSFORMATION TRACK

1. J. C. Ryle, *Holiness,* Centenary Edition (Welwyn, UK: Evangelical Press, 1979), pp. 317, 460.

CHAPTER TEN:
POOR HEALTH

1. Philip Edgcumbe Hughes, *Paul's Second Epistle to the Corinthians* (NICNT; Grand Rapids: Eerdmans, 1962), *ad loc.*